LEARNING IN THE GLOBAL ERA

LEARNING IN THE GLOBAL ERA

INTERNATIONAL PERSPECTIVES ON
GLOBALIZATION AND EDUCATION

Edited by

Marcelo M. Suárez-Orozco

UNIVERSITY OF CALIFORNIA PRESS

BERKELEY   LOS ANGELES   LONDON

ROSS INSTITUTE

University of California Press, one of the most
distinguished university presses in the United States,
enriches lives around the world by advancing scholarship in the humanities, social sciences, and natural
sciences. Its activities are supported by the UC Press
Foundation and by philanthropic contributions from
individuals and institutions. For more information,
visit www.ucpress.edu.

University of California Press
Berkeley and Los Angeles, California

University of California Press, Ltd.
London, England

Library of Congress Cataloging-in-Publication Data

Learning in the global era : international perspectives
on globalization and education / Marcelo M. Suárez-
Orozco, ed.
  p.   cm.
  Includes bibliographical references and index.
  ISBN: 978-0-520-25436-7 (pbk. : alk. paper)
  1. Education and globalization.   2. Education and
state.   3. Educational change.   4. Educational equal-
ization.   5. Education—Effect of technological innovations on.   6. Learning.   I. Suárez-Orozco, Marcelo M.,
1956–.

LC191.L367   2007
306.43—dc22   2007018638

Manufactured in the United States of America

16 15 14 13 12 11 10
10 9 8 7 6 5 4 3 2

The paper used in this publication meets the minimum
requirements of ANSI/NISO Z39.48-1992 (R 1997)
(Permanence of Paper).

For Carola

Contents

Tables

Illustrations

Acknowledgments

The origins of this book can be traced to the First International Conference on Globalization and Learning (FICGL), which was held in Hässelby Castle, outside the old city of Stockholm deep into the Swedish winter of 2005.

The FICGL was generously supported by grants from the Ross Institute of New York. I would like to thank Courtney Sale Ross, founder of the Ross Institute, for her generosity, wise counsel, and unwavering support of this initiative. Courtney Ross is well known in the field of education as the cofounder with her late husband Steve Ross, of the Ross School, an incubator for innovation in globalization and learning. Courtney has been decades ahead of the curve in her visionary work at the Ross School, whose faculty endeavors to teach "the whole child for the whole world," as one often hears at the breathtakingly beautiful campus in the East End of Long Island.

I am happy to acknowledge additional grants from New York University, the Globalization and Learning Council in Stockholm, the Royal Institute of Technology in Stockholm (Kungliga Tekniska Högskolan [KTH], with special thanks to Anders Flodström, rector), the Stockholm Institute of Education (Lärarhögskolan [LHS], with special thanks to Eskil Franck, rector), the Royal College of Music in Stockholm (Kungliga Musikhögskolan [KMH], with special thanks to Gunilla von Bahr, rector), the Bank of Sweden Tercentenary Foundation (Stiftelsen Riksbankens Jubileumsfond, with special thanks to Dan Brändström, managing director), the Electrum Foundation/Kista Science City, Microsoft Sweden, and the Swedish Research Council. Their support enabled us to engage a truly international and interdisciplinary group of scholars, policy makers, and practitioners in a gorgeous and tranquil setting away from the daily demands we all face.

The FICGL was formally hosted by the city of Stockholm, which provided an unforgettable dinner banquet for all participants in its magnificent building in the heart of the old city—the site where the royal dinner for the Nobel ceremonies is held every year. It is safe to say that more than one of the invited scholars fantasized about being invited to *that* banquet one day. The FICGL was also hosted by the Tensta Gymnasium, a secondary school outside the old city of Stockholm. During our visit, Tensta served as an open laboratory for participants to witness firsthand one school's efforts to better educate a very diverse student body (80 percent of its students come from immigrant and refugee-origin homes) while integrating state-of-the-art information, communication, and media technologies to impart twenty-first-century skills to the young learners. The consensus among the participating scholars was that the visit to the gymnasium and the presentation of the Tensta case study by the school leadership team was a conference highlight. We are thankful to the leadership team, Principal Inger Nyrell and Vice Principal Kerstin Friborg, for their warm and sincere welcome. Opening their doors to a large number of international visitors took courage and conviction. They addressed all inquiries, pointed questions, and requests for clarification made by the visiting scholars during our time at the school with care, rigor, and transparency, revealing the leadership's complete devotion to the education of all the children in their school. The well-known and well-liked Swedish journalist Bim Clinell acted as conference MC, keeping us all on time and on track with firmness and disarming humor.

In addition to the authors of the various chapters in the book, the following scholars, policy makers, practitioners, and foundation leaders participated in the FICGL. The papers they presented, discussion groups they led, pointed questions they asked, countless exchanges—formal and informal—during our four days in Sweden have shaped this book in innumerable ways. It is a pleasure to acknowledge them. Lawrence Aber of New York University; Kenneth Abrahamsson of Luleå University of Technology; Gunilla von Bahr, rector of the Royal College of Music, Stockholm; Barbro Berg of the city of Stockholm; Kjell Blückert of the Bank of Sweden Tercentenary Foundation; Dan Brändström, managing director of Stiftelsen Riksbankens Jubileumsfond (Bank of Sweden Tercentenary Foundation); William Brunson of the Royal College of Music, Stockholm; Annie Maccoby Berglöf of Stockholm; Erik Berglöf of the Stockholm School of Economics; Jennifer Chidsey (then of the Ross School); Kirsten Drotner of the University of Southern Denmark; Olle Edqvist of the Royal Institute of Technology; Bo Ekman of the Tällberg Foundation; Per Engback of the City of Stockholm Schools; Walter Feinberg of the University of Illinois; Anita Ferm of the City of Stockholm Schools; Anders Flodström, rector of the Royal Institute of Technology in Stockholm (Kungliga Tekniska Högskolan); Eskil Franck, rector of the Stockholm Institute of Education (Lärarhögskolan); Karen Symms Gallagher, dean, Rossier School of Education, University of Southern California; Birgitte Holm-Sørensen, Danish University of Education; Peter Holmstedt of the Globalization and Learning Council in Stockholm; Anders Holst (then of the Ross Institute); Ambjörn Hugardt of the Royal College of Music, Stockholm, Torkel Klingberg of the Karolinska Institute at Astrid Lindgrens Children's Hospital; Bengt Kristensson Uggla of Åbo Akademi University; Gunther Kress of the University of London; Theo van Leeuwen of Cardiff University; Johan Leman of the Catholic University of Leuven; Anders Lönnberg of the Globalization and Learning Council in Stockholm; Joseph McDonald of New York University; Mirta Michilli, general director of the Digital Youth Consortium in Rome; Slavko Milekic of the University of the Arts; Bengt Molander of NTNU Norwegian University of Science and Technology; Alfonso Molina of the University of Edinburgh; Christal Morehouse, then of the offices of the Hon. Rita Süssmuth (now of the Bertelsmann Foundation); the Hon. Erik Nilsson of the city of Stockholm; Pedro Noguera of New York University; Eva Pethrus of the Microsoft Corporation; Lauren B. Resnick of the University of Pittsburgh; David Rose of Harvard University and the Center for Applied Special Technology; Klas Roth of the Stockholm Institute of Education; Roger Säljö of Göteborg University; H. E. Marcelo Sanchez Sorondo, chancellor of the Pontifical Academy of Sciences; Michael Schrage of the Massachusetts Institute of Technology; Staffan Selander of the Stockholm Institute of Education; Christer Wiklund, dean of the School of Music in Piteå, Luleå University of Technology; Stanton Wortham of the University of Pennsylvania, and Jim Wynn of Microsoft Corporation.

Naomi Schneider of the University of California Press joined us at the FICGL as an active participant and followed the development of the manuscript from its very inception with enthusiasm, energy, and care. Her wise counsel was essential at every turning point in the making of this book. Carola Suárez-Orozco participated in the FICGL and read various iterations of this volume. As usual, Carola's feedback was understated and brilliant. Over the last thirty years I have learned more about "love and work" from Carola than she will ever know. This book is for her.

INTRODUCTION

Marcelo M. Suárez-Orozco
and Carolyn Sattin

LEARNING IN THE GLOBAL ERA

Human societies, in all their breathtaking differences, face a common task: to transfer a range of skills, values, and sensibilities to the next generation. Socialization of the young is culturally defined and highly varied and is constantly evolving. All societies organize formal institutions to nurture in the next generation the qualities to carry forth the work of culture. For the first time in human history, basic education in formal schools has become a normative ideal the world over. Indeed, over the last five decades formal schooling has emerged globally as one of the most important societal institution for the education of the next generation.

Education, broadly conceived as formally structured, socially organized directed teaching and learning, has always been connected to, yet purposefully set apart from, the other institutions of society. Furthermore, the research literature has clearly established the multiple discontinuities between teaching and learning within versus out of schools.[1] Teaching and learning in schools tend to be highly formalized—for example, around strict time, subject, and level or grade demarcations—while learning outside of schools tends to be more fluid and informal (see Cheng, this volume). Schools usually privilege acontextual learning, whereas learning outside of schools is nearly always context-dependent and hands-on. Learning in schools is often organized to achieve increasing levels of abstraction, whereas learning outside school tends to be applied and designed to solve concrete problems. In general the focus in schools is predominantly on *teaching,* whereas the focus outside of school is on *learning.* Of course, these dichotomies are heuristic and do not represent strict binary oppositions: in reality, there is fluidity in all human learning whether in or out of school.

While formal schooling is frequently set apart from other institutions in society—such as systems of kinship or religion or that of production and distribution of goods and services—some degree of calibration and convergence between what goes on in schools and what awaits youth in the posteducational opportunity structure is of course vital. Whether it is by shaping the sensibilities and habits of mind and heart of future citizens or by imparting skills to prepare them for the labor market, schooling is deeply interconnected with the economies and societies that encompass them. Schools should reflect—and reflect upon—the cultural and socioeconomic realities of the communities of which they form an essential part.[2] The main idea animating this book is that the schooling of youth today is largely out of sync with the realities of a global world. Precisely at a time when more is asked of formal education than ever before and when youth the world over need more cultural sophistication, better communication and collaboration skills, and higher-order cognitive skills for critical thinking, as well as the metacognitive abilities for reflecting on their own learning so as to become lifelong learners, most schools around the world risk anachronism and redundancy. Twenty-first-century economies and societies are predicated on increasing complexity and diversity—the twin corollaries of an ever more globally interconnected world. The lack of fit between what education *is* and what it *needs to be* is implicated in the three most important failures of schools today.

First, too many schools today are failing to engage youth in learning. In both the wealthy advanced postindustrial nations and in many developing countries, the predominant schooling experience for most youth today is one of boredom. Do a simple test: go to an average school in any of the global cites in the world and have students complete the sentence "School is ____." The most common response to that sentence is likely to be "boring." Schools have had to work hard to make children and youth epidemically bored and emotionally disengaged from the activity in school. It is indeed a considerable achievement, given the fact that the human brain is biologically programmed to take in the world, manipulate it, transform it—that is, to learn and to act upon what is learned (see Damasio and Damasio; and Katzir, Immordino-Yang, and Fischer, both this volume).

The second glaring failure of formal education is happening at the very vital global link between the wealthy global cities in the Northern Hemisphere and the developing world. Schools are failing to properly educate and ease the transition and integration of large and growing numbers of immigrant youth arriving in Europe and North America; many quickly become marginalized as racially, ethnically, religiously, and linguistically marked minority groups. In Europe, the failure to properly educate the children of Muslim immigrants became clear as the results of the Program for International Student Assessment (PISA) study sent shockwaves[3] and as countries such as Germany confronted their poor records in educating their neediest pupils—those originating in refugee- and immigrant-headed homes (see Hugonnier; Süssmuth; Crul; Wikan, all this volume). In the United States, the enduring racial achievement gap,[4] as well as the very uneven educational trajectories of the children of Latin American, Caribbean, and some Asian immigrants—now the fastest growing sector of the U.S. child population—augurs trouble ahead as the so-called new economy is increasingly unforgiving of those without the skills and credentials required for functioning in the knowledge-intensive sector of the opportunity structure, and as a high-school diploma has yielded steadily diminishing returns (see, for example, Suárez-Orozco, Suárez-Orozco, & Todorova 2007; see also Myers 1998). The results of these general trends are painfully obvious in multiple measurable ways: from the high dropout rates among immigrant, ethnic, and racial minorities in many wealthy countries, to stark differences in achievement patterns between native and racialized minorities (see Crul; and Süssmuth, both this volume). The furious rioting in French suburbs in November 2005, where second-generation children of immigrants performed for the global stage their alienation from and anomie in relation to French social institutions is but one recent example of the consequences.

Third, the persistent under-enrollment of children in schools in poorer regions of the developing world, as well as the variable quality of many of these schools, is among the most alarming failures of schooling in the twenty-first century. Approximately 200 million children and youth are not enrolled in primary and secondary schools today.[5] For those who are enrolled, the education they are likely to receive will be vital (see LeVine, this volume) but for most of them, perversely, not enough to thrive in the era of globalization (see Cheng, this volume). These children and youth are falling further and further behind their peers in the wealthy nations.[6]

Education faces new challenges in a world more globally connected yet ever more unequal, divided, and asymmetrical.[7] For many youth

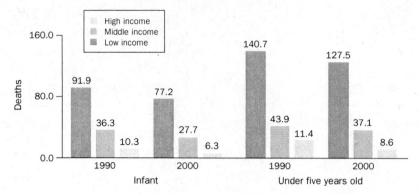

Figure I.1 Infant and under-five mortality rates in high-, middle-, and low-income countries (per 1,000 live births). SOURCE: University of California Atlas of Global Inequality.

growing up in the developing world, crippling poverty continues to define everyday life. It is estimated that every 3.6 seconds, a person dies of starvation: that person is usually a child under the age of five. The infant and under-five mortality rate in low-income countries is over fourteen times greater than in high-income countries.[8] (See figure I.1; see also www.world-bank.org/depweb/english/beyond/global/glossary.html). About 600 million children in the developing world live on less than one U.S. dollar a day (UNESCO 2006). A recent World Bank study suggests that a large proportion of children growing up in India may be cognitively impaired—largely because of malnutrition—before they ever reach school (see Pritchet & Pande 2006).[9] Global poverty deprives one billion children of the basic resources for life: clean water, proper nutrition, safe shelter, and the proper supervision required for survival and positive human development (UNESCO 2006). As a consequence, life expectancy at birth in low-income countries is on average more than twenty years less than in high-income countries (see figure I.2). Individual country comparisons reveal even more striking inequalities: the average life expectancy at birth in Malawi is 38.8 year versus 78.9 years in Canada. In other words, the average Canadian born in 2000 is expected to live forty years longer than the average Malawian born in the same year (see the appendix to this introduction for additional data on global comparisons of birth, death, and fertility rates).

Basic primary and secondary education remains an elusive luxury for millions and millions of children (see figure I.3; see also Cohen, Bloom, & Malin 2006); illiteracy remains a worldwide epidemic (see figure I.4).

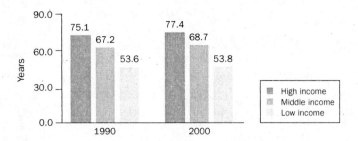

Figure I.2 Life expectancy at birth in high-, middle-, and low-income countries. SOURCE: University of California Atlas of Global Inequality; *see also www.worldbank.org/depweb/english/beyond/global/glossary.html.*

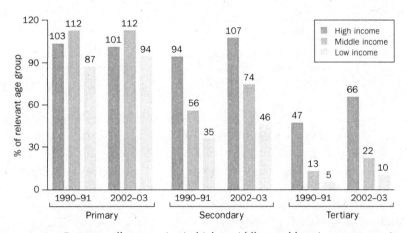

Figure I.3 Gross enrollment ratios in high-, middle-, and low-income countries. SOURCE: University of California Atlas of Global Inequality; *see also www.worldbank.org/depweb/english/beyond/global/glossary.html.*

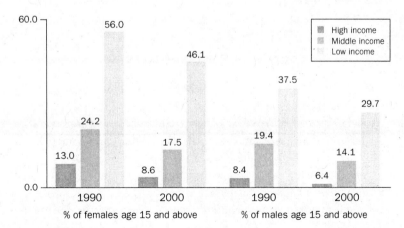

Figure I.4 Illiteracy rates in high-, middle-, and low-income countries. SOURCE: University of California Atlas of Global Inequality; *see also www.worldbank.org/depweb/english/beyond/global/glossary.html.*

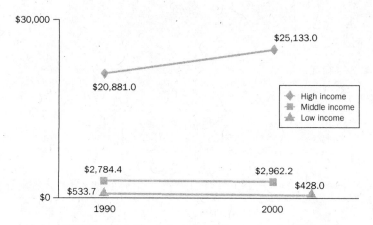

Figure I.5 GDP per capita by income level (constant 1995 U.S. dollars). SOURCE: University of California Atlas of Global Inequality; *see also www.worldbank .org/depweb/english/beyond/global/glossary.html.*

Yet everywhere today, more is asked of education. It is the Camino Real for development and a powerful engine of wellness. The data presented by Robert LeVine (this volume) suggest that education—almost any form of education that inculcates and supports basic literacy—generates powerful virtuous cycles. A recent UNICEF study concludes: "Education is perhaps a child's strongest barrier against poverty, especially for girls. Educated girls are likely to marry later and have healthier children. They are more productive at home and better paid in the workplace, better able to protect themselves against HIV/AIDS and more able to participate in decision-making at all levels" (UNICEF 2004, 1; see also Bloom 2004). The worldwide disparities in health and education mimic a massive and growing gap in income distribution worldwide (see figure I.5).

SCHOOLING AS USUAL

In the meantime, schools in most parts of the world continue business as usual. In some parts of the developing world, ministries of education continue to uncritically borrow and copy materials from the developed world that are at once irrelevant to their own realities and controversial and anachronistic in the source countries—the testing craze is but a recent example.[10] Throughout the world most schools tend to share a general orientation toward an earlier era of social organization: the early industrial moment of mass production, with the promise of lifelong jobs, in the context of bounded and homogeneous nation-states. These formations are increasingly irrelevant to the realities of both the developing nations and the wealthier nations of the North. Schools are conservative by nature: they privilege established traditions, precedent, and long-honored pedagogies. Furthermore, they are both averse and slow to change (see Hugonnier, this volume). And when change happens inside schools, it is often reactive and slow to take hold. Howard Gardner has argued that education typically changes because of shifts in values (such as from a religious to a secular orientation); new scientific breakthroughs that reorient our understanding of the human mind and learning such as the development of the new field of mind, brain, and education (see Damasio & Damasio; and Katzir, Immordino-Yang, & Fischer, both this volume); or broad historical and social forces, such as globalization. Gardner further claims that there is a new tension between the glacial pace of institutional change in ministries of education and schools and the rapid social, economic, and cultural transformations brought about by the forces of globalization (Gardner 2004).

But what is globalization? Why does it matter to education?

Globalization is the ongoing process of intensifying economic, social, and cultural exchanges across the planet. It is an ancient dynamic that perhaps originated sixty thousand years ago when humans first embarked on a journey that would take us, as a species, out of the African savanna to explore and transform the globe. Globalization is about the increasing integration and coordination of markets, of production, and of consumption. These global economic forces are stimulating the migrations of people in unprecedented numbers from and to every corner of earth. Globalization is about exchanges of cultures that make the old boundaries, as well as the aspired cultural coherence and homogeneity of the nation-state, increasingly untenable. These new global realities are challenging schools everywhere and in multiple ways. In this book we focus on two interrelated domains of rapid global change: new socioeconomic formations and new global migrations. As Kai-ming Cheng argues in this volume, there has always been a synergism between schooling and local socioeconomic realities. But economies are now global in scope and are generating unique opportunities, challenges, and constraints.

Indeed there is a rapidly expanding internationalization of production, distribution, and consumption of goods and services. Local economies are becoming integrated into complex webs of global relations. First, new global networks of production—fueled by increasing levels of international trade, foreign direct investment, migrant remittances, and capital flows, which now approximate a trillion dollars a day—set the pace for socioeconomic life in every continent of earth. Second, production is increasingly deterritorialized as certain jobs can be done nearly anywhere on earth (see Levy & Murnane, this volume). Third, over the past two decades the insertion of China, India, and the former Soviet Union into the global system of production, distribution, and consumption has added approximately 1.47 billion workers to the worldwide labor force.[11] As a result, today there are 300 to 400 million highly educated Indians, Chinese, and Russians competing for jobs with graduates from the elite research universities in the Western world. Local economic realities are now thoroughly embedded in ever expanding global networks.

Global patterns of mobile capital and mobile production, distribution, and consumption of goods and services are stimulating and accelerating international migration. With between 185 and 200 million transnational migrants, migration is now a global phenomenon involving every region of the world (see Süssmuth, this volume). Some regions are becoming important centers of out-migration (the so-called sending countries of emigration). For example, over the past decade, on average one million Latin Americans have left the subcontinent every year. Asia, likewise, is experiencing the largest human migration in history. In these regions, migration is the single most important source of foreign exchange via the international remittances sent back by workers in the diaspora. Data from multiple sources, including the International Monetary Fund (IMF), suggest that remittances to developing countries have been rising steadily. Currently, "they are almost comparable to FDI [foreign direct investment], and exceed both non-FDI private capital inflows and official aid in magnitude" (International Monetary Fund 2006).[12] For the countries of "Lesotho, Vanuatu, Jordan, and Bosnia and Herzegovina remittances represent nearly 25 percent of their GDP. The main sources of recorded remittances are the United States, Saudi Arabia, Switzerland, Germany, and France" (International Monetary Fund 2006). Indians and Mexicans in the United States, Turks in Germany, and Filipinos and Egyptians in Saudi Arabia are now the economic lungs of the countries they leave behind. Their remittances are the economic oxygen keeping countless individuals, families, and communities in their home countries from asphyxiating.

Mexico is a prime example of how some parts of the world are becoming important transit regions. (Of course, over the past century, Mexico has also emerged as an important country of emigration.) Now migrants from every continent on earth routinely choose Mexico as the

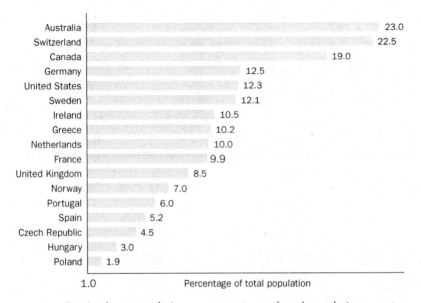

Australia 23.0
Switzerland 22.5
Canada 19.0
Germany 12.5
United States 12.3
Sweden 12.1
Ireland 10.5
Greece 10.2
Netherlands 10.0
France 9.9
United Kingdom 8.5
Norway 7.0
Portugal 6.0
Spain 5.2
Czech Republic 4.5
Hungary 3.0
Poland 1.9

1.0   Percentage of total population

Figure I.6 Foreign-born population as a percentage of total population, 2006.
SOURCE: *EuroStat 2006 (http://epp.eurostat.ec.eu).*

favored route to enter the United States—mostly without legal documentation. Yet other regions of the world—notably the wealthier,
advanced postindustrial democracies of the North but also countries like
Australia and Argentina—continue to attract millions and millions of
immigrants year after year (see Süssmuth, this volume). The United
States is in the midst of the largest wave of immigration in its history, with
over a million new immigrants per year for a total foreign-born population of over 35 million people, equaling 12 percent of its total population. In Canada, Switzerland, and Australia the rates of immigration
are nearly double the U.S. rate (see figure I.6).

In Europe a particular demographic predicament—rapidly aging populations combined with below-replacement fertility rates—are producing the threat of a deep demographic winter (see Süssmuth, this volume).
New estimates suggest that the countries of the European Union might
need an estimated 50 million new immigrant workers over the next five
generations, or otherwise face enormous labor shortages (see figure I.7)
—at a time when the immensely generous European welfare system will
need more productive workers to pay for the projected massive retirements
of the aging population. More immigration, not less, is in the future of
most European nations.

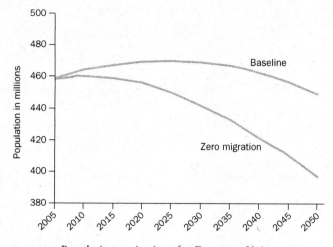

Figure I.7 Population projections for European Union twenty-five member states. SOURCE: *EuroStat 2006 (http://epp.erostat.ec.eu).*

Likewise in the United States, where immigration always generates deep ambivalence at present even as it is celebrated looking backward, further immigration is likely to be needed in the decades ahead because of a demographic predicament unfolding before our eyes.[13] As the nearly 80 million baby boomers continue to retire in growing numbers over the next generation and as the population of white European origins continues to show lower fertility rates than Hispanic minorities, the United States will face complex options. In the words of President George W. Bush, "The retirement of the baby-boom generation will put unprecedented strains on the federal government. By 2030, spending for Social Security, Medicare, and Medicaid alone will be almost 60% of the entire federal budget. And that will present future Congresses with impossible choices—staggering tax increases, immense deficits, or deep cuts in every category of spending." By then, the United States very likely will once more turn to immigration to deal with its "impossible choices."[14] Immigrant workers will once again be summoned, this time to take care of retired citizens, to pay into the social security system, and to help the country maintain its economic vitality.

Other regions of the world are also experiencing massive population movements because of globalization. The insertion of China into the global economy has led to one of the largest migratory chains in human history: over 150 million Chinese are now migrants, some migrating to other nations but most from the rural hinterlands into the rapidly globalizing coastal cities.[15]

With global migrations come new challenges to schools. The children of immigrants are the fastest-growing sector of the child and youth population in a variety of advanced postindustrial nations, including Australia, Canada, and the United States as well as Sweden, Germany, the Netherlands, and France. These new demographic realities have immense implications for education and schooling in sending, transit, and receiving countries.

But schools in many countries of immigration have been slow to respond to the challenge of managing the transition of immigrant youth. Inertia in the face of rapid change has led to many missed opportunities and outright failures. Is teaching the glories of the Gallo-Roman period to students in the Paris suburbs, most of whom originated in the former colonies of the Maghreb, the best way to engage them? Might there be more agile ways to engage immigrant students, many of whom are deeply alienated, are leaving schools without the tools to function in postindustrial France, and are increasingly gravitating to the underground economy or a life of petty crime? Maurice Crul and Rita Süssmuth (this volume) offer important insights into Europe's uneven record of managing the education of new immigrants and the transition of their children to the labor market.

New global realities increasingly define the contexts in which youth growing up live, learn, love, and work. Indeed, globalization in its various manifestations—economic, demographic, sociocultural—is a quotidian part of the experience of youth today. Theirs is a world in flux where the rate of change is of an order never seen before.[16] In cities like Frankfurt, London, and New York, youth live where global cultural flows are increasingly normative. North and South, East and West, youth are creating and exchanging ideas with others originating in faraway places; whether living in Bangalore, Brussels, or Buenos Aires, they wear similar clothing, share tastes in music, follow the achievements of today's global sports heroes— such as soccer stars Ronaldinho (a Brazilian who plays in Spain) and Crespo (an Argentine who plays in England)—and gravitate toward the same websites. This is the first generation in human history in which the fortunes of youth growing up far apart will be demonstrably linked by ever more powerful global socioeconomic and demographic realities.[17]

In addition to transnational economics and mass migrations, the high-octane fuel that gives global interdependence speed includes the information, communication, and media technologies that connect youth through exchanges of ideas, symbols, and tastes across the world instantaneously. These communication networks, especially high-speed, low-cost connections and the digitization of data, have another global effect with deep consequences for formal education: they are putting a huge premium on knowledge-intensive work and making possible the deterritorialization of entire economic sectors. Indeed, schools today need to inculcate information and media literacy skills that were not on educators' radar screens even a decade ago. As Levy and Murnane argue (this volume), from now on, tasks that are rule-based and easily broken down into constituent units can be done anywhere in the world: complex data for a tax company based in Boston can be entered in Bangalore, X-rays for a hospital in Brussels can be read and analyzed in Buenos Aires—at a fraction of the cost.[18]

Yet the ethos in most schools is anachronistic relative to the new realities animating the world of youth. Precious few schools today are organized to nurture the habits of mind, higher-order cognitive and metacognitive skills, communication skills, interpersonal sensibilities, values, and cultural sophistication needed to engage an ever more complex globally linked world. Schools continue to teach sclerotic facts and have no way of coping with the increasing ambiguity, complexity, and linguistic, religious, and ethnic diversity that defines the world. The work of education in the twenty-first century will be to nurture and stimulate cognitive skills, interpersonal sensibilities, and cultural sophistication of children and youth whose lives will be engaged in local contexts and yet will be suffused with larger transnational realities. Schools that are neither anachronistic nor irrelevant will be necessary to teach today's youth to thrive in the complexity and diversity that define the global era (see M. Suárez-Orozco & Qin-Hilliard 2004).

In March 2005 the contributors to this book convened with many other scholars, policy makers, and leaders of various teacher education programs in an international conference in Hässelby Castle outside the old city of Stockholm in Sweden. The First International Conference on Globalization and Learning (FICGL) brought together leading scholars, researchers, educators, and policy makers from around the world to examine the future of education in the global era.[19] The presentations and exchanges at the conference endeavored to clarify the educational challenges and opportunities presented by globalization and to articulate a long-term research agenda addressing these concerns. Conference participants identified research themes, and researchers in anthropology, cognitive science, communication, economics, education, neuroscience, psychology, and other fields formed collaborative, interdisciplinary discussion teams.

The conference hosted over seventy researchers, senior scholars, policy makers, and educators from around the world. These participants brought to the conference an extraordinary wealth of experience, expertise, and international stature. Conference presenters included such esteemed policy makers as Rita Süssmuth, former Speaker of the German Bundestag and former minister of youth, family, health, and women's issues; Hanna Damasio and Antonio Damasio, among the world's leading neuroscientists; Kai-ming Cheng, vice rector of the University of Hong Kong and renowned authority on education and its relationship to changing economic landscapes; Robert LeVine, senior anthropologist at Harvard and one of the world's leading scholars on the anthropology of socialization.

We purposefully chose to meet in Stockholm because, by all accounts, Sweden has come to embody many of the fundamental traits we associate with globalism: it is one of the world's most open economies, it is leading the way in new information and communication (especially wireless) technologies, it is increasingly a multicultural society with growing numbers of highly visible immigrants and refugees from virtually every corner of earth, and historically it has been one of the most equitable countries in the world. How, then, is this globally open democracy that privileges equality dealing with the profound and often destabilizing changes associated with globalization? How is it managing its extraordinary new demographic diversity? Are its schools meeting the challenge of educating all children and imparting to them twenty-first-century skills and sensibilities? To explore these and other questions, we decided that part of the conference should take place in a local school dealing with complex global realities.

In addition to the scholarly and scientific work typical of international conferences—including the development of new scholarly papers addressing clearly demarcated research problems, presentation of new and heretofore unpublished data, special keynote addresses, panel presentations, and group discussions—a working visit to a local school would allow us, we hoped, a window into the concrete realities of globalization and education that we were to discuss in more abstract scholarly exchanges. The visiting group included senior international scholars of education with research experience in Africa, Asia, the Americas, the Caribbean, Europe, and the Middle East. We spent half a day at the Tensta Gymnasium, an experimental high school outside Stockholm located in a highly segregated immigrant enclave situated next to Kista, the area known as "Sweden's Silicon Valley" for its cutting-edge information and communication technology (ICT) research and development facilities.

A SMALL UNITED NATIONS: THE STORY OF TENSTA

We chose Tensta because of its location (next to a twenty-first-century-science city), demography (children of displaced peoples from nearly every troubled spot on earth are now enrolled in the school), its global outlook and ethos, and most important, its proactive efforts to transform itself to meet the challenges of providing a twenty-first-century education to its ever more diverse student body. We visited with teachers and students and heard from the school leadership about their experiences with school change. Tensta staff and students were also invited as special guests to the conference. Our visit to Tensta helped frame and inform many discussions and exchanges during the conference, as reflected in various chapters in the book.

The Tensta Gymnasium, like many multiethnic schools in global cities, had been struggling with declining enrollments (because Sweden is an all-voucher system, some students choose to take their vouchers to more academically rigorous schools in central Stockholm), a persistent dropout problem, and an epidemic of student disengagement and boredom. At Tensta, globalization took the form of rapidly changing demographic and cultural realities. Each wave of immigrants and refugees brought with them new issues and challenges. Gymnasium principal Inger Nyrell noted in a subsequent interview: "Immigration in Stockholm has been increasing very rapidly in the past ten to fifteen years. But the groups that come here have changed. Earlier on it was people from South America, Turkey, Iran, and Europe, depending on different crises in different countries. Now we have immigrants and refugees from other parts of the world—mostly from Asia but also from Africa. These groups have different characteristics from the earlier immigrants. We now have a big group of immigrants from Somalia that is very noticeable in Tensta. They come from a very simple life in country villages in Somalia straight into the modern city life."[20]

A new reality played out in school, including a chorus of multiple languages heard in the hallways, new customs, and veiled girls in nearly all classrooms, but also comprising different cultural practices such as female genital mutilation and arranged marriages—practices that unsettle Swedish sensibilities and gender norms and push the limits of tolerance in one of the most tolerant societies ever known (see Wikan, this volume). How then is a school to create an inclusive, engaging environment to nurture its tremendously diverse new students so they may thrive in a twenty-first century global society?

The story of Tensta's transformation is itself a story of global cooperation —in this case with its sister institution, the Ross School in New York. One of the lessons of this experience is that schools do not need to reinvent the wheel: innovation can sometimes travel across oceans, languages, and cultures. An ambitious new Ross-Tensta program of collaboration had begun three years prior to our visit. Over the course of those three years, teachers and administrators from the Ross School worked closely with their counterparts in Tensta to introduce a series of curricular, pedagogical, and architectural innovations designed to enhance student engagement. Tensta chose to partner with the Ross School because the leadership was intrigued by Ross's integrated curriculum, its efforts to privilege interdisciplinary thinking and global understanding, its focus on cultural history, and its sophisticated deployment of state-of-the-art media and information technologies. Since 2003, teachers and administrators from the Ross School have worked closely with their Tensta counterparts. They visited each other's schools, and together they developed a series of workshops to guide the development of the new Tensta Gymnasium model. Over time, Tensta's curriculum, learning spaces, and approaches to wellness and nutrition began to change—a process whereby the imported ideas and practices from the Ross School were adapted to local Swedish sensibilities, traditions, and current realities and the changing student body's needs.

Infusing technology into every aspect of the school was a cornerstone of Tensta's restructuring. Each student was provided with a state-of-the-art laptop computer and access to a wireless connection network during the school day. A series of integrated units was developed, along with a new cafeteria serving balanced and ethnically appropriate meals, and interdisciplinary team teaching was introduced, requiring the cooperation of teachers whose main disciplines had been artificially separated. Intensive teacher training was provided, and teams of teachers were assigned to jointly teach cohorts of students. Partnerships with local universities and businesses began to take root. As the ethos of Tensta began to change, students began to feel the difference.

During a prior visit, a group of us spent time in various Tensta class-rooms. One of the biology classes we observed included students from Iran, Iraq, Somalia, Ethiopia, the former Yugoslavia, and Chile and a few from mainstream native Swedish homes. Nearly 80 percent of the students at the Tensta Gymnasium are of immigrant or refugee origin. (Approx-imately 40 percent of all students in Stockholm schools are foreign-born or children of foreign-born parents). The students in this classroom all spoke some English, in addition to their own home languages such as Somali, Arabic, Farsi, and Spanish, as well as Swedish. They all had their wireless PCs out and were engaged in an Internet-based research project, using their wireless computers to visit sites in multiple languages and e-mail each other across the aisles, as well as peers around the world.

The Swedish teacher told us how she had worked to integrate the biol-ogy unit with cultural, historical, and geographic materials relating to the origins of agriculture in Mesopotamia—the area of the world where many of the students originated. What struck us about this classroom was how an experienced teacher working in a media-rich environment enabled a highly heterogeneous group of students to deeply engage with complex interdisciplinary materials. The computers were a critical part of engen-dering and maintaining student focus and engagement. A student from Chile who was working closely with a classmate from the former Yugoslavia and another from Iran was excited to show one of us (Marcelo Suárez-Orozco) how she found in a Spanish-language website new data for their joint research project that they had not been able to find on Swedish-language sites. During our visit, the teacher encouraged the students to work in teams and scaffolded their knowledge so as to achieve a higher-order understanding of the problem at hand. She also encouraged the students to reflect on their own learning by subtly sug-gesting how they could apply what they had learned in other units to the new problem—hence nurturing their metacognitive abilities.

Toward the end of yet another visit to the school, we asked a (con-venience) sample of students what they thought about the new program at Tensta. The laptops, they said, were a great idea, certainly at the top of their list—along with the better food (i.e., ethnic foods) in the cafete-ria and the team teaching among the faculty. A young man from Soma-lia said, "Now we learn better because we go over similar problems from many different perspectives with different teachers." Another Somali student, wearing a veil and carrying a full load of books under one arm and her brand-new laptop under the other, responded: "We, the students, are now at the center of the school. I like the new computers, the cafeteria, and integration of subjects." By the end of the third year, word of mouth was that Tensta was becoming a "hot" school with an innovative program. Enrollment was up, and teachers and students seemed to agree that the changes were beginning to engage a highly diverse group of students in ways not seen before. When I asked a teacher how she knew her students were more engaged now, her answer said it all: "They stay working on their project during recess and don't want to go home at the end of the day."

The wholesale reform of the Tensta Gymnasium was reflected not only in students' comments and visible engagement and teachers' assessments but also in the significant increase in demand for enrollment. During a final visit, the school leadership reiterated, with the muted Lutheran pride so typical of Sweden, that Tensta, as a result of the Swedish voucher system, had been losing its brightest and best students to other schools. Now, the principal said, the school was seeing a twofold increase in the number of students who selected it as their first choice—and not just immigrant students from the neighborhood but growing numbers of native Swedish students as well. Over time, teachers began to sense a new kind of student engagement and performance displacing the former boredom and anomie that is a deadly reality in diverse student bodies in global city schools. As a result of Tensta's innovations, the school now offers regular tours to visiting delegations from all over Sweden and from other European countries dealing with changing student populations and hence with the new cultural realities of the twenty-first century.[21]

Classrooms such as Tensta's are beginning to emerge in a number of the world's global cities. Tensta testifies to the main pillars that define learning for the global era: increasing diversity; increasing complexity; premiums placed on collaboration and interdisciplinary work, taking multiple perspectives on problems, and moving across language and cultural boundaries; and the sophisticated use of state-of-the-art technologies to enhance student engagement.

Schools like Tensta are an important experiment in Europe as the old continent continues to struggle with the adaptation of its rapidly changing new immigrant and refugee populations. Whereas most earlier immigrants immediately following World War II originated in Europe and Turkey—such as Portuguese in France, Italians in Belgium, Spaniards in Switzerland, and Turks in Germany—the most recent immigrant and refugee waves have largely come from the Middle East (e.g., Iran and Iraq), central Asia (Pakistan, Afghanistan), and Africa (Somalia, Ethiopia). The new arrivals challenged Tensta Gymnasium in multiple ways. A senior administrator explained: "What happens is that when immigrants from, for example, Somalia immigrate to Sweden, it is like traveling two hundred years in time for them. The expectations and the need for education are extremely different now compared to ten years ago, when the immigrant groups were composed differently. The people coming from Eastern and Southern Europe (as well as those from South America) had a completely different kind of educational background. The new waves of immigrants from Africa have a big impact on Sweden, both in the high schools and the elementary schools. During the last ten years the composition of the immigrant students at Tensta has definitely shifted to a different kind of school background. They have a different experience, which we need to pay attention to. In many cases the students had maybe just three years of village school" (December 2005 interview conducted at Tensta).

Further, whereas earlier immigrants and refugees found plentiful work at good wages in rapidly growing postwar European industries, those jobs had evaporated by the early 1970s, and the unemployment rates in the immigrant enclaves began to soar, reaching more than 40 percent in some immigrant neighborhoods. Today and moving forward, the Swedish economy, like those of other advanced postindustrial nations, will increasingly depend on innovation in the knowledge-intensive sector; that is, in the creation of jobs that can stimulate status mobility. Formal education, therefore, will have a much more profound influence on the way children of immigrants and refugees make the transition to their new societies and, we hope, become productive and engaged citizens contributing to the collective good.

FOSTERING CULTURES OF ENGAGEMENT

Children and youth growing up today are more likely than in any previous generation to face a life of working and networking, loving and living with others from different national, linguistic, religious, and racial backgrounds. The Tensta classroom is a microcosm of the global classrooms of today. They are challenged to engage and, in new ways, work through competing and contrasting cultural models and social practices that include gender, language, and the complicated relationships between race, ethnicity, and inequality. Transcultural communication, understanding, empathy, and collaboration are no longer abstract ideals but now have a premium. It is not as simple as the one-way assimilation and accommodation models according to which ethnic, racial, linguistic, and religious minorities learn the codes of the majority society to get along and get ahead. Much more is needed: majority children, too, will benefit by mastering other cultural sensibilities and codes.[22]

An intellectually curious, cognitively autonomous, socially responsible, democratically engaged, productive, and globally conscious member of the human family in the twenty-first century cannot be educated in the twentieth-century factory model of education. The regimented mastery, internalization, and mechanical regurgitation of atomized facts and rules that served the industrial era are anachronistic. The redundancy in much of today's schooling is surely the elephant in the (class)room in the rich societies of the North, reflected in the pandemic of boredom and emotional detachment from school among children and youth in European and U.S. schools.[23] But there are even more alarming problems in schools than boredom.

The failure to properly engage, educate, and integrate large and growing numbers of racial and ethnic minorities including immigrant and refugee-origin youth is creating new threats (see Wikan, this volume). The devastating "home grown" terrorist plots and attack in London (July 2005 and August 2006) and the subsequent "home grown" terrorist plots in Canada (June 2006) suggest just what is at stake when the children of immigrants are alienated from their new societies. The fact that nearly half of the French prison population is of North African Muslim origin (a similar statistic applies to the Netherlands), a number well out of proportion to this group's representation in the general population, reveals a pattern of enormous gravity that casts an ominous shadow on Europe's future.[24]

This book is predicated on the claim that an education for the global era is an education for lifelong cognitive, behavioral, and relational engagement with the world.[25] The skills, sensibilities, and competencies needed for identifying, analyzing, and solving problems from multiple perspectives will require nurturing students who are curious and cognitively flexible, can tolerate ambiguity, and can synthesize knowledge within and across disciplines. They will need the cultural sophistication to empathize with their peers, who will likely be of different racial, religious, linguistic, and social origins. They will need to be able to learn with and from them, to work collaboratively and communicate effectively in groups made up of diverse individuals.[26] An education for globalization should aim at nothing more nor less than to educate "the whole child for the whole world."[27]

Globalization will continue to demand more of schools at a time when formal education is facing a deep malaise. In rich countries, millions of children are bored and large numbers of ethnic and immigrant minorities are leaving school without the tools to become engaged citizens in their new countries (Suárez-Orozco, Suárez-Orozco, & Todorova 2007). In the developing world, millions and millions of children and youth who should go to primary and secondary schools will not be enrolled. Devastating as these numbers are, more worrisome yet is the fact that millions of children are enrolled in what can only be called "schools of hatred," where they are mostly learning pre-scientific, pre-rational habits of mind that will do nothing to help them cultivate the skills and competencies required for productive and critical citizenship in the global era. How then should we think of learning and education in these troubled times?

PART ONE: INTERDISCIPLINARY APPROACHES TO LEARNING AND UNDERSTANDING IN THE GLOBAL ERA

In Part 1 of this book, we examine the function and responsibilities of schools to equip all youth with the skills and knowledge required to lead successful lives in increasingly complex, globally linked twenty-first-century societies. By and large, the wealthy advanced postindustrial democracies continue to fail to satisfactorily address the needs of all students, particularly the needs of immigrant, refugee, and racial-minority students. We need a new agenda for the institutional and cultural reforms that school administrators, educators, and policy makers must undertake in order to respond to the demands and challenges of globalization. We start Part 1 with a portrait of promising educational practices employed by an exemplary group of teachers in Massachusetts, and an exploration of the difficulties they encounter in their attempts to engage students in the study of globalization. This chapter offers a view of what effective twenty-first-century classrooms might look like and points to important areas of research needed to improve current understanding of students' experiences in living and learning within the context of globalization.

In the chapter "From Teaching Globalization to Nurturing Global Consciousness," Veronica Boix Mansilla and Howard Gardner of Harvard University's Project Zero share their experiences and insights about successful practice in the teaching of globalization and illuminate the obstacles that teachers may confront when endeavoring to broach such complex, often charged topics in the classroom. Through their work with students and teachers in Massachusetts schools, the authors witnessed and participated in innovative forms of student learning on focused topics of globalization. They identify strategies that educators may incorporate to facilitate students' development of "global consciousness," a term Boix Mansilla and Gardner introduce and define in this chapter. Citing specific examples, the authors claim that interdisciplinary lessons that "put students in the center of contemporary debates" and require them to investigate "real-life forces shaping the planet" nurture a grounded understanding of the meaning and processes of globalization and how it directly relates to their lives, in turn leading to their development of "global consciousness." The idea of putting the child at the center of learning resonates powerfully with what we witnessed in the Tensta Gymnasium.

Boix Mansilla and Gardner, identifying teachers' own limited understanding of globalization as an important challenge to successful teaching, delineate four core aspects of globalization that may help teachers focus their perspectives and lessons: economic integration, environmental stewardship, cultural encounters, and governance and citizenship. The goal of such lessons is "to engage students affectively in a reflection about their role as key actors in a dynamic, often uneven, matrix of economic and cultural exchanges . . . [and] to stimulate [them] to use this emerging sense of self to guide their commitments as consumers or to reinterpret their immigrant family history as part of a larger contemporary phenomenon." Thus, ultimately, the authors believe that educators must understand their responsibilities and "the purpose of the enterprise as one of nurturing *global consciousness.*"

Boix Mansilla and Gardner devote a significant part of their essay to a discussion of how various academic disciplines engage with the concept of consciousness, historical consciousness in particular. They claim that consciousness functions, inter alia, to orient humans in the place and time in which they live. This background serves to inform the authors' thorough explanation of global consciousness and schools' role in helping students develop their own. The authors' detailed breakdown of the cognitive-affective capacities of global sensitivity, global understanding, and global self provides readers with a valuable map for understanding the concept of global consciousness. Their comprehensive definition and various examples strengthen their call to teachers and schools to reinvent their roles and take ownership of the new need to assist all students in their transition to becoming worldly, interconnected, responsible global citizens of the twenty-first century.

A growing corpus of basic research on learning and understanding is emerging from the nascent field of mind, brain, and education, which promises to revolutionize our thinking about learning and its relationships to cognition and emotion. Moving forward, this new work should inform educational practices to be better synchronized with changing understandings of how humans learn. In the chapter "Understanding Cultural Patterns," Peter Gärdenfors of Lund University's Cognitive Science Department examines the processes by which humans make meaning and thereby illuminates how students learn and how to best structure lessons to achieve maximum understanding. Gärdenfors cites scientific data to support his main claim that the perception of patterns is a fundamental cognitive building block of understanding. He recommends teaching students to identify and interpret patterns rather than to learn isolated facts. Further, he stresses the importance of developing familiarity with different cultures as an indisputable reality in globally connected twenty-first-century societies. Gärdenfors's emphasis on teaching through patterns is in part a response to what he views as one of the major challenges of globalization—students' inability to make sense of and connect to other cultures.

Gärdenfors also develops a powerful argument for the use of instructional technologies to provide students with real-life simulation experiences, opportunities for visualization, and individual tutoring. He is skeptical of theories that place student exploration and independent discovery at the center of all learning. Instead he stresses that in order for students to most effectively learn to recognize patterns "that have taken scientists and professionals centuries to uncover," they must receive instruction and scaffolding from skilled and knowledgeable teachers. Gärdenfors advocates incorporating instructional technologies as a way to make patterns meaningful by anchoring them in concrete experiences for students. He closes the chapter with a reference to the ongoing debate about the appropriate role of advanced technologies in education. For Gärdenfors, this debate is a symptom of the need for increased research on student learning processes in order to further develop pedagogy based on the needs and learning styles of students in the global world. Gärdenfors's contribution highlights the value of advanced research on learning and understanding—especially new research that is becoming the cornerstone of scientific exploration in the age of new technologies and globalization.

New imaging technologies are rapidly changing our understanding of the human brain and its relationships to learning, emotions, and understanding. The connection between children's neurological makeup and their ability to learn has important implications for the structure of classrooms and for the development and implementation of pedagogy. How might research in the field of mind, brain, and education (MBE) contribute to educational innovations and provide new insights into the education of children in the globalized classroom? In their chapter, "Mind, Brain, and Education in the Era of Globalization," researchers Tami Katzir, Mary Helen Immordino-Yang, and Kurt W. Fischer discuss the historical development of the field and present two detailed case studies to demonstrate the value of MBE in illuminating children's learning and in identifying effective pedagogical strategies for the age of globalization.

An overview of MBE's growth and development sheds light on the interdisciplinary nature of the work that MBE researchers are doing to connect cognition, biology (especially neuroscience and genetics), culture, and educational practice. The authors claim that new interdisciplinary research is critical to overcoming what they identify as a key challenge in educating youth in the era of globalization: distinguishing aspects of learning that are universal from those that are unique to individual learners. Using data from two case studies—one involving reading acquisition and the other, a cross-cultural study of brain hemispherectomies in two adolescent boys—the authors conclude that "in bringing information about the neuropsychological organization of skills to bear on the design of learning environments, researchers and practitioners can improve education by understanding both the kinds of tasks presented to students and the various possible ways a learner can transform and interpret these tasks." This serves as an important call to action for scientists and educators to improve communication and increase collaborative efforts in order to put theories into practice and improve student learning in the globalized world.[28]

In their chapter, "Social Conduct, Neurobiology, and Education," renowned University of Southern California neuroscientists Hanna Damasio and Antonio Damasio explore the role of genetics and education in the patterning of social conduct. To test the prevailing assumption that both neurobiological processes and sociocultural factors are implicated in the development of appropriate social behaviors, the authors conduct an in-depth comparative study of the intellectual and emotional capacities in two groups of subjects with identical brain damage occurring at different points in life, adulthood versus childhood.

The Damasios' study includes a series of intelligence tests as well as psychological and neurological assessments used to gauge the subjects' emotional and social responses in simulated real-life situations. It advances our understanding of how the age at which brain damage occurs may affect cognition and the brain systems needed to support social knowledge and skills. In addition, this chapter's valuable data reveal how "emotions play an indispensable role in the acquisition of social knowledge *and* in the ultimate practice to which the acquisition leads." The work of the Damasios in the field of mind, brain, and education demonstrates the power of brain science to influence both educational and social policy making. It also emphasizes the immense need for continued research to better understand the link between neurobiology and education, and to create classrooms that best serve all students' diverse learning needs and styles.

PART TWO: LEARNING AND THE FUNCTIONS OF EDUCATION IN A CHANGING GLOBAL ECONOMY

In the second part of the book, we turn to a sample of basic research on the relationships between education in formal settings and rapidly changing economies and societies in the twenty-first century. In his chapter, "The Global Spread of Women's Schooling: Effects on Learning, Literacy, Health, and Children," Robert A. LeVine, an anthropologist at Harvard University, considers women's access to education in the developing world and examines the impact of women's education through a novel conceptual framework. His study of the effects of women's schooling in four countries—Mexico, Nepal, Zambia, and Venezuela—during the second half of the twentieth century focuses specifically on literacy and language acquisition and its consequences for girls and their families.

Building on the existing corpus of scholarship on the role of women's schooling for achieving gender equity and addressing health, population, and family problems (e.g., in UN declarations and UNICEF and World Bank publications), LeVine delves deep into the matter of just how school experience for girls and women actually affects socially desirable outcomes such as health, fertility, and child development. He develops a contextual and historical framework for understanding the impact of women's education in four continents. His analysis of the rapid expansion of schooling in the developing world, particularly during the last half of the twentieth century, and his thoughtful explanation of the familial and environmental circumstances that, in addition to education, may contribute to changes in health, reproduction, and child development patterns are important contributions to our understanding of global educational challenges.

LeVine's exploration of literacy and language acquisition as distinct variables in assessing the impact of women's schooling augments the earlier work of demographers and sociologists in this field. In this study, LeVine develops data that reveal, contrary to the assumptions of many social scientists, real academic skill development and retention among female students, even in the face of seemingly low-quality schools and limited school attendance. LeVine identifies specific literacy and language skills, including familiarity with the "academic register" (language peculiar to schooling and bureaucratic environments), that have far-reaching benefits for women and their families. The study develops empirical evidence that the literacy and language skills women learn in school have an impact on their ability to understand public health messages and navigate complex bureaucratic institutions, specifically hospitals. LeVine thus demonstrates a potential pathway from school attendance to changes in health, family, and child outcomes in developing countries. His argument, bolstered by an impressive data set on the impact of literacy, supports expanding the number of primary and secondary schools and increasing access to education as means of equipping women in the developing world with some of the skills they and their families will need to survive in the increasingly complex, demanding world.

Variable school quality and, especially, unequal access to quality schooling are pervasive problems that disadvantage citizens in both Western and developing countries. Bernard Hugonnier, deputy director of education at the Organization for Economic Co-operation and Development (OECD), claims that the importance of human capital in the knowledge-based economies of the twenty-first century necessitates rapid and extensive reform of education systems worldwide. In his chapter, "Globalization and Education: Can the World Meet the Challenge?" he calls for significant improvements in education and training and provides a thorough comparative analysis of the current state of education worldwide. Furthermore, he explores where the global economy is headed and what nations and international stakeholders must do to compel sluggish school systems to match the pace of global economic, technological, and cultural change. Dr. Hugonnier's premise is that the process of globalization, characterized in part by the increasing replacement of physical labor by knowledge-based skills, has direct consequences for education. Local, national, and international leaders have a responsibility to act accordingly. This chapter provides data on a variety of indicators such as lagging student performance in certain domains and the disastrous effects of persistent inequality in schooling. Hugonnier emphasizes the need for collaboration among institutions of higher learning in order to assist the global population in reaping the greatest benefits from globalization via education.

The OECD has led much of the research to determine what skills, training, and education people worldwide will require to survive and thrive in the knowledge-intensive economies of the twenty-first century. Hugonnier examines a number of OECD studies, including ones on countries leading the way in training citizens for "lifelong learning" and others on the ongoing disparities between native-born and immigrant student performance on standardized tests. These studies provide evidence of existing efforts to meet the challenges of education in a global world, and demonstrate the serious need for significantly more work. The author describes what he sees as the five major challenges of globalization for education: the need for higher-level skill development and opportunities for continuous learning; the demands of increased cultural interconnectedness; increasing social and income disparities; the responsibilities of global citizenship; and the impact of education in the developing world. He offers a sobering caveat about the dire consequences for all if countries fail to respond in a timely manner to the pressing educational demands of the twenty-first century: "Limited educational endowment and inequality in the world distribution of educational opportunities can only limit their [countries'] ability to reap the full benefits of globalization." Hugonnier ends on a hopeful note by providing government leaders, educators, and citizens with a series of thought-provoking questions to stimulate conversation and action regarding possible changes to educational practices and policies on an international level.

According to Sigmund Freud's wise maxim, love and work constitute a happy life. But the nature of work is rapidly changing under the new realities of globalization. Analyses of labor market trends and job growth sectors are critical for identifying the specific types of skills and knowledge people will need in order to compete in the global economies and societies of the twenty-first century. Considerable improvements will be required for schooling to meet the demands of global economies. Yet because formal education systems are so averse to change, an orchestrated campaign based on reliable data and conceptual rigor will be required to promote comprehensive reform in educational policy and pedagogy at all levels. The work of economists Frank Levy of MIT and Richard Murnane of Harvard University plays a pivotal role in moving this discussion forward. In their chapter, "How Computerized Work and Globalization Shape Human Skill Demand," the authors explain the major shifts in the global marketplace and advocate more widespread and diverse training in higher-level skills. Through their investigation into the impact of globalization and the computerization of work on labor markets, they answer a number of basic questions about the role of computerized work in substituting human work and identify the educational implications of today's changing economic conditions.

Levy and Murnane begin with the claim that "globalization and computerized work currently substitute for workers in similar occupations—they reinforce each other—and this reinforcement occurs in both the United States and other advanced economies." The authors then discuss the different categories of work and the specific skills required to complete work-related tasks in various domains. By dissecting work into its discrete constituents, the authors are able to explain how certain jobs—so-called rules-based jobs, governed by deductive rules and easily recognizable patterns—are easily taken over by computers, or outsourced to workers in another country, or both. At the same time, Levy and Murnane rebuff the idea that computers will eventually replace human labor entirely; they describe uniquely human skills, intellectual and emotional capabilities that include the ability to perform "expert thinking" and to manage "complex communication" tasks and that will never be supplanted by computational technologies. The authors warn against the continuation of pedagogical practices that do not help students develop "expert thinking" and "complex communication" skills, and condemn the current overemphasis on standardized testing. Alarmed by "growing inequality as significant numbers of moderately skilled workers are displaced and must compete for lower-skill jobs," they endorse a far-reaching campaign to train all citizens to compete and succeed in the global economies of the new millennium.

Kai-ming Cheng of the University of Hong Kong builds on Levy and Murnane's analysis of labor market shifts and their implications for education by looking at the changing structure and organization of work through an anthropological lens. In his chapter, "The Postindustrial Workplace and Challenges to Education," Cheng describes the nature of work in global societies and explains how new working environments and management structures and different skill requirements for workers contradict much of the training and organizational theory of the past. He focuses on the large-scale shift from the large-factory business model characterized by hierarchical management to smaller, more flexible work-places in which employees are required to work autonomously across multiple domains and to use high-level communication, problem-solving, and decision-making skills.

Cheng dedicates the second part of the chapter to identifying the main underlying assumptions that govern school structure and curriculum: labor market demands, specialization, and the importance of academic study. He effectively identifies the flaws of each assumption by pointing to data on new societal demands for postsecondary education, on how specialization causes an enormous mismatch between education and work, and on how the world of work now requires individuals to possess a new set of skills and capabilities learned both inside and outside the classroom. The author claims that "preparing young people for a definite occupation is not always a positive contribution to their future" and that "people's capacities have to go beyond occupational specificities." Emphasizing the need for "soft skill" development, Cheng points to the increasing relevance of communication and expert thinking and makes various explicit suggestions for school reform. His anthropological assessment of work and schooling adds to the growing body of research on the reforms needed for students to emerge from school equipped with the knowledge and diverse skills needed for social, academic, and professional success in the twenty-first century. Cheng concludes, "Changes in workplace structure will eventually result in fewer available *jobs*. At the same time, however, there will be almost limitless space for *freelancing and entrepreneurship*."

PART THREE: LEARNING, IMMIGRATION, AND INTEGRATION

Global demographics are shifting, and in many countries, native populations are decreasing while immigrant populations continue to grow apace. This is increasingly the case in the advanced postindustrial democracies of the Northern Hemisphere. These changes represent an important challenge and have implications not only for immigration controls but also for social, economic, and educational integration policies. Everyone, native and nonnative alike, must learn to adapt to the new, heterogeneous face that globalization is painting throughout the global cities of the world. Rita Süssmuth, former president of the German Bundestag (parliament), deploys various demographic projections and up-to-date data on migration trends to emphasize teaching all students the "intercultural skills" they need to work, communicate, and interact successfully with the diverse people they are likely to come into contact with, either in person or digitally, in today's highly integrated, technology-dependent world. In Süssmuth's view, most educational institutions are failing to adequately prepare their students to navigate in new, heterogeneous, multicultural environments, and the content and delivery of school curricula are in desperate need of revision and modernization.

Rita Süssmuth is a seasoned and widely admired senior policy player in German and European politics. She frames the general disconnect between the new demographic reality on the ground in Europe and the timid, anemic policy interventions as a matter of political will. She explains: "Based mainly on immediate economic concerns and cultural fears, issues such as investment in education and integration policies often take a back seat in order to avoid risking political capital in the short run." She cites data from the OECD's PISA study, which identified a significant gap in the educational attainment of immigrant students in many OECD countries, to illustrate how a dysfunctional educational policy has profound consequences in everyday life. The author focuses much of the chapter on defining the "intercultural skills" that she believes are critical to student development in the twenty-first century. She concentrates on the cognitive, digital, social, and emotional skills needed in today's global economies and societies and offers concrete ways in which to integrate skill-building interventions into the classroom. Turning to the Tensta Gymnasium in Stockholm, Dr. Süssmuth argues that it can serve as a model example of how a school may undergo extensive structural, pedagogical, and philosophical changes in order to adjust to the shifting demands of a highly diverse global student population. She reflects on Tensta's experiment and its many successes in meeting the challenges of preparing all students to fulfill their roles as global citizens. She closes with an urgent call for more time, investment, and research on intercultural curricula, pedagogy, and practice in order to expedite the educational reforms needed for schooling to catch up with global economic, demographic, social, and political changes.

While much works remains to be done, the experience with large-scale migration to and within Europe over the last half century has of course led to experimentation with policies and practices aimed at facilitating the social transition and integration of immigrants to their new countries. Some of this work has focused on education. In his chapter, "Globalization and Education: Integration of Immigrant Youth," Maurice Crul of the Institute for Migration and Ethnic Studies at the University of Amsterdam examines various European educational policies and initiatives designed with immigrant students in mind. Furthermore, he identifies practices that serve immigrant students as well as those that have failed and indeed may be derailing immigrant student achievement.

The successful integration of immigrants can never be a matter of simply implementing top-down policies. Hence Dr. Crul explores ways in which immigrants are using their own knowledge and expertise to develop networks and resources aimed to help ease their children's transition and meet the social, cultural, and educational challenges they might experience in the host society. This chapter compiles data about the work being done in Europe, both inside and outside schools, to respond to major changes in the demographic makeup of many cities and towns; changes requiring resources and strategies to assist immigrant youth's mastery of new languages, cultures, and educational and social environments.

In his essay, Crul develops the argument that the skills, knowledge, and "human capital" that immigrant students and their parents bring with them from their country of origin have profound implications for their successful transition to their adoptive country. He conducts an in-depth comparison of the experiences and academic outcomes of second-generation Turkish youth above age fifteen in Germany, the Netherlands, France, Austria, and Belgium and isolates the factors that are contributing to or hindering their educational advancement. Beyond the human capital the immigrants bring with them, Crul specifically argues that the following variables are important factors in the transition of their youth: the age at which schooling begins (which is different in all the countries); the number of contact hours between pupils and teachers; the school selection mechanism; the age at which students are put into an academic versus a career track; the stigma attached to vocational programs; and the availability of apprenticeship programs. Each of these shapes the likelihood of an immigrant student's success or failure. Disparities in the countries' educational structures and policies related to these factors account for varying student outcomes. The author also describes a number of community-based initiatives aimed at nurturing immigrant student engagement in school and achievement. He argues that "the capital (knowledge and experience) of successful students with a migrant background should be put to use more effectively." Concluding with a reflection on the Tensta Gymnasium in Stockholm, Crul points to the increase in student-teacher contact, rather than improved technology, structure, or pedagogy (emphasized by other scholars in this book), as the defining element of change that may have helped turn a failing school into a model success story for immigrant students and families.

Immigration nearly always generates ambivalence in a society: immigrants are seen as needed for labor, but their presence raises concern about their cultural adaptation and the changes large-scale immigration causes in host societies. Are immigrants learning the new language, or are they linguistically balkanized? Are they giving up cultural practices that are incompatible with the new societies—such as female genital mutilation, arranged marriages, and inheritance by primogeniture? Controversy over appropriate and equitable responses to the social, cultural, linguistic, economic, and educational impact of large-scale immigration is not a new phenomenon. As Marie McAndrew of the University of Montreal argues in the chapter "The Education of Immigrant Students in a Globalized World: Policy Debates in a Comparative Perspective," disputes over how to best educate immigrant youngsters have emerged repeatedly during periods of globalization and large-scale immigration over the past century. Professor McAndrew focuses on three major public policy debates regarding the education of immigrant students today. She provides historical context for each of them in order to "ascertain to what extent the challenges we face today are specific to the present or can be enlightened by the lessons of past experiences, whether positive or negative." She examines three issues: the role of common schooling versus ethnocultural institutions in the integration of newcomers; the place of majority and immigrant minority languages in the curriculum; and the extent to which public schools should adapt their norms and regulations to religious and cultural diversity. She concludes that the last area is the most controversial and, in many ways, most challenging for liberal democracies increasingly confronting unsettling cultural clashes for the first time (see also Wikan, this volume).

An overview of the ethnospecific institutions of the nineteenth and early twentieth century and of today leads McAndrew to conclude that the existence of separate schools for immigrant minorities has in general tended to benefit immigrant students, through the propagation of cultural values and language (especially in earlier historical phases of large-scale migration) and, in more recent times, through the provision of academic classes at a higher level than provided by the low-performing public schools to which immigrant students are otherwise often relegated. She identifies a corpus of scholarly work demonstrating the positive impact of interventions nurturing the development of a strong self-identity as an effective road to integration. In response to ongoing discussions about the value of teaching immigrant languages in schools, McAndrew presents a host of policy options for consideration. She emphasizes the importance of keeping the conversation focused on the needs of immigrant students, but mentions the possibility of "collateral benefits" of learning a new language for native students as well. McAndrew does not attempt to provide guidelines for how to resolve the contentious debates surrounding cultural and religious diversity in European societies. Instead, she offers scholars, policy makers, and practitioners a valuable overview of five practices on a continuum and carefully reflects on those policy options that could be most damaging to immigrant children and the societies in which they live. McAndrew closes the chapter with an important caveat about the treatment of immigrant students: "They can live in two different worlds as long as they are not forced to choose one over the other or made to feel that some cultural or religious characteristics are linked to socially devalued individuals." It is critical that all members of these changing societies and, particularly, public institutions that work with immigrants understand the fragile balance that immigrant students strive to achieve, and support their transition to the new country.

The social, cultural, and economic equilibrium that liberal European democracies worked hard to achieve in the aftermath of World War II and the Cold War has begun to show signs of deep destabilization. Immigration is at the core of this new dynamic. There is a new clamor, originating in both immigrant and native communities alike, demanding new responses to the obvious failures of the status quo. There is a huge premium on creating the conditions for the coexistence of immigrants and native citizens and their effective adaptation to Europe's new linguistic, cultural, and demographic realities. Eugeen Roosens, Belgian anthropologist of immigration at the Catholic University of Leuven, examines the question of first language and culture in Flanders, Belgium, and highlights one of a series of pivotal issues regarding the interplay between effective integration of immigrant youth and respect for immigrant languages and cultures. In his chapter, "First Language and Culture Learning in Light of Globalization: Muslims in Flanders, Belgium," Roosens describes the current state of what he terms "intercultural education" in Belgium and distinguishes between the reality of current efforts and the ideal content and pedagogy advocated by the immigrant community via the Flanders Forum of Ethno-Cultural Minorities. His careful dissection of the flaws of current work to assist immigrant students' identity formation through language and culture classes has broader implications for all efforts within this arena. He offers important recommendations for how to reach the fine balance of teaching students both native and second language and culture.

Dr. Roosens examines the current xenophobic attitudes in European politics and media—a dynamic significantly shaping policy debates on immigration and integration while also obscuring important issues such as the most appropriate options for immigrant education. He describes the fall from grace of such concepts as "multiculturalism" and paints a worrisome picture of a climate quite hostile to the reforms and innovation urgently needed in immigrant education. Pointing to polarization that has led to a lack of cultural critique in Flanders, something he attributes to the persistence of a liberal fear of offending any culture, Roosens concludes that a general failure to seriously discuss cultural identity and rights, particularly in a time of interethnic tension, is doing considerably more harm than good. The author's discussion of the value of cultural critique has particular significance in light of his recommendations for first-language and culture courses, given the Flemish government's multiple missteps in this area. He criticizes the use of teachers from immigrant students' countries of origin, who are often ill prepared, have limited knowledge of the Dutch language or of Flemish traditions, and typically lack familiarity with the students' local social realities in Northern Europe. Furthermore, he blames federal and regional policy makers who "continue to leave the youngsters in the hands of the imported traditional sectors as far as knowledge of their culture, language, and history of their religion is concerned, . . . [with] no rational, critical counterweight whatsoever." For Roosens, developing a means for the integration of immigrants that helps them to both preserve and critique cultural traditions is no longer a choice for countries whose immigrant populations continue to grow. He presents ideas for moving this agenda forward and warns of the potential consequences if politicians and other members of society continue to turn away from the cultural realities in which they live.

Unni Wikan of the University of Oslo takes Roosens's warnings one step further in her chapter, "Rethinking Honor in Regard to Human Rights: An Educational Imperative in Troubled Times." What is at stake if we fail to integrate immigrant youngsters? In her contribution, Dr. Wikan describes the deadly results of the failure to seriously engage, critique, and outlaw cultural practices that violate an individual's human rights. Wikan, an eminent Norwegian anthropologist with extensive fieldwork experience in the Middle East, Asia, and Europe, examines the "honor killing" of Fadime Sahindal as a cultural paradigm of a death foretold, illustrating the deep ideological conflicts that many liberal European democracies have been forced to contend with—and that they have increasing difficulties in managing as a result of growing immigrant populations with foreign cultural practices that are unsettling to local sensibilities. Wikan, in an ethnographic *j'accuse,* decries the Scandinavian governments' prolonged passivity and lack of response to repeated violations of individual rights in the form of forced arranged marriages and even honor killings, and uses Fadime's own testimony prior to her death to highlight the enormous failure to integrate immigrants into European society. In this chapter, the author claims that a fear of cultural critique, lack of effective legislation in response to unfamiliar cultural practices, and anemic efforts to facilitate immigrant integration and adaptation are the primary causes of an estimated twenty-five honor-killing deaths over the past twenty years.

Wikan's extensive experience as a social anthropologist working with Muslims in multiple settings in many countries frames her deep understanding of an "honor code" as the basis of the right of the collective over the individual in many societies in Eastern Europe, the Middle East, North Africa, and South Asia. She thoroughly describes the cultural models and social practices at the heart of the honor code and explains how immigration to modern liberal democracies such as Sweden, where Fadime lived for a long time before being murdered by family members, does not mean that these deep cultural formations are automatically or easily shed. In fact, globalization in the form of inexpensive, widely available, and instantaneous Internet communication technologies has contributed to the perpetuation of clan hierarchies, transnational decision making, and enforcement of certain traditions, including honor killings and forced marriages.

Wikan uses Fadime's case, in part because it is a particularly poignant example for illustrating the complexities of current European struggles with cultural contact and transculturation—and lack thereof. Indeed, the case suggests that even in seemingly integrated communities the gulf marking cultural divides can be enormous. Fadime's cultural tragedy suggests that the continuation of tribal practices such as honor killings does not simply occur in immigrant families that appear to be cut off from "mainstream" society and economically marginalized. Fadime's family lived in an integrated city, not an immigrant enclave, and her father had worked for a small Swedish company with Swedish colleagues for almost twenty years. The case demonstrates that socioeconomic integration does not automatically translate into cultural integration. Fadime ominously identified this very issue early on and emphasized the need for policies and practices aimed at improving outreach and integration of immigrants in order to bridge a deep cultural divide. For Wikan, at the root of the problem is that cultural practices that value the collective good over individual freedom and liberty have been left unopposed by European governments for too long. Although certain governments have begun legislating to protect individual rights and to respond aggressively to illegal activities, change is often slowed by fear of cultural insensitivity. Wikan offers a formula for overcoming the apparent obstacles to outlawing certain traditional cultural practices: "By delinking honor from violence and reconnecting it with human rights, we can transcend barriers between cultures and form an agenda for our time." In shifting the discussion from collective rights to human rights, Wikan hopes to galvanize individuals and policy makers to take action to prevent further loss of individual life and liberty. All stakeholders working on immigrant and refugee education in the advanced postindustrial democracies of the West should read her chapter carefully.

This book contributes to the nascent body of scholarly research on globalization and education. Its broad scope paints for readers the breadth and depth of globalization's challenge to education and its impact on nations, communities, and individuals. All global citizens are now implicated in the struggle to create better-integrated, more egalitarian and just societies. Furthermore, each chapter identifies research questions vital to advancing understanding of the implications of globalization. The volume calls on scholars across academic disciplines to take on these issues at a most critical time in history.

Learning in the Global Era is the result of a long-standing intellectual debate and of multiple exchanges that originated at the FICGL in March 2005 and continue in various forms today. This project has brought together scholars, researchers, educators, and policy makers from around the world to examine how globalization is changing the educational landscape and discuss what schools and allied institutions can and must do to prepare youth to live in the global era. The chapters that constitute this volume were originally presented as lectures or presentations at the conference, and were chosen for inclusion for their particular relevance in advancing the conference's mission to clarify the educational challenges and opportunities presented by globalization and to generate a long-term international research agenda that directly addresses these concerns.

The Tensta Gymnasium served as a learning laboratory where conference participants came to reflect in situ and in conversations with students, teachers, and administrators about one school's struggles to redefine education for all in light of new global realities. That experience left a powerful impression on all participants; indeed, many of the contributing authors cite the Tensta Gymnasium in their work, each commenting from her or his own scholarly vantage point and each reflecting on a different aspect of the school's design, focus, pedagogy, or philosophy. Tensta is a work in progress that already stands as a beacon of hope and possibility for effectively educating all students and especially facilitating the integration of immigrant and refugee-origin youth in their adoptive country; however, the stark contrast between this school and the school environment and forms of instruction the majority of students, particularly refugees and immigrants, currently receive the world over reminds us of just how much work is ahead.

Reforming education to be more in tune with global reality will require focused energy, commitment, creativity, political will, and resources on local, national, and international levels. The political class, policy makers, opinion shapers, business leaders, teachers, parents, and concerned citizens alike must be inspired and galvanized to take on the arduous work of dismantling an increasingly anachronistic system and creating educational systems in sync with the realities of the global era. The Tensta experience described here suggests that there is no educational reform on the cheap: educating poor, immigrant, and refugee-origin youth for the global era cannot be done without the political consensus to support expensive interventions such as longer school days, significant technological investment, and intensive teacher training and mentoring. This is the Achilles' heel of the No Child Left Behind Act in the United States, a largely unfunded federal mandate. However, our children cannot wait for the political will and much needed funds to catch up with the current demands of the global society. Schools can and must begin to take the necessary steps to provide all students with the learning and skill-building opportunities they need to survive and thrive in the twenty-first century.

The challenges to implementing a resource-intensive model such as Tensta are numerous, and the unique commitment on the part of Sweden's political, business, and education leadership to provide additional resources to schools serving lower-income and high-need student populations is not likely to be duplicated in other countries, at least in the short term. There are, however, a number of core elements common among many promising school models—some of which have been discussed in depth by the contributors to this volume—that are more easily replicated by school staff and require less up-front financial investment. Specifically, restructuring curriculum and pedagogy to place student engagement at the very center of learning offers one potentially effective remedy to the overwhelming issue of student boredom that pervades classrooms across the globe. Lessons that are grounded in events and issues relevant to students' lives and built on key concepts and pattern recognition, as suggested by Boix Mansilla and Gardner and by Gärdenfors in this volume, signify one concrete change educators can implement collaboratively across the school. Ongoing and nearly instantaneous feedback has proven to be another successful and relatively inexpensive technique that teachers can use to promote and maintain students' engagement in their learning and in their progress. Using a host of evaluation and communication methods, teachers, parents, and students can partner in tracking a student's development and collaborate in devising strategies to support continued academic growth. Finally, a clear narrative of the school's basic mission and a shared sense of purpose among students and school personnel have been cited as major factors likely to generate successful results with immigrant, refugee, and other minority youth. These practices represent just some of the countless adjustments schools can begin to make in their journey to providing a twenty-first-century education.

Research on the dynamic relationship between globalization and education and its consequences for society at large is critical to fostering public debate and stimulating work grounded in empirical evidence, conceptual clarity, and an empathic vision of a more just, equitable, and humane global world. This book represents, we hope, a step toward beginning this journey by identifying important issues and laying the groundwork for the development of a reform agenda. All stakeholders must understand their roles and responsibilities in effecting fundamental changes in education worldwide and must embrace the opportunities this monumental task offers.

GLOBAL COMPARISONS OF FERTILITY, BIRTH, AND DEATH RATES

Table I.1 Fertility rates in high-, middle-, and low-income countries

	1990	2000
High income	2.1	1.9
Middle income	3.5	2.8
Low income	5.5	4.6

SOURCES: *University of California Atlas of Global Inequality*; World Bank Development Report 2000; World Bank Development Indicators 2002.
NOTE: Total births per 1,000 women.

Table I.2 Birth and death rates in high-, middle-, and low-income countries

	Birth rate		Death rate	
	1990	2000	1990	2000
High income	16.5	13.5	7.7	7.6
Middle income	26.8	21.9	8.2	8.1
Low income	39.9	34.3	14.3	13.7

SOURCES: *University of California Atlas of Global Inequality*; World Bank Development Report 2000; World Bank Development Indicators 2002.
NOTE: Crude figures per 1,000 people.

NOTES

We are thankful to Juliana Pakes of the Institute of Globalization and Education for Metropolitan Settings (IGEMS) at New York University for her masterful work in developing the graphs and charts for this chapter.

1. See, for example, Benedict 1938; Ogbu 1982.
2. See Noguera 2003, p. 2
3. PISA is an internationally standardized assessment jointly developed by participating OECD countries and administered to fifteen-year-olds in schools. The survey was implemented in forty-three countries in the first assessment in 2000, forty-one countries in the second assessment in 2003, and nearly sixty countries in the third assessment in 2006. Tests are typically administered to between 4,500 and 10,000 students in each country.
4. See Noguera & Wing 2006.

5. The Global Fund for Children estimates that approximately one in five children worldwide are not enrolled in school; see www.globalfundforchildren
.org/pdfs/gfc_schools_scholar.pdf.

6. Joel Cohen writes, "It is difficult to estimate how many school-age children
are being educated well. The available educational statistics are so poor that the
World Bank does not even attempt to estimate primary or secondary net enrollment ratios for the world as a whole. The best guesses suggest that late in the
twentieth century, about three-quarters of the children eligible to attend primary
schools in the poor countries did so. The 130 million children who were not
enrolled in primary schools were disproportionately girls and were mainly illiterate. A much smaller fraction of secondary-school-age students are enrolled in
school or receiving other education. In 1999 the World Bank estimated that among
people 15 to 24 years of age in the low-income countries, 23 percent of males
and 41 percent of females are illiterate. These young adults are not well equipped
for a rewarding life." See www.amacad.org/blvlivn2/blvlivn2_28b.aspx. In addition, an untold number of youth are educated in formal settings, such as the
madrassas in central Asia and the Middle East, where they are, at best, learning
stereotypes and pre-rational and pre-scientific ideas and, at worst, hatred.

7. Inequality is growing both within and across many countries. For example, *The Economist* reported that "since 2001 the pay of the typical worker in
the United States has been stuck, with real wages growing less than half as fast
as productivity. By contrast, the executive types gathering for the World Economic
Forum in Davos in Switzerland next week have enjoyed a . . . bonanza. If you look
back 20 years, the total pay of the typical top American manager has increased
from roughly 40 times the average—the level for four decades—to 110 times the
average now." See Globalisation and the rise of inequality: Rich man, poor man
(2007).

8. See appendix A for definitions and lists of countries.

9. Pritchett & Pande 2006.

10 In the United States, for example, the No Child Left Behind Act has put
high-stakes testing at the center of everyday practices in schools. Testing is no
longer a means but an end in the current education ethos.

11. See Freeman 2006.

12. See International Monetary Fund 2006.

13. See, for example, Glendon 2006.

14. Quoted in ibid.

15. See Murphy 2002. See also Huang & Zhan 2005.

16. Giddens 2000.

17. While much of the concern in globalization and education is over competition—how the United States, for example, can maintain its global edge—competition is in fundamental ways the least of our problems. In today's globally
interconnected world, issues that place youth at risk in Baghdad or Kabul can lead
to disaster in Madrid or New York. Competition is yesterday's problem; collaboration in solving global problems that do not respect national boundaries takes
new urgency in the era of globalization.

18. For a journalistic account, see Friedman 2005.

19. The FICGL built on the momentum generated by the Harvard-Ross Seminar on Globalization and Education held in Cambridge, Massachusetts, in 2002 and the accompanying book, *Globalization: Culture and Education in the New Millennium* (University of California Press and Ross Institute, 2004). In that work, the contributors identified the four ways in which globalization is impacting precollegiate education: (1) by stimulating large-scale migrant flows that result in growing numbers of immigrant and refugee-origin children worldwide (see M. Suárez-Orozco and Qin-Hilliard 2004; C. Suárez-Orozco 2004); (2) by stimulating economic changes that integrate production and distribution of goods and services into ever more complex networks of relationships (see Coatsworth 2004; Bloom 2004); (3) by the now ubiquitous information, communication, and media technologies that are reshaping how children and youth learn and place a high premium on knowledge-intensive work (see Turkle 2004; Battro 2004); and (4) by stimulating cultural flows and counterflows that deterritorialize cultural practices from their traditional moorings in nation-states (see Watson 2004; Jenkins 2004; Maira 2004; C. Suárez-Orozco 2004). That work focused closely on the scholarship of U.S. social scientists and involved mainly the perspectives of academics at Harvard and MIT.

The FICGL expanded our understanding of globalization and learning in various ways. First, it involved a more international chorus of voices informed by basic interdisciplinary scholarly work in a range of settings including Africa, the Americas, Asia, Europe, and the Middle East. Second, it involved the voices and perspectives of policy makers who face difficult choices when dealing with ever more complex educational options. Third, it included perspectives informed by the experiences of a high school, the Tensta Gymnasium in Sweden. The Tensta case is a paradigm of the challenges that globalization poses to learning and education in an advanced postindustrial democracy that privileges equality and quality in learning opportunities and an ethos of egalitarianism. Tensta is also an open laboratory for examining one school's efforts to better educate a vastly diverse student body (80 percent of its students come from immigrant and refugee-origin homes) while attempting to integrate state-of-the-art information, communication, and media technologies to impart twenty-first-century skills to the student body. It is also a setting proactively working to make cultural difference an asset for rather than a threat to learning. The consensus among the participating scholars was that the visit to the gymnasium and presentation of the Tensta case study were among the highlights of the conference.

20. From interviews conducted in Swedish at Tensta School over several days in December 2005. Marcelo M. Suárez-Orozco developed the interviews, which were translated by Marianne Nielsson, then of the Ross Institute.

21. Innovations such as Tensta's are quite expensive. In the case of Tensta, a particularly Swedish model of consensus between stakeholders—the school's leadership, the political class, and the business community—came together to develop a formula whereby one of the neediest schools receive more funding.

22. See Sommer 2002.

23. See C. Suárez-Orozco & M. Suárez-Orozco 1994.

24. See C. Suárez-Orozco & M. Suárez-Orozco 2001. See also Süssmuth 2005. For a journalistic account of the schooling of immigrant and refuge-origin youth in Germany, see Robelen 2005.

25. See C. Suárez-Orozco, M. Suárez-Orozco, & Todorova 2007.

26. See Gardner 2004 and Organization for Economic Co-operation and Development 2005.

27. These are the very words George Lakoff used to describe the Ross School in New York.

28. The authors also offer a thoughtful caveat about the dangers of public misunderstanding and misuse of MBE research. In calling for improved public dissemination of scientific findings, they caution that, while this emerging field promises to advance knowledge, a significant amount of research remains to be done and increased collaborative and practical work is necessary between teachers and neuroscientists before the new data and conceptual work can be widely applied to practice.

REFERENCES

Battro, A. (2004). Digital skills, globalization, and education. In *Globalization: Culture and education in the new millennium*. M. Suárez-Orozco and D. Qin-Hilliard, eds. Berkeley and Los Angeles: University of California Press; Cambridge, MA: Ross Institute.

Benedict, R. (1938). Continuities and discontinuities in cultural conditioning. *Psychiatry* 1, 161–167.

Bloom, D. (2004). Globalization and education: An economic perspective. In *Globalization: Culture and education in the new millennium*. M. Suárez-Orozco and D. Qin-Hilliard, eds. Berkeley and Los Angeles: University of California Press; Cambridge, MA: Ross Institute.

Coatsworth, J. (2004). Globalization, growth, and welfare in history. In *Globalization: Culture and education in the new millennium*. M. Suárez-Orozco and D. Qin-Hilliard, eds. Berkeley and Los Angeles: University of California Press; Cambridge, MA: Ross Institute.

Cohen, J., D. Bloom, and M. Malin (2006). *Educating all children: A global agenda*. Cambridge, MA: MIT Press.

EuroStat (2006). Europe in figures. http://epp.eurostat.ec.europa.eu/portal/page?_pageid_1090,30070682,1090_33076576&_dad=portal&schema=PORTAL.

Freeman, R. (2006). What really ails Europe (and America): The doubling of the global workforce. *The Globalist* (Fall). www.theglobalist.com.

Friedman, T. (2005). *The world is flat: A brief history of the twenty-first century*. New York: Farrar, Straus and Giroux.

Gardner, H. (2004). How education changes: Considerations of history, science, and values. *Globalization: Culture and education in the new millennium*. M. Suárez-Orozco and D. Qin-Hilliard, eds. Berkeley and Los Angeles: University of California Press; Cambridge, MA: Ross Institute.

Gardner, H. (2005). Organization for cooperation and economic development. In *Education at a glance*. Paris.

Giddens, A. (2000). *Runaway world: How globalization is reshaping our lives.* New York: Routledge.

Glendon, M. (2006). Principled immigration. *First Things,* no. 164 (June–July): 23–26.

Globalisation and the rise of inequality: Rich man, poor man (2007). *The Economist,* Jan. 18, p. 1.

Huang P. and Zhan S. (2005). Internal migration in China: Linking it with development. Paper presented at the IOM-DFID-CASS Regional Conference on Migration and Development in Asia, Lanzhou, China, March.

International Monetary Fund (2006). Remittances statistics. www.imf.org/external/np/sta/bop/remitt.htm.

Jenkins, H. (2004). Pop cosmopolitanism: Mapping cultural flows in an age of media convergence. In *Globalization: Culture and education in the new millennium.* M. Suárez-Orozco and D. Qin-Hilliard, eds. Berkeley and Los Angeles: University of California Press; Cambridge, MA: Ross Institute.

Maira, S. (2004). Imperial feelings: Youth culture, citizenship, and globalization. In *Globalization: Culture and education in the new millennium.* M. Suárez-Orozco and D. Qin-Hilliard, eds. Berkeley and Los Angeles: University of California Press; Cambridge, MA: Ross Institute.

Murphy, R. (2002). *How migrant labor is changing rural China.* Cambridge: Cambridge University Press.

Myers, D. (1998). The economic adaptation of Mexican-origin men, with commentary by Nathan Glazer. In *Crossings: Mexican immigration in interdisciplinary perspectives.* M. Suárez-Orozco, ed. Pp. 159–203. Cambridge, MA: David Rockefeller Center for Latin American Studies, Harvard University, 1998.

National Center on Education and the Economy (2006). *Tough choices or tough times: The report of the new commission on the skills of the American workforce.* San Francisco: Jossey-Bass.

Noguera, P. (2003). *City schools and the American dream: Reclaiming the promise of public education.* New York: Teachers College Press.

Noguera, P., and J. N. Wing, eds. (2006). *Unfinished business: Closing the racial achievement gap in our schools.* San Francisco: Jossey-Bass.

Ogbu, J. (1982). Cultural discontinuities and schooling. *Anthropology and Education Quarterly* 13(4) (Winter): 290–307.

Pritchett, L., and V. Pande (2006). Making primary education work for India's rural poor. Social Development Papers, South Asia Series, no. 95. June 2006. Washington, DC: World Bank.

Robelen, E. (2005). The great divide. *Education Week* 24(36) (May 11): 31–35.

Sommer, D. (2002). American projections. In *Latinos: Remaking America.* M. Suárez-Orozco and M. Páez, eds. Berkeley and Los Angeles: University of California Press.

Suárez-Orozco, C. (2004). Formulating identity in a globalized world. In *Globalization: Culture and education in the new millennium.* M. Suárez-Orozco and D. Qin-Hilliard, eds. Berkeley and Los Angeles: University of California Press; Cambridge, MA: Ross Institute.

Suárez-Orozco, C., and M. Suárez-Orozco (1994). *Transformations: Immigration, family life, and achievement motivation among Latino adolescents.* Stanford, CA: Stanford University Press.

Suárez-Orozco, C., and M. Suárez-Orozco (2001). *Children of immigration.* Cambridge, MA: Harvard University Press.

Suárez-Orozco, M., and D. Qin-Hilliard, eds. (2004). *Globalization: Culture and education in the new millennium.* Berkeley and Los Angeles: University of California Press; Cambridge, MA: Ross Institute.

Suárez-Orozco, M., C. Suárez-Orozco, and I. Todorova (2007). *Learning in a new land: The children of immigrants in American schools.* Cambridge, MA: Harvard University Press.

Süssmuth, R. (2005). Globalization and learning. Keynote address at First International Conference on Globalization and Learning, Stockholm, Sweden, March 17–18.

Turkle, S. (2004). The fellowship of the microchip: Global technologies as evocative objects. In *Globalization: Culture and education in the new millennium.* M. Suárez-Orozco and D. Qin-Hilliard, eds. Berkeley and Los Angeles: University of California Press; Cambridge, MA: Ross Institute.

UNESCO. See United Nations Educational, Scientific, and Cultural Organization.

UNICEF (2004). *The state of the world's children.* www.unicef.org/media/media _15444.html.

United Nations Educational, Scientific, and Cultural Organization (2006). *Poverty: The human rights approach.* http://portal.unesco.org/shs/en/ev .php-URL_ID=3905&URL_DO=Do_TOPIC&URL_SECTION=201.html.

University of California Atlas of Global Inequality. http://ucatlas.ucsc.edu/.

Watson, J. (2004). Globalization in Asia: Anthropological perspectives. In *Globalization: Culture and education in the new millennium.* M. Suárez-Orozco and D. Qin-Hilliard, eds. Berkeley and Los Angeles: University of California Press; Cambridge, MA: Ross Institute.

PART ONE

LEARNING AND UNDERSTANDING IN THE GLOBAL ERA

Interdisciplinary Approaches

ONE

**Veronica Boix Mansilla
and Howard Gardner**

FROM TEACHING GLOBALIZATION TO NURTURING GLOBAL CONSCIOUSNESS

INTRODUCTION

Over the past decade, scholarship on globalization and education has shed light on multiple ways to prepare youth to meet current challenges. It has examined the impact of immigration on children's cognitive, emotional, and linguistic development in migrant and receiving communities (C. Suárez-Orozco & M. Suárez-Orozco 1995, 2001; M. Suárez-Orozco & Qin-Hilliard 2004; M. Suárez-Orozco, C. Suárez-Orozco, & Qin-Hilliard 2005). It has mapped the cognitive and socioemotional competencies at a premium in postindustrial market economies (Levy & Murnane 2004; OECD-PISA 2005). It has advanced educational policies to narrow the opportunity gap across nations. It has revealed the potential of information technologies to enhance cross-cultural learning (Battro 2004; Negroponte 2005; Turkle 2004; Rose 2005), redefined long-standing conceptions of "international education" and "cosmopolitanism," and assessed the impact of an "education abroad" (Fail, Thompson, & Walker 2004; Gunesch 2004).

Informed by these approaches, we explore a different means of preparing the young for our fast-changing times. Working in classrooms, we give students the opportunity to examine key forces shaping lives on the planet—for example, how the accelerated traffic of capital is transforming cultural values and economies in the developing world, and how cultural identities blend and collide as migrants respond to demographic, economic, and cultural impulses. We argue that, to thrive in a globalized world, young people must understand key patterns and dilemmas facing our planet. Indeed, student learning about globalization should include more than the acquisition of knowledge about world history and cultures. Learning should be inspired by the goal of developing *global consciousness* —a mindful way of *being* in the world today.

Our observations stem from an empirical study in which twelve exemplary Massachusetts high-school teachers, with the support of peers and researchers in the study, designed model experimental units of instruction on globalization. Teachers were identified through a multiphase process: Faculty, school principals, and teacher leaders affiliated with research and development programs at the Harvard Graduate School of Education offered initial recommendations. Forty-five potential candidates were interviewed over the phone to yield a subset of twenty teachers whom we interviewed in person after classroom observation in order to select twelve.

Selection criteria included a demonstrated commitment to excellence in interdisciplinary teaching, a clear constructivist approach to instruction, diversity in the sample in terms of disciplinary background, a reflective stance toward teaching and learning, and willingness to attend a biweekly seminar and design experimental units of instruction. Ten of the teachers were or became teaching award recipients (e.g., Massachusetts teacher of the year, biology teacher of the year, Abbot Scholars award). Such awards did not inform our initial selection. The teachers served a variety of student populations in their schools. Five teachers worked in urban public schools, four in suburban public schools, two in a rural charter school, and one in a suburban public school. Seven teachers were male, and five female.

Close documentation of teacher-seminar discussions and classroom practice, supplemented with in-depth interviews and examination of selected student work, shed light on the dilemmas these educators confronted when teaching globalization, and on the need to reconceptualize the purpose of the enterprise as one of nurturing global consciousness. In what follows, we begin with a portrait of good practice in teaching globalization and an outline of the pedagogical challenges it presents. We then introduce the concept of global consciousness as a desirable long-term goal for contemporary education. In conclusion we discuss implications of an education for global consciousness and propose lines for further study.

UNDERSTANDING GLOBALIZATION:
SNAPSHOTS OF PRACTICE

For two years (2003–05) our research group at Harvard's Project Zero worked closely with twelve teachers representing a range of disciplines and serving various socioeconomic and ethnic communities. Collaboratively, we developed experimental units on globalization that were woven into teachers' regular courses and designed to expand students' learning by inviting them to examine our changing world. In a humanities course, a study of late-nineteenth-century immigration was extended to consider contemporary migration and the reshaping of cultural identities taking place in increasingly cosmopolitan cities. Students historicized their own experience of migration, borrowing insights from literature and anthropology to understand themselves and others in their largely immigrant community. In a science class, students moved beyond understanding why the climate is changing to considering local and global approaches to redistributing the indirect costs of greenhouse gas emissions. A course in dance reframed a focus on hip-hop and the use of Laban notation to spotlight an examination of transnational youth cultures. Students discussed the homogenization and localization forces at play when youth in Brazil, Japan, and the United States re-create movements and meaning in the dance. Similarly, a course in photography led students to explore how to create visual portraits that depict hybrid identities and ambient signs of globalization.

Michael K, a tenth-grade history teacher in a suburban public school, led a unit on the impact of outsourcing on developing countries. The idea for his unit emerged at an early seminar meeting in which teachers and researchers were assessing the value and viability of globalization as a focus of instruction. "Globalization is everywhere!" Michael pointed out. "It is changing our lives and the lives of our students in every way." Pointing to the label of a plastic orange juice bottle standing on the table, he read: "Orange juice concentrate from USA, Brazil, and Mexico. . . . Customer information 1-800- . . . website. . . . Se habla español."

Who picked the oranges for our juice? Michael passionately asked the seminar members. Under what working conditions and with what new opportunities? Who benefits from new patterns of trade production and consumption? Does knowing about Mexican farmers demand a new form of consumer responsibility? With these questions in mind, Michael prompted his students to investigate the transnational production of a familiar object of their choice (e.g., Apple iPods, Motorola cell phones,

Reebok sneakers, Fender guitars). Over six weeks, students investigated the impact (positive and negative) that job migration is having on job-receiving communities in Mexico, India, and China.

Group presentations provided a climactic ending to the unit. Before an audience charged with deciding whether the community should approve a new sneaker plant, each team presented the promise and the risk of building a new plant in the group's region. When the group that studied Reebok in the province of Guangdong took the floor, three students representing corporate interests sought to charm their audience with detailed descriptions of job opportunities, working conditions, and health standards. They emphasized the company's compliance with articles 4 and 5 of the Universal Declaration of Human Rights—(banning slavery and maltreatment), as well as its voluntary compliance with European standards for greenhouse gas emissions. Preempting citizens' concerns, the corporate spokespersons spoke of the hardships of Chinese migrant workers facing shifting values in society, and introduced the company's programs to help them maintain mental and physical health.

A student representing an environmental NGO's perspective explained short- and long-term consequences of deforestation on nutrition cycles and the extinction risk for endangered species such as the giant panda and golden monkey. Another student was quick to denounce Reebok's labor violations in the early 1990s, including cases of child labor, compulsory overtime, and limited freedom of speech. Her critique, that corporate principles of conduct were not being enforced on the ground, met the energetic response of a student who outlined the measures taken by Reebok to prevent new violations. The latter student described monitoring procedures in detail and Reebok's labor standards, recognized by UNICEF, *Time* magazine, and the *Boston Globe* as corporate models. Members of the audience challenged presenters with questions about the prospects for small local businesses, long-distance relationships in families, inter-generational tensions, and the impact of urban development on rural China.

After deliberations, the class approved the construction of the new plant but requested that local authorities develop stricter monitoring procedures (e.g., surprise visits) to enforce compliance with labor standards. They proposed the involvement of independent monitors represented by NGOs. In a shift from several students' initial orientation, environmental degradation was a minor concern when considered in light of economic development and social mobility. In feedback to the class, Michael pointed out this change of heart.

Michael's unit placed his students at the center of globalization's core dilemma—the inescapable association between economic growth afforded by the transnationalization of production and the destabilization of social, cultural, and natural capital that puts social cohesion and sustainable development at risk. Students' assumptions were challenged: "I always kind of thought globalization was a good thing, a sharing of ideas, lowering boundaries," one student (Jenna) said halfway through the unit. "Something most of the world had in common. Everyone has a stake in [the] world economy. But it is much more complicated. The strong, like the U.S., can easily use the weak and manipulate them . . . for higher profit, without thinking about the person working hard for pennies. In part because the person working for pennies feels he got a great deal with a new job anyway! It's a catch-22 and it will *never* get better! . . . That's it."

Michael was pleased with students' grounded understanding of the promise and perils of off-shoring. Students addressed matters of economic growth, environmental survival, and cultural and social cohesion sensibly, employing concepts and modes of thinking novel to them—from considering indicators of the investment climate and a country's GDP, to interpreting data on social mobility and biodiversity. What was striking about this unit is how effectively it raised students' awareness of the global connections present in their daily lives. "They owned the problems that they studied in a deep way," Michael explained as he described the unit as being about today, about the products the students buy, the world in which they live, and ultimately about themselves as participants in such a world.

"I went right home, turned over all the dishes in my house, and found that they were all made in Malaysia. Pretty much everything in my house seems made in Malaysia!" commented one student, exhibiting a new sensitivity for transnational production and lamenting knowing "almost nothing" about the people who made the dishes on which she eats. Another student noticed that her father's latest issue of *Time* magazine had a special report on China's record economic development. "It was exciting —I was feeling like reading *Time* magazine cover to cover. I asked Dad if I could borrow the magazine . . . he was surprised and glad."

TEACHING GLOBALIZATION:
OPPORTUNITIES AND CHALLENGES

As Michael's example illustrates, teaching globalization places students at the center of contemporary debates—the immediacy of which they begin to recognize in the products they purchase and the newsstands they walk past. Globalization is in the air, and by treating it explicitly as a phenomenon for exploration, students learn to recognize the symptoms of a changing planet. They reflect on their experiences outside of school with the aid of conceptual tools and perspectives that challenge or expand their initial commonsense intuitions. Teachers in our group recognized the opportunity to enhance the contemporary relevance of their curricula. Although exciting, designing quality instruction about globalization presented abundant pedagogical conundrums.

Finding Focus in a Ubiquitous Phenomenon

At multiple points, teachers' experience of globalization was complicated by its hyperconnectivity. As a member of the group put it, "It relates to all disciplines, all places, and all cultures . . . all sections of the *New York Times*." Identifying a feasible focus for instruction became teachers' first challenge. What about globalization, exactly, was worth teaching and why? The problem of finding a workable focus was exacerbated by teachers' partial and unsystematic understanding of globalization. Members of the group spoke past one another as different teachers emphasized distinct focal points: the post–Cold War zeitgeist, the decline of the nation-state, imperialism, McDonaldization, the Internet, migration, outsourcing, and so forth.

To support teachers' decisions about focus and offer a common ground for exchange, our group developed a conceptual map highlighting four core problem areas that embody globalization's central tensions and dilemmas for inquiry: *Economic integration* emphasized the opportunities and costs for economies, societies, cultures, and individuals associated with the flux of capital and production around the globe. (Michael's unit focused on this quadrant of our conceptual map.) *Environmental stewardship* concerned the state of the global environment (including global health) and what we can and should do to ensure its long-term sustainability and well-being. *Cultural encounters* focused on the forces of homogenization, hybridity, and localization that shape how nations, cultures, and smaller groups exchange ideas, people, and cultural products. *Governance and citizenship* referred to emerging tensions between national and supranational forms of government, as well as the extent to which individuals enjoy global rights and bear responsibilities as a function of their humanity.

Scholarly work on globalization in economics, anthropology, sociology, law, and philosophy informed our understanding of each problem area. By placing their unit designs primarily within one problem space, teachers were able to locate their interests and instructional emphasis in relation to those of others on a common conceptual landscape. They were also able in each unit to focus selectively on aspects of everyday experience (e.g., consumer products, migrant friends, hip-hop music).

Helping Students Understand Culture

Cultural globalization is a familiar experience for teachers and students alike, even though it is unrecognized as such. Visibly present in urban centers around the globe, Coca-Cola, McDonalds, Reebok, and Motorola billboards stand as reminders of the impulse toward cultural homogenization. Yet helping students understand how individuals in various cultural contexts make sense of these icons differently presented an unprecedented challenge for teachers.

The difficulty had multiple roots: Students were often anxious as they addressed issues of "culture." They tended either to minimize cultural differences or to feel paralyzed by the fear of producing politically incorrect accounts. Teachers felt anxious about helping students understand human experience in cultural contexts with which they were themselves unfamiliar. In their work, competing definitions of "culture"—often echoing debates in anthropology (Borofsky 1994)—led them to ponder whether we can we talk about a "Chinese culture," equating one culture with one society, seeking coherence across clearly dissimilar subsystems of beliefs. Conversely, can students understand the personal meaning-making act by which hip-hop dancers perform in the Brazilian *favelas* or workers punch their timecards at a Guangdong Reebok factory without placing the *favela* and the factory in a broader context—a more stable and cohesive set of beliefs and values? In watching their students learn, teachers also considered the degree to which intercultural understanding means *having information* about how others lead their lives and whether it should also require engaging affectively with others' experience. And if the latter is the case, is emotional engagement an illusion of understanding?

Fostering intercultural understanding presented visible difficulties to the teachers in our group; the solutions that we considered only partially addressed the issue. The more successful teachers often met the challenge by leading students to wear an anthropologist's hat. For some, the cultural frameworks under study were visibly represented in students' immigrant communities. Teachers invited students to observe familiar phenomena—a family dinner, the photographs on display at a friend's house—in search of indicators of cultural affiliation and hybridity. Students interviewed migrant friends and neighbors, inquiring about the motivations, emotional trade-offs, and experiences of immigration and uncovering the meaning that family dinners or photographs had for them. While some students embraced the discovery of such an "interpretive approach" to familiar phenomena with excitement—often overusing their budding interpretive skills—others found the task daunting.

Teachers charged with helping students understand how individuals make sense of globalization in far-flung contexts (e.g., Guangdong, São Paulo, or Oaxaca) lacked occasions to engage students in palpable intercultural interactions. Hoping to advance textured understandings of these cultural actors' experiences, they supplemented information about social structure, cultural values, and practices with close analysis of regional films and works of literature. Our analysis of student work and interviews with students revealed the power of film and literature to inform students' cultural imagination. In some cases, it also revealed the risks of confusing fact and fiction.

Helping Students Construct Membership

In studying globalization, students often felt overwhelmed by the magnitude of the phenomenon under study, its ubiquity, and the human drama that characterizes a world where two-thirds of the population live on less than two dollars a day and where the rise in atmospheric temperature approaches a point of no return. Feeling unable to respond individually or locally in constructive ways, students were often inclined to defer responsibility for action to others (e.g., governments, the UN, other nations and cultures, the international criminal court). Teachers struggled to help students position themselves in a global matrix somewhere between disengagement and paralyzing overload. Jenna's aforementioned perception of the impact and process of outsourcing as a "catch-22" for which "nothing can be done" illustrates the point.

Responding to this challenge, teachers in our study chose to present concrete options for participation. A schoolwide exhibit of art addressing "inequality and the global supermarket" allowed students in one class to use art to make a statement "about the things we take for granted and the people who make them." Another group studying global climate change sought ways to reduce energy consumption in daily life. Team members examined the possibility of lending home and school computer power to a group of global climate scientists in Britain who use distributed computing to make future climate projections (Bohannon 2005; www.climatepredictions.net). "Being part of it" was their reward. In a unit on human rights, students learned to post their thoughts on a public website—"making them visible to the world"—and to design memorials that invited visitors to remember past abuses and achieve reconciliation. The options that Michael's students generated ranged from contacting a corporate CEO to discussing the tensions between economic growth and working conditions, to revising their personal consumption patterns.

THE CONSCIOUSNESS TURN

Units of study like the ones here described present students with opportunities to examine a particular aspect of globalization in depth. Their instructional designs called on students to employ disciplinary concepts and modes of thinking to learn not only *that* Motorola's factories in India are transforming local economies but also *how* and *why* this transformation is taking place. Attending to key dimensions of analysis (e.g., corporate interests, economic growth, social-cultural cohesion, the environment), students used economics concepts to understand how incentives shape corporate behavior; alternatively, they borrowed methods from anthropology to explore how people in cultures other than their own perceive change. By offering a way of reasoning about outsourcing, Michael and his colleagues furnished students with interpretive frameworks with which to move beyond the particular case in question (e.g., Reebok in China) and ask informed questions when confronted with comparable phenomena (e.g., outsourcing in India).

Yet units like Michael's went beyond careful analysis of aspects of globalization, the deployment of disciplinary constructs, and the construction of complex explanations. By focusing on consumer products students hold dear and problematizing their roots in transnational production, Michael's unit drastically redrew the line that divides schoolwork from the work of life. It alerted students to a changing reality around them, sharpening their sensitivity for the ways the global economy is increasingly present locally. The unit engaged students affectively in a reflection about their role as key actors in a dynamic, often uneven matrix of economic and cultural exchanges. In doing so, the unit challenged students to begin to place them-selves (their individual life stories, their likes and dislikes) in a broader global context; they were stimulated to use this emerging sense of self to guide their commitments as consumers or to reinterpret their immigrant family history as part of a larger contemporary phenomenon.

We came to a key realization. Beyond its stated goal of advancing stu-dents' *understanding* of globalization, Michael's unit embodied a more ambitious, if tacit, aspiration: to nurture students' *global consciousness* —a disposition to place their immediate experience in the broader matrix of developments that shape life worldwide, to construct their identities as members of world societies, and at least in some instances, to orient their actions accordingly. Tacitly, our teachers sought to prepare students to be reflective agents and actors—citizens of today and tomorrow. But what is consciousness? How can global consciousness best be defined? How can such a private phenomenon be made visible in contemporary classrooms?

THE PROBLEM OF CONSCIOUSNESS

Conceived as a capacity that defines us as a species, consciousness has cap-tured the inquisitive imagination of scholars in philosophy, psychology, history, and neurobiology alike (Damasio 1999; Dennet 1991, Rüssen 2004; Seixas 2004, Wineburg 2001). Neuroscientist Antonio Damasio describes the higher order of human consciousness as a complex mental capacity that enables the construction of an autobiographical self.[1] In Damasio's view, such capacity develops throughout our lifespan as we encounter objects and experiences in our environment such as another person, a melody, a toothache, or a state of bliss. We generate mental rep-resentations of these objects and rearrange them in the form of concep-tual frameworks that organize what we know. We also record our experience of such encounters—the feeling of them. In doing so, we become increasingly aware of the relationship between these objects and our self—coming to understand ourselves, autobiographically, as know-ers, feelers, and actors in interaction with our environment (e.g., our likes and dislikes, how we tend to experience an opera, how we tend to engage in relationships). This autobiographical consciousness serves as a compass to orient our future engagements by making knowledge about ourselves available when we confront novel objects or situations. Con-sciousness, Damasio summarizes, "places the person at a point in individual historical time richly aware of the lived past and of the anticipated future and keenly cognizant of the world beside it."

Clearly a private mind-brain enterprise, consciousness could be seen in Michael's class as Jenna commented on her "changing mind" about the promise of globalization, or as another student described herself as feeling anxious about learning macroeconomics. In both cases, perceptions of self learned over time and engraved in the student's mind/brain, informed the ways students confronted a new example of globalization or engaged in a lesson on foreign investment.

While Damasio examines the foundations of consciousness at the individual neuropsychological level, the budding field of *historical consciousness* places this capacity beyond the scope of the individual lifespan. This historical perspective focuses on how our representation of a past unfolding before our birth informs our knowledge of self in the present and orients us toward the future. Scholars in this field do not look into the brain to build biopsychological accounts of this phenomenon. Rather, they describe consciousness using units of analysis that stem from history (historical time, historical actors); the philosophy of history (memory, narrative structure); and psychology (mental representation and identity). As expressed by philosopher Jörn Rüssen: "History is the mirror of past actuality into which the present peers in order to learn something about its future. Historical consciousness should be conceptualized as an operation of human intellect rendering present actuality intelligible while fashioning its future perspectives. . . . By means of historical identity, the human self expands its temporal extension beyond the limits of birth and death, beyond mere mortality" (Rüssen 2004, pp. 67–68).

Historical consciousness places objects, events, beliefs, and people in a broader temporal framework, thereby reframing the autobiographical self. In doing so, historical consciousness serves an orienting function. Nowhere is this function more evident than in the construction of national historical identities. Consider, for instance, two ways our autobiographical self can be placed within the broader context of the American narrative of manifest destiny. We may come to view ourselves as bearers of a long-standing tradition of manifest destiny that we choose to uphold under most circumstances. Alternatively, we may view this national narrative more skeptically as entailing imperial domination and place ourselves as critics favoring compensatory actions. Historical consciousness orients us not by proposing a determined course of action but by forcing us to confront our thoughts and actions in the light of earlier events and framings thereof.

In our work with teachers, this historicization was exemplified in our ongoing discussions. We came to recognize that the wave of globalization we were exploring made it impossible for us to know, today, what our descendants will think tomorrow about the implications of the times in which we live. Such placement of our daily activities within the flux of time led one teacher to describe herself as a "pioneer" in education—a term at once embodying individual agency and shared historical time.

Whether examined within the parameters of an individual lifespan or in its historically informed reconceptualization, consciousness entails three core competencies: First is *sensitivity* toward objects in our environment (e.g., people, places, melodies, landscapes) with which the self comes into contact. Historical consciousness entails selective sensitivity for objects and circumstances that link us to past and future (an inscription on a wall, the shape of urban streets, a monument). Second, consciousness entails the competency of *organization*—the capacity to arrange such mental representations. Autobiographic consciousness distills patterns that reveal defining qualities of self. Historical consciousness, on the other hand, employs historical understanding to reinterpret experience along a continuum of past, present, and future, conferring new meaning on our experiences. Finally, consciousness entails the competency of *self-representation*—the reflective capacity to understand ourselves as knowers and feelers—and as historical actors. Through this latter competency, consciousness exercises its orienting function. Knowledge of ourselves, of what we value, of what makes us anxious, as well as knowledge of how we stand vis-à-vis the experience of generations before and ahead of us, necessarily shape the repertoire of options, commitments, and opportunities that we perceive.

GLOBAL CONSCIOUSNESS: EXPANDING OUR SENSE OF THE WORLD WE INHABIT

We define *global consciousness* as the capacity and the inclination to place our self and the people, objects, and situations with which we come into contact within the broader matrix of our contemporary world. An individual exhibits global consciousness when she is attuned to daily encounters with world cultures, landscapes, and products (e.g., through the Internet and other media and through migration); places such encounters in a broader narrative or explanatory framework of contemporary global processes (e.g., the traffic of people, capital, and ideas; shifting economic, demographic, and cultural interdependence); and perceives herself as an actor in such a global context (e.g., acting locally on global issues, using channels of transnational participation, resisting geopolitical change). In our formulation, global consciousness places the self along an axis of contemporary *space* in ways comparable to the way historical consciousness places it along an axis of *time* (Seixas 2004).

Three cognitive-affective capacities lie at the heart of global consciousness as here defined: *global sensitivity*, or our awareness of local experience as a manifestation of broader developments in the planet; *global understanding*, or our capacity to think in flexible and informed ways about contemporary worldwide developments; and *global self*, or a perception of ourselves as global actors, a sense of planetary belonging and membership in humanity that guides our actions and prompts our civic commitments.

Global Sensitivity

No person experiences globalization in its fullest complexity, but the daily lives of billions of individuals around the world are affected by this contemporary process in concrete ways. Changes in diet, work, neighbors, disease, consumption, and communications reflect novel forms of production, governance, and cultural exchange. Global sensitivity entails selective attention to issues markedly shaped by, or shaping, global interconnectedness. Daily experiences are viewed as instances of the larger world's increasing local presence.

Michael exhibited global sensitivity when he reinterpreted a bottle of juice standing on a seminar table in Cambridge, Massachusetts, as mixing physical oranges picked by workers in Florida, Mexico, and Brazil and symbolically containing stories of individual opportunity and social inequality. Michael's attention to transnational production alerts him to the lives of Mexican and Brazilian farmers whose existence unfolds well beyond his immediate reality. A globally conscious mind is attuned to such local expressions of global phenomena whether "local" is one's own doorstep or a town multiple time zones away.

Opportunities for global sensitivity abound. Cultural diversity dominates everyday life in postindustrial and developing nations alike. Film, music, advertising, and other media transport cultural symbols transnationally, rendering popular culture as a central agent in the selection and representation of things global. By redistributing jobs around the planet, transnational production is creating new inter- and intranational inequalities and social unrest, which are in turn projected on television screens worldwide. The globally conscious mind notices these, selectively, as experiences of increasing interconnectedness and tension.

Global Understanding

In addition to sensitivity, global consciousness requires an informed understanding of contemporary developments on the planet—within a framework whereby daily practices and products are interpreted and organized. Global consciousness does not mindlessly absorb, consume, or resist the products and practices yielded by accelerated global exchange. Rather, it seeks to locate them, reflectively, within credible explanations of how the world works, trustworthy narratives about how it came to be this way, and informed consideration of how local cultures mediate experiences of global transformations. Just as historical consciousness is unattainable without an understanding of history, global consciousness is impossible without an unfolding understanding of the world and the ways it is rapidly changing.

To promote students' understanding, Michael focused on student's capacity to use information in novel contexts (Cheng 2005; Gärdenfors 2005; Wiske 1999). Indeed he approached the study of outsourcing armed with intellectual resources that his students lacked. He recognized the unprecedented macroeconomic growth in countries like China and India. India alone averaged a 5.9 percent annual economic growth rate between 1996 and 2002. He recognized India's overall poverty reduction rate, which exceeds the UN's Millennium Development Goal of eradicating extreme poverty and hunger by the year 2015 (United Nations 1999). He tempered this observation by describing the distribution of wealth and opportunity. For example, in 2000, 79 percent of India's population was still living on less than two dollars a day (World Bank 2004a), and only 20 percent of the nation's poor children completed the eighth grade (compared to 82 percent of their richer peers) (Stern 2001; World Bank 2002b). Michael recognized that an account of the impact of outsourcing needs to move beyond purely economic indicators to capture changes in the overall well-being of the affected populations.[2] Examination of Motorola cell phones, Reebok shoes, or Fender guitars when placed against interpretive frameworks of this kind informs at once our understanding of the objects and our relationships with them.

Global Self-Representation

Finally, global consciousness is characterized by its power to construct a representation of the self as an actor in the global matrix. As we come into contact with people, products, or daily situations contextualized in a broader global framework, we take note of these experiences—advancing at once our understanding of the world and of ourselves in relation to it. We become aware of the inclinations, relationships, commitments, and concerns that link us to the planet and to others in it (M. Suárez-Orozco, C. Suárez-Orozco, and Qin-Hilliard 2005). Global consciousness provides the self with a renewed sense of relationship to people and issues across personal, family, local, cultural, national, regional, and global landscapes—whether such relationship proves to be harmonic or problematic (Haste 2004; Hayden & Thompson 1989; Nussbaum 2000; Youniss et al. 2002; Walker 2002).[3]

It is by construing the self as a global actor that this form of consciousness performs its orienting function. Particular ways of positioning ourselves in our rapidly globalizing world will channel our actions in one direction or another. We may have come to view ourselves as actors promoting economic liberalization or as compensatory agents in a world of growing inequality. Such perceptions of self and world in interaction will inform how we meet novel situations in everyday life: from considering the additional cost of fair-trade products to envisioning our heightened or reduced professional opportunities.

Global consciousness does not yield *one* necessary normative path to guide practical action. Understanding the conditions leading an immigrant to move into our neighborhood does not indicate whether cultural differences or human commonalities will be privileged in our forthcoming neighborly interactions. Similarly, understanding the circumstances that enabled a foreign company to establish a new manufacturing plant in Maharashtra, India, offers workers no direct advice as to whether to seek employment there. Neither does it directly instruct Michael's students about what should be done, nationally or individually, to maximize the benefits and curtail the costs of outsourcing. Instead, our sensitivity toward, understanding of, and personal engagement with global matters provide a platform from which multiple possible courses of action can be assessed, including the option of no action at all.

A deeper understanding of economic integration and reflections on himself as a global actor led Michael to expand the perception of his own role as a teacher and of the curricular content for which he feels responsible. "I used to have things that I read for pleasure [outside the classroom] (literature, news) and things I read for [for class] (works in history and sociology)," he explained. "Now everything I read seems to be relevant in the classroom!" By teaching globalization, he argued, he is teaching about "our world, here, today, and how we live our lives." For Michael, teaching about globalization, fostering global consciousness among youth, has become a channel for global participation in its own right.

In sum, as here defined, global consciousness captures the capacity to attend to global dimensions of our contemporary experience; to reflect on its tensions, issues, and opportunities by bringing informed categories and modes of thinking to bear; and to define our identities as members of complex global political, social, economic, and environmental spheres.

AN EDUCATION FOR GLOBAL CONSCIOUSNESS: IMPLICATIONS FOR PRACTICE AND RESEARCH

We began this essay by describing our experience with a small group of exemplary teachers in Massachusetts determined to teach globalization. Then we defined global consciousness as a desirable aim of contemporary education and suggested a structure of cognitive-affective competencies on which it stands. Preparing students to thrive as members of world societies calls for teachers who view themselves as brokers between children and their rapidly changing environments—not mere conveyors of certified information. In the best case scenarios, students are exposed to a school culture of global consciousness—one in which global influences in our daily lives, the eradication of global poverty, or the puzzles of interculturality permeate hallway posters, cafeteria discussions, and student organizations.[4] In most school realities, however, not all teachers will embrace the new demand—nor should they, in our view, be obligated to do so. The postindustrial educational systems of today call for a new distribution of areas and levels of expertise in schools where a small number of trained "teacher-brokers" and a collaborative institutional ethos may be more reasonable goals, as we strive to "bring what we teach and how we teach into the twenty-first century" (Wallis & Steptoe 2006).

Admittedly culturally positioned, our observations about global consciousness as a goal for contemporary education call for further study. Advancing our understanding of global consciousness as a cognitive-affective construct demands that we come to understand its important variations.[5] For example, we hypothesize that individuals hold more or less stable *forms* of global consciousness—that is, particular ways of understanding our changing world and orienting oneself in it. For instance, some may tend to place particular experiences within stable narrative plots of single leading forces of change (e.g., the success of free markets), finding themselves as participants in this movement. Others may understand our contemporary world as one of tensions and resistances and find themselves oriented as critical of ongoing change. A psychological examination of types of global consciousness may inform the degree to which the beliefs and orientations that constitute particular forms of global consciousness operate as well-articulated belief systems or as a loose collection of sometimes contradictory ideas.

We also hypothesize that the content and orientation of global consciousness varies across cultures and regions as people situate themselves differently in geopolitical, cultural, and environmental landscapes. Thus a study of global consciousness must be cross-cultural. In the same vein, we may expect global consciousness to vary developmentally. We would anticipate that youth who have been directly exposed to experiences of globalization (as through migration, formal learning, or social entrepreneurship) may exhibit greater global sensitivity, more informed understanding, and a more nuanced sense of global self. An empirical study of young individuals of demonstrated global consciousness (e.g., those receiving awards from Oxfam, the World Bank, and Netaid) would help us understand variations in students' beliefs and commitments as we make comparisons based on age, region, and level of formal education.

To conclude, whether we peer at global consciousness through the normative lens of education or we examine it empirically as a developing psychological capacity, the most important function of global consciousness for today's individuals is to give coherence to otherwise fragmented experience. Ongoing breaking news from around the world, a fast-changing job market, accelerating intercultural exchanges, and communications innovations prove profoundly disorienting for students and adults alike. Global consciousness situates us—not without tension—in unifying narratives and explanations that help us make sense of daily developments on the planet. In doing so, global consciousness expands our human self beyond the limits of our here and now, revealing new aspects of our identity in connection to others and to the planet.

NOTES

We would like to thank the Atlantic Philanthropies for their generous funding of the Interdisciplinary Studies Project. We thank the teachers and students participating in our study and the members of our research team, who contributed to the development of experimental teaching cases. We are especially thankful to Marcelo Suárez-Orozco and Carola Suárez-Orozco for comments on this manuscript and for their shared vision about the urgency of new educational models suited to our times.

1. Damasio distinguishes this higher-order consciousness from "core" consciousness—a more fundamental capacity that, as self and object interact, provides an organism with a sense of self in the present moment and immediate place.

2. Note that in our formulation, and that of a strong tradition of domain-specific cognition, capacities such as learning to learn, problem definition, problem solving, and pattern finding are inextricable from their substantive knowledge base.

3. Like long-standing notions of internationalism and cosmopolitanism, the concept of global consciousness attends to matters of identity, awareness of cultural difference, and transnational interconnectedness. It differs from those traditional educational constructs in its selective emphasis on contemporary globalization-related issues that lie beyond a focus on the nation-state or on an ability to "feel at home" anywhere around the world.

4. For an example of current efforts toward such enculturation, see the description of the Tensta Gymnasium, the public school in Stockholm Sweden, in the introduction of this volume.

5. For comparable reflections taking place in the area of historical consciousness, see Seixas 2004.

REFERENCES

Battro, A. (2004). Digital skills, globalization, and education. In *Globalization Culture and Education in the New Millennium*. M. Suárez-Orozco and D. Qin-Hilliard, eds. Berkeley and Los Angeles: University of California Press; Cambridge, MA: Ross Institute.

Bohannon, J. (2005). Distributed computing grassroots supercomputing. Special section. *Science* 308(5723): 810–813.

Borofsky, R. (1994). *Assessing cultural anthropology*. New York: McGraw Hill.

Climate*prediction*.net. Oxford University, UK. www.climateprediction.net.

Damasio, A. (1999). *The feeling of what happens: Body and emotion in the making of consciousness*. San Diego: Harcourt.

Dennet, D. (1991). *Consciousness explained*. New York: Little, Brown.

Fail, H., J. Thompson, and G. Walker (2004). Belonging, identity and third culture kids. *Journal of Research in International Education* 3(3): 319–338.

Gunesch, K. (2004). "Education for cosmopolitanism: Cosmopolitanism as a personal cultural identity model to and within international education." In *Journal of Research in International Education* 3(3): 251–275.

Haste, H. (2004). Constructing the citizen. *Political Psychology* 25(3): 413–439.

Hayden, M., and J. Thompson (1989). *International education: Principles and practices*. London: Kogan Page.

Levy, F., and R. Murnane (2004). *The new division of labor: How computers are creating the new job market*. Princeton, NJ: Princeton University Press.

Negroponte, N. (2005). $100 laptop initiative. Paper presented at the World Economic Forum. Davos, Switzerland, January 2005.

Nussbaum, M. (2000). *Cultivating humanity: A classical defense of reform in liberal education*. Cambridge, MA: Harvard University Press.

OECD-PISA. See Organization for Economic Cooperation and Development, Program for International Student Assessment.

Organisation for Economic Co-operation and Development, Program for International Student Assessment. *Definition and selection of key competencies*. Report, June 30, 2005.

Rose, D. (2005). Teaching Every Student in the Digital Age. Paper presented at the First International Conference on Globalization and Learning, Stockholm, Sweden, March 2005.

Rüssen, J. (2004). "Historical Consciousness, Narrative Structure, Moral Function, and Ontogenetic Development." In *Theorizing historical consciousness*. P. Seixas, ed. Toronto: University of Toronto Press.

Seixas, P., ed. (2004). *Theorizing historical consciousness*. Toronto: University of Toronto Press.

Stern, N. (2001). Building a climate for investment growth and poverty reduction in India. Report presented to the Export-Import Bank of India, Mumbai, March 22. World Bank.

Suárez Orozco, C., and M. Suárez Orozco. (2001). *Children of Immigration*. Cambridge, MA: Harvard University Press.

Suárez-Orozco, C. and M. Suárez-Orozco (1995). *Transformations: Immigration, family life, and achievement motivation among Latino adolescents*. Stanford, CA: Stanford University Press.

Suárez-Orozco, M., and D. Qin-Hilliard, eds. (2004). *Globalization: Culture and education for a new millennium*. Berkeley and Los Angeles: University of California Press; Cambridge, MA: Ross Institute.

Suárez-Orozco, M., C. Suárez-Orozco, D. Qin-Hilliard, eds. (2005). *The new immigration: An interdisciplinary reader*. New York: Routledge.

Turkle, S. (2004). The fellowship of the microchip: Global technologies as evocative objects. In *Globalization: Culture and education in the new millennium*. M. Suárez-Orozco and D. Qin-Hilliard, eds. Berkeley and Los Angeles: University of California Press; Cambridge, MA: Ross Institute.

United Nations (1999). *We the peoples: The role of the UN in the 21st century*. New York.

United Nations (2005). *UN Millennium Development Goals 2005*. New York.

Wallis, C., and S. Steptoe (2006). How to bring schools out of the 20th century. *Time*, December 18, 2006.

Walker, G. (2002). International education and national systems. Paper presented at the Interpreting International Education conference of the Center for the Study of Education in International Contexts, University of Bath (CEIC/BAICE), September 11–12, Geneva.

Wineburg, S. (2001). *Historical thinking and other unnatural acts: Charting the future of teaching the past.* Philadelphia: Temple University Press.

Wiske, M. S. (1998). *Teaching for understanding: Research into practice.* San Francisco: Jossey-Bass

World Bank (2002a). Country summary: India. Research report.

World Bank (2002b). "Education enrollment and dropout." Education Labor and Employment Report, May 31 2002.

Youniss, J., et al. (2002). Youth civic engagement in the twenty-first century. *Journal of Research on Adolescence* 12(1): 121–148.

TWO

Peter Gärdenfors

UNDERSTANDING
CULTURAL PATTERNS

Nothing in education is so astonishing as the amount
of ignorance it accumulates in the form of inert facts.

—Henry B. Adams

This chapter focuses on the role of understanding in learning and, more
specifically, on the use of abstract theories to make sense of the world.
Learning a given set of facts about the world is one thing, and learning
abstract theories is another, but learning to understand how the theories
make sense of the world should be the obvious goal of education.

As a working hypothesis, I argue that *understanding consists of seeing patterns*. We find a range of abstract patterns at all levels of thinking. Some of the patterns we perceive are based on our biological
constitution, some are learned during our childhood and in formal education, and some are provided by the culture in which we live. I argue
that perception of patterns is one of humans' most central cognitive
processes. However, while relying on patterns increases our efficiency, it
can also hamper our ability to approach situations—especially multicultural encounters—with an open mind.

Providing students with information or facts is a superficial form of
education. Helping them to create knowledge by teaching them how to
interpret and evaluate information is a much deeper form of education.
The best form of education, however, is one that results in the students
understanding the material they study. This is achieved by helping them
to see patterns that they cannot discover on their own.

One problem of globalization is the difficulty in perceiving the patterns
of other cultures. Since these patterns do not fit those of our own culture,

we often experience them as "strange," "odd," or simply foreign. Cultural educational programs tend to focus too much on teaching facts about other cultures and too little on understanding the basic patterns underlying cultural practices or belief systems. I discuss possible educational techniques, some of which utilize global information technologies, to guide students in recognizing and comprehending the patterns of other cultures.

THE ROLE OF UNDERSTANDING IN LEARNING

It is a miracle that curiosity survives formal education.

—Albert Einstein

Surprisingly, the very concept of understanding has often been overlooked or mistreated in educational and psychological research. The tradition of hermeneutics focuses on *Verstehen*, but in that case the primary objects of study are literary works or objects of art. When it comes to investigating, for example, the role of quotidian insights in student learning and in general learning processes, research is still in its nascent stage. This is a remarkable lacuna in contemporary scientific research. A focal theme for educational science should be to identify those pedagogical practices that foster in-depth student understanding.

Cognitive neuroscience is also interested in understanding what happens in the brain when, for example, a student experiences an "Aha!" insight and what emotional and motivational responses correlate with that insight. Few researchers have investigated these processes (recent examples include Jung-Beeman et al. 2004). Although I lack the empirical data to support my position, I am convinced that the more often one experiences true understanding, the more *motivated* one will be to pursue one's studies. In brief, understanding is a key motivational factor in education.

From the cognitive point of view, I propose that understanding is seeing a pattern among all the items within a specific knowledge domain. For example, a child who realizes that the letters in a text correspond to separate speech sounds has cracked the reading code. The rest is practice. Or a music student who suddenly understands how a Bach fugue is composed immediately has a richer experience of the fugues. The insight, the "Aha!" moment, occurs when the pieces fall into place in the pattern.

We know that experts differ from novices in the way each group solves problems, but we know very little about the cognitive processes that make experts so efficient. Presumably, this is connected with the experts having a better understanding of their knowledge domain. They have built up a rich repertoire of patterns they can use in their problem solving. They can *transfer* their knowledge to new types of situations (see Mayer 1992).

The great advantage of pattern recognition is that it can be applied to new problems that go beyond the training set. A student who understands can not only answer questions taken from the textbook but also solve new problems. The deeper one's understanding, the more one can generalize one's knowledge. And when one has understood, one can also much more easily explain this knowledge to others. In other words, one who understands can teach. Every student recognizes the joy of suddenly understanding a difficult problem or seeing a pattern in a new complicated domain. And an experienced teacher can easily perceive when a student has understood. Because of multiple complex questions, research on the process of understanding does not fall within traditional academic borders. Rather, understanding the process demands new kinds of interdisciplinary initiatives. I believe that improved comprehension of the process of understanding from various perspectives within the cognitive sciences will have a great impact on the design of educational programs.

A PARADOX OF EDUCATION

Education's purpose is to replace an empty mind with an open one.

—Malcolm Forbes

There is a saying that education is what is left when you have forgotten what you have learnt. This seems paradoxical because it is difficult to fathom how there can be any knowledge left when one has forgotten it. The paradox arises from the way we generally appreciate the concepts *information* and *knowledge*. To make these abstract notions more tangible, we use *metaphorical* language, often without being aware of it. The dominating metaphor for information is the "conduit," which depicts information as something that can be "conducted" in "channels" from a "sender" to a "receiver" (Reddy 1979). Information is transmitted in some form of "code" that is "unpacked" by the receiver. According to the conduit metaphor, learning something means that you "store" information somewhere in your head. We have access to the information in the same way that we have shoes in the wardrobe, apples in the cellar, or files on a computer. Forgetting something consequently means "removing" it from storage. For this reason, it sounds paradoxical to say that education is what is left when one has forgotten everything.

My solution to the paradox is that *education consists of the patterns we assimilate during life*. A pattern can remain even if the facts used to discover it are forgotten. The patterns are more important than the facts, since the former can be used for solving new problems.

DISCOVERING PATTERNS

We don't see things as they are; we see them as we are.

—Anaïs Nin

After attending a concert or visiting an art exhibition, we often say we are left with an impression. But it is a myth that our sensory experiences are "impressions" in the sense that something is pressed into our brains. Our brain is not a passive receiver of images and sounds from the surrounding world. It actively seeks patterns and *interprets* what it receives. This continuously running process is the basis for all understanding.

Our cognition searches for patterns, whether we want to or not, at a variety of levels. At the basis of our understanding are biologically determined mechanisms that strongly control the way we perceive the surrounding world. At the top level, one finds the cultural codes required to interpret works of poetry, music, dance, and other arts. However, when we master the codes, they also influence our perception of the cultural products. As a consequence, we do not all see and hear the same things— there is no "objective" experience of the world.

At the bottom levels of pattern searching, an example of a biologically controlled mechanism illustrates that the search for patterns is ubiquitous. At an early stage of the visual process, the brain tries to find patterns among all the dots in figure 2.1. Presumably, you perceive circles of different sizes in the figure. Interestingly, one circle is soon replaced by another that suppresses the first, and so forth. The figure "lives," even though not a single dot is moving. You may even discover Maltese crosses in the figure. If you do, the crosses will block the perception of the circles, and vice versa. Although the figure has no global meaning, our visual system searches incessantly for patterns. There is therefore no unequivocal answer to how one "perceives" the figure.

The brain is full of mechanisms that *fill in* what falls on the retina, eardrum, or other sensors. From an evolutionary perspective, these mechanisms are important: Bad lighting conditions or occluding objects

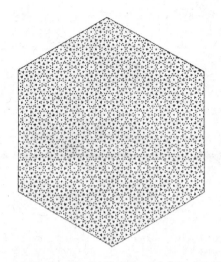

Figure 2.1 Six-sided patterned figure.
SOURCE: *Marroquin 1982. Reprinted by permission.*

do not prevent us from discovering danger or food, thus clearly increasing our chances for survival. If one sees the tail of a tiger, one surely understands that a whole tiger lurks in the vicinity. Our brains have constructed a large repertoire of patterns. Although we are often unaware of them, they can be elicited by various tests. For example, look at the two pictures in figure 2.2. What do they depict? One may easily see that the left is a picture of a violin, but for many observers a clue is needed for the picture to the right. It is of an elephant (with its head to the left). Suddenly the pieces fall into their places and one can *interpret* the picture— it becomes a gestalt. The discrete parts become *meaningful*. For instance, one of the black blotches suddenly becomes the tip of the trunk. An interesting feature of such Gestalt experiences is that once one has seen the pattern, one cannot forget it.

Early in the twentieth century, Gestalt psychology attempted to formulate the "laws" that govern the organization of our perceptions. This branch of psychology was suppressed mid-century by behaviorism. Gestalt-related ideas have become relevant again, however, and are now securely grounded in modern knowledge of cognitive brain mechanisms.

Cognitive mechanisms actively seek patterns in the world. Some of the mechanisms are organic, others are learned, and still others are directly associated with language. Still other patterns belong to our culture, and

Figure 2.2 Incomplete depictions of objects. SOURCE: *Leeper 1935. Reprinted with permission of the Helen Dwight Reid Educational Foundation. Published by Heldref Publications, 1319 18th Street NW, Washington, DC 20036-1802. www.heldref.org. © 1935.*

it takes an interaction and sometimes a clash with another culture to realize that certain patterns are not universal.

CATEGORICAL PERCEPTION

Es hört doch jeder nur, was er versteht.

—Johann Wolfgang von Goethe

For some category systems, the effects of categorization are *amplified* by our perceptual systems so that distances within a category are perceived as smaller and distances between categories are perceived as larger than they "really" are. This phenomenon is called *categorical perception* (see, for example, Harnad 1987). This finding implies that a reality in which there are no sharp borders is sorted into distinct slots by our cognitive mechanisms. The categories can be seen as a kind of pattern. They are normally a product of learning, most of which is implicit.

Found in many domains, categorical perception has been studied in particular in phonetic systems (see, for example, Petitot 1989). Even though a set of sounds may be produced by an articulatory parameter (output variable) that varies continuously, the auditory system perceives this variable in a categorical way, so that when the articulatory parameter is varied along its scale, the perceived sound (input variable) seems to remain constant for a long interval and then suddenly jumps to a new sound that is also relatively stable.

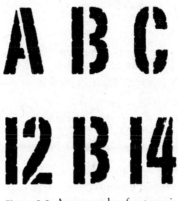

Figure 2.3 An example of categorical perception.

Figure 2.3 provides a simple illustration of categorical perception. If you focus on the upper row, the sign in the middle is seen as a B, whereas if you focus on the lower row, the very same sign is seen as 13. The example illustrates that the context determines how we interpret information our senses receive. This mechanism makes our processing more efficient, but it also locks us into certain interpretations. The patterns in the figure are culturally transferred: they form part of basic Western education, which uses Latin letters and (adapted) Arabic numerals.

Musical scales are clear examples of cultural patterns that actually influence perception itself. When Westerners listen to Arabic or Indian music, they perceive many of the tones as being out of tune. The reason is that the Western music scale is based on twelve tones, whereas in Arabic music the scale can contain seventeen tones, and in Indian twenty-one. Western ears fail to sort the tones from an Indian raga or an Arabic love song into the twelve slots of the standard scale. The tones do not fit the categorical pattern of Western music. An alternative pattern in the form of a different scale must be picked up before the music can be fully appreciated.

Cultural patterns can be subtle. A striking example of hidden categorical perception is the way a pharmaceutical company attempted to sell headache medicine to a new market. Seeking to globalize its business, the company launched an advertising campaign in North Africa. Because a large proportion of the inhabitants were analphabets, the message was presented in the form of a three-panel cartoon. In the left-most panel, a frowning human figure holds its head in its hands. In the middle panel, the figure pops a pill into its open mouth. In the right-most panel, the figure is smiling, with open hands outstretched to either side.

The campaign was a fiasco. Those who could read, read Arabic, which is read from *right to left,* would only conclude that the medicine caused the headache. The cartoon was thus interpreted in the opposite way from what the company intended. Those who could not read interpreted the cartoon as three separate figures and could not understand the intended causal connection between the pictures. In Western cultures, people are so used to reading a cartoon from left to right that it does not occur to them that this could be a culturally induced pattern.

In much the same vein, culturally dependent behavioral patterns can seem strange to an outsider. This phenomenon poses particular difficulty for an immigrant who moves to a country with different cultural patterns that he or she has problems identifying. Conversely, confusion and tension often arise among nonimmigrants who do not understand the immigrant's behavior nor why he or she cannot adapt to the culture of the new country. The cultural patterns that do not fit often result in misunderstanding and a potentially detrimental sense of "otherness." I should emphasize that it is not sufficient to give the immigrant "facts" about the new country; more is required to facilitate her or his comprehension of the underlying cultural patterns.

Because the human brain is programmed for categorical perception, whenever we distinguish between "us" and "them," problems often arise. This neurological function can lead to dangerous results. In fact, one may even argue that there is a genetic foundation for xenophobia. Once we have determined the in-group and out-group—whether based on family membership, town residence, religion, or citizenship status—strong mechanisms with powerful emotional loadings categorically define the in-group as good and the out-group as bad. To avoid this trap of categorical perception, we must make a conscious effort to spell out exactly why a certain group is judged as the right in-group. Often, however, there are no reasons, just prejudice. As Charlotte Brontë aptly put it, "Prejudices, it is well known, are most difficult to eradicate from the heart whose soil has never been loosened or fertilized by education; they grow there, firm as weeds among rocks."

CULTURAL PATTERNS IN LANGUAGE AND NARRATIVE

There are strong ties between the patterns we perceive and the language we use. Patterns give meaning to the concepts we use when structuring the world. Language then names the patterns, not the single sensory experiences.

Linguistic differences in cultural patterns often create mismatched expectations. For example, *breakfast* is translated as *prima colazione* in Italian. Yet the concept stands for radically different phenomena. An Italian seeing a full English (or American) breakfast for the first time would probably be as taken aback as an Englishman would be disappointed when first encountering the minuscule *prima colazione* at an Italian hotel. Such examples are common in translations between any two languages and can even occur within a language when it is used in two culturally different regions.

Unni Wikan describes "honor," a much more charged example of culturally distinct patterns and their linguistic divergences, in her contribution to this volume. In parts of the Middle East, North Africa, and South Asia an honor code is central to the culture. In some cases the honor code has implications that violate human rights as described by the UN declaration. In many Western societies it may be difficult for students to grasp this alternative definition of honor.

Bartlett (1932) described the role of cultural patterns in the transmission and understanding of narratives. In one experiment, he used the story "The War of the Ghost," a standard Native American folktale. His subjects were all English. A subject read the story and was then asked to write it down for another subject to read. That person would then repeat his version to a third, and so on to the tenth individual. After these ten rounds the story became constant in an abbreviated form that had been adjusted to fit the culturally normative English way of telling stories. In the process, subjects added and dropped elements for which there was no apparent causal connection in an effort to make the story better fit the English pattern. In particular, subjects had difficulty understanding why some characters were ghosts and why the Indian dies at the end. These two facts were especially subject to change in their memories. The upshot is that what one remembers of a narrative is what fits into the expectations of one's cultural patterns. (Bartlett used the term *schema* instead of *pattern* in defining what we remember as based on our cultural patterns.)

Bartlett's experiments using this repeated-storytelling technique to observe changes that correspond to expectations of certain shared cultural patterns provided important evidence that narratives occur in specific cultural frames. The frame consists of a *canonical form* for narration, determining which causal relations are comprehensible and which individuals and objects may appear and which actions may occur in a story.

If one is not familiar with another culture's canonical form, one likely will not understand its stories. Bartlett's investigations show that someone not familiar with the culture in which a story originates will not likely remember the story correctly, but will tend to adapt it to her own cultural canon. Such canonical forms are prime examples of cultural patterns.

In their contribution to this volume, Veronica Boix Mansilla and Howard Gardner discuss the importance of "global consciousness" in our increasingly interconnected global world. Perceiving and understanding cultural patterns is a sine qua non for global consciousness. Becoming aware of and understanding cultural patterns helps establish the three faculties on which Boix Mansilla and Gardner focus: awareness of global issues, a reflective stance on these issues, and a personal orientation toward them.

EDUCATIONAL TECHNIQUES FOR UNDERSTANDING CULTURAL PATTERNS

Human beings, who are almost unique in having the
ability to learn from the experience of others, are also
remarkable for their apparent disinclination to do so.

—Douglas Adams

Effective pedagogical techniques that facilitate students' discovery of relevant patterns within a knowledge domain are critical to their reaching true understanding. According to some Piagetian constructivist views of education, students should not be taught the patterns; they should discover them on their own through independent exploration. The teacher, or the cognitively more developed mentor, should simply provide scaffolding and the appropriate materials for this autonomous process to unfold. However, practical educational experiences show this method to be far from optimal. An orthodox constructivist viewpoint demands too much of the students: they are supposed to discover the patterns that took scientists and professionals centuries to uncover.

A different approach, one in which a teacher introduces the theoretical structure within a knowledge domain and presents abstract patterns to the students, is also insufficient. The theoretical structure can, for example, be a grammatical rule, a mathematical equation, or a method of composing music. The pattern is often constructed from theoretical variables that are not found in experience. However, many students, even at the college level, often do not understand the theoretical elements beyond mechanically manipulating the formulas. For example, they pass their exams in physics by putting in the right numbers in the equations without understanding what the equations represent. In this way, they hardly achieve any deeper knowledge, let alone an understanding of physics.

The dilemma lies in the fact that making meaning out of a theoretical pattern requires applying it to some more tangible domain. Students must be given a rich experiential background to accommodate the theoretical structure (compare Schwartz, Martin, & Nasir 2005). The patterns are made meaningful when anchored in concrete activities. Understanding depends on an intricate alliance between experience and theoretical knowledge.

In a sense, a culture is a particular theory about the world. The question then becomes, How can a student be made to understand the perspective of a foreign culture? In my view, learning another language is always beneficial for understanding cultural patterns. The earlier one learns it, the better (see also Süssmuth, this volume). Marie McAndrew (this volume) discusses different policies concerning the language training of immigrant students. It is fairly obvious that by learning the "heritage language," a student can better understand his or her background. Against this it has been claimed that a bilingual education rather leads to semilingualism. I want to emphasize, however, that learning another language, whether the student's "heritage language" or not, expands his access to cultural patterns and also his metacognitive awareness of conflicts between such patterns (see also Roosens, this volume; Leman 1999). As McAndrew notes: "Children are extraordinarily flexible human beings: they can live in two different worlds as long as they are not forced to choose one over the other or made to feel that some cultural or religious characteristics are linked to socially devalued individuals (especially if the latter are their parents)."

Obviously, the best method for identifying and understanding the patterns of other cultures would be to immerse oneself in the culture while working with a tutor who explains the relevant cultural, religious, or social codes needed to make sense of new experiences. However, for various reasons, this form of education can seldom be arranged. Surrogates for the real experiences must be sought.

Exploiting the variety of media tools available today is one possibility. We currently rely on books, TV, movies, recordings, and the like to learn about other cultures. These media give us vital *substitute* experiences. But there are other ways of creating learning experiences. In language education, *role-playing* has been used successfully. Unlike traditional media, role-playing requires students to incorporate physical as well as verbal exercises into the learning process. This practice of physical engagement has turned out to be an important factor in promoting efficient and effective learning, in part because when someone can role-play or act out the seemingly odd aspects of the culture in a way that brings out a pattern, students more easily see and understand their rationale. Because role-playing also involves *interactivity*, it is much more engaging than using traditional media.

THE ROLE OF INFORMATION TECHNOLOGY TOOLS

> I have the information; now I want to know what is going on.
>
> **—Henrik Tikkanen**

Computers, as we saw in the Tensta Gymnasium, are quickly becoming standard in many educational settings. Many have tended to believe that if only enough computers could be installed in schools, a number of educational problems would be solved. However, students as well as teachers are increasingly questioning the value of information technologies (IT) in education. Even if computers are frequently used for word processing, searching for information in the Internet, e-mailing, and chatting, there is concern over whether these tools really improve student learning and understanding.

What is missing from much of the current debate is a theoretical perspective on learning processes that can undergird creative recommendations for constructing pedagogically valuable tools based on IT. Such a perspective will also result in grounded recommendations on how learning processes, with or without IT support, should be evaluated. In particular, theories concerning how learning can be mediated by IT ought to build on what is known about human cognitive processes (Gärdenfors & Johansson 2005).

The standard method for evaluating the effects of an educational IT tool is to make a comparative study. In such a study, two groups of students are first presented with a pretest within some knowledge domain. Then one group learns about the knowledge domain using the IT tool, while the other group learns the same material in a more traditional way. Both groups are given a posttest, and the learning outcomes of the two methods are compared. Of course, it can be difficult to assess whether the two groups are effectively presented with the same material. This method is not optimal, since it provides no direct information about the cognitive (or emotional) processes involved in the two ways of studying the material.

Acquiring knowledge, rather than just obtaining information, should be a goal of learning. The information found in computers does not turn into knowledge by itself—the student must work actively with the material in order to construct meaning. Knowledge is information that has been interpreted, evaluated, and put in context. Computers are hardly helpful in this process. Undervaluing the ability to interpret information is one of the negative consequences of the current information society. How can a student sitting alone in front of the computer learn to distinguish information from disinformation? Computers cannot help, because they do not understand. On the other hand, certain educational IT tools, in the hands of an experienced teacher or mentor, can be effective in promoting understanding. In particular, I point to tools for *visualizing* abstract data and correlations and to programs for *simulating* various cognitive processes.

Visualization

Above all, we perceive patterns visually. When a teacher wants to convey an abstract theory, visualization is an excellent method for promoting understanding. In mathematics a third-degree equation suddenly becomes comprehensible when drawn as a graph, the connection between supply and demand in economics becomes apparent when drawn as intersecting curves in a graph, and the development of a historic battle is easier to remember if presented by blocks and arrows on a map. Presenting theoretical patterns visually makes it easier for students to connect them to their own experiences, thereby enhancing their understanding considerably.

IT offers many opportunities for creating visualizations within most knowledge domains. Multimedia, which has already had considerable impact in educational settings, incorporates several types of information simultaneously. For example, a student can use the computer to view a text-based document, graphic illustrations complementing the text, and a video that illustrates the text and simultaneously listen to the video commentary. Some multimedia encyclopedias deploy this technique. For example, an entry about a bird may consist of text and pictures, as in a traditional book, and be complemented with a video showing the bird's flight patterns and a soundtrack with its song.

In light of the difficulties in conveying cultural patterns, visualization can be an excellent tool in second-language education. In traditional lexica, words are explained by other words. But "pictionaries" explain words with the aid of pictures. For example, the difference between breakfast and *prima colazione* could quite easily be expressed using pictures. IT can also be used to develop even more advanced multimedia lexica, "mictionaries," where words are explained with the aid of the most suitable medium—whether other words, pictures, videos, or sounds. To give but one example, Romance languages are poor in motion verbs, while English is extremely rich. So if an Italian student wants to understand the differences between *strut, stroll, stride,* and *saunter,* it is unhelpful to say that they are different kinds of walking, all translating more or less as *camminare.* Small, stylized video clips illustrating the verbs would be more efficient for conveying the differences in meaning.

Simulations

A second example of an IT-based education tool that promotes understanding is *simulation.* A simulation replaces a real course of events through the use of a dynamic model that accounts for the most important variables. Simulation programs are visualizations of dynamic systems. The computer game industry has produced a number of advanced simulation programs. One interesting example is SimCity, where the player constructs a complex virtual city with its own water supply, electricity, streets, schools, industries, and so forth. The goal is not to shoot at moving targets or conquer anything, but to keep the dynamic system representing the city in balance so that the city can develop harmoniously. The player must prevent shortages of electricity or water and avoid excessively expensive streets. Even though SimCity offers a stylized model of a real city, youngsters learn much from playing the game that they cannot learn by just reading books. The simulations do not give players real experience in city planning, but they do provide *virtual experiences.* And when it comes to understanding a process, such experiences are valuable substitutes. Because the student can *interactively control* a number of variables, she may acquire a rather rich experience of different causal connections in the system and thereby achieve a better understanding of it.

A disadvantage of SimCity is that the equations that drive the simulation model are not transparent. If the students could have access to the equations and manipulate their values, an even deeper understanding of the system could be achieved. In a more recent simulation program, The Sims, one follows the lives of various artificial persons on the screen. Again, the user can control a number of variables concerning the environment and the individual's personal characteristics. While this program currently restricts the characters' nationality to American, The Sims might be used as a tool for presenting diverse cultural patterns. For example, in a Japanese version of The Sims, the user would have to learn to grasp Japanese cultural patterns in order to interact successfully with the simulation program. This way of practicing everyday interaction with the Japanese could be attractive to many young students. Again, to maximize learning and enhance understanding, the equations behind the simulations should be made transparent.

The virtual world of a simulator can complement the real one by depicting a variety of situations that a student, for various reasons—ethical, economic, physical, or temporal—cannot experience directly. Such virtual experiences become much more corporeal and powerful than those derived from just studying a text or abstract equations. Textbook learning should not be discarded altogether, as the theories presented in textbooks can support interpretation of the experiences. Understanding a knowledge domain builds on the interplay between theory and experience.

Creating simulations does not require the use of computers. Role-playing, mentioned above in connection with language learning, offers simulations of social interactions that can also provide students with valuable virtual experiences that they can later exploit in real life. If the students enact situations involving people from other cultures, the clashes between the cultures may become tangible without being embarrassing and without causing real problems. After such experiences, analysis of the clashes conducted with the support of a teacher or supervisor could efficiently achieve understanding of the underlying cultural patterns. Furthermore, the students will be more motivated for such an analysis after playing a role in a game.

Tutoring Systems

A computer program can never replace a good teacher. She or he is not needed so much for conveying facts, as the conduit metaphor would have it, as for explaining connections—to *expose* the patterns the students need to understand what they are learning. Furthermore, an experienced teacher can *see* whether a student understands—a computer cannot. He or she is also needed to follow the learning process of the students and to intervene when necessary. The *tutoring* role of the teacher cannot be overvalued.

When human resources are scarce, however, *some* of the tutoring functions can be taken over by computer programs. The British educational researcher Diane Laurillard describes "intelligent tutoring systems" in her book *Rethinking University Education* (1993). These computer programs function as virtual tutors, albeit in rather limited form. Laurillard conceives of such a system as consisting of three parts. First, an educational program (e.g., a simulation program) introduces a knowledge domain to the student. A second program keeps track of the mistakes the student makes. Most mistakes have been made before by other students, and much of an experienced teacher's professionalism consists in knowing *how* a student has made a particular mistake. On the basis of this experience, the teacher can then choose the right way to explain the mistake and to guide the student in the right direction. Laurillard's idea is that a tutoring system should be able to handle the most frequent types of errors so that the program can identify the mistake and give advice concerning the right method to solve the problem. A third program tracks the student's *individual learning style*. This program should learn what kinds of tasks the student finds difficult and what mode of presentation is optimal for the student, and should adapt to the student's interaction with the tutoring system. Such tutoring systems can become rather complex, however, and their construction demands significant resources.

CONCLUSION

The test and the use of man's education is that he finds pleasure in the exercise of his mind.

—Jacques Martin Barzun

This chapter focuses on the role of understanding in education. My central tenet is that understanding is seeing a pattern. On this basis, I outline educational techniques, some of which use IT, that help students understand by perceiving relevant patterns.

Additional research is needed concerning the way students achieve understanding and how the experience of understanding affects students. Among other things, there is a lack of psychological tests to measure understanding as it occurs during a learning process. We need to find out much more about how to learn to understand and, perhaps more important, how understanding motivates students.

A culture is not just people in an environment, but a particular way of interpreting the world. Each culture brings with it a different set of patterns of interpretation. For this reason, education that strives to bridge cultures should focus on conveying the relevant patterns rather than simply facts about other cultures.

With this perspective on understanding other cultures, I see some areas of future research concerning educational tools as particularly promising. One is the study of role-playing. By enacting aspects of a culture that is different from their own, the student can engage in a deeper understanding of that culture's fundamental patterns. We need to know more about what kinds of role-playing are most effective for this purpose. IT can be a useful complementary tool here. By playing a highly interactive computer-supported game that requires understanding a culture to win, students will be motivated to learn about the culture. However, further research is needed to find the best format for such culture games.

Along the same lines, so-called *virtual animated agents* can provide useful pedagogical tools (Gulz 2004). Such agents can serve as virtual mentors in a tutoring system of the kind I describe in the previous section. Again, further research should investigate how the understanding and metacognitive skills of students are affected by virtual animated agents.

REFERENCES

Bartlett, F. (1932). *Remembering: A study in experimental and social psychology.* Cambridge: Cambridge University Press.

Gärdenfors, P., and P. Johansson, eds. (2005). *Cognition, education, and communication technology.* Mahwah, NJ: Lawrence Erlbaum.

Gulz, A. (2004). Benefits of virtual characters in computer based learning environments: Claims and evidences. *International Journal of Artificial Intelligence in Education* 14: 313–334.

Harnad, S., ed. (1987). *Categorical perception: The groundwork of cognition.* Cambridge: Cambridge University Press.

Jung-Beeman, M., E. M. Bowden, J. Haberman, J. L. Frymiare, S. Arambel-Liu, R. Greenblatt, P. J. Reber, and J. Kounios (2004). Neural activity when people solve verbal problems with insight. *PLoS Biology* 2(4), e97 doi:10.1371/journal.pbio.0020097:.

Laurillard, D. (1993). *Rethinking university education: A framework for the effective use of educational technology.* New York: Routledge.

Leeper, R. (1935). A study of a neglected portion of the field of learning: The development of sensory organization. *Journal of Genetic Psychology* 46 (1935): 41–75.

Leman, J. (1999). Cultural hybridism and self-categorization: Trilingually and biculturally scholarized adolescents in Brussels. *International Journal of Educational Research* 31: 317–326.

Marroquin, J. L. (1982). Human visual perception of structure. Master's thesis, Department of Electrical Engineering and Computer Science, Massachusetts Institute of Technology, Boston.

Mayer, R. E. (1992). *Thinking, problem solving, cognition.* 2nd ed. New York: Freeman & Co.

Petitot, J. (1989). Morphodynamics and the categorical perception of phonological units. *Theoretical Linguistics* 15: 25–71.

Reddy, M. (1979). The conduit metaphor. In *Metaphor and thought.* A. Ortony, ed. Pp. 284–324. Cambridge: Cambridge University Press.

Schwartz, D., T. Martin, and N. Nasir (2005). Designs for knowledge evolution: Towards a prescriptive theory for integrating first- and second-hand knowledge." In *Cognition, Education and Communication Technology.* P. Gärdenfors and P. Johansson, eds. Pp. 21–54. Mahwah, NJ: Lawrence Erlbaum.

THREE

Tami Katzir, Mary Helen Immordino-Yang, and Kurt W. Fischer

MIND, BRAIN, AND EDUCATION
IN THE ERA OF GLOBALIZATION

In the early twenty-first century the newly emerging field of mind, brain, and education (MBE) has garnered much attention as both a framework for scientifically grounding educational practice and a way of bringing a developmental-educational perspective to neuroscience. As with most innovations, however, there has been an initial period of overuse and unrealistic expectation, as evidenced in the frequent use of the phrase *brain-based education* in the popular press, the marketing of various "brain-based" children's products, and the misguided, state-mandated provision of classical music CDs to mothers of newborns in Georgia because of research about the "Mozart effect" on some cognitive test items in college students. While the idea of connecting the study of mind and brain to the practice of education has generated much legitimate excitement, it will take time to develop a productive and responsible partnership suited to the needs of an increasingly globalized society. Researchers and practitioners are just beginning to come together to clearly formulate a field that will greatly influence education.

A principal challenge to education in the twenty-first century is to shift from a localized factory model to one that prepares citizens to function in an increasingly interconnected and rapidly changing globalized world (Suárez-Orozco & Qin-Hilliard 2004). As our visit to the Tensta Gymnasium in Stockholm revealed, for postindustrial nations, integrating the large and growing numbers of youth from highly diverse linguistic, ethnic, religious, racial, and cultural backgrounds into their societies and economies is the greatest challenge as borders and markets become more fluid. The schooling and integration of immigrant youth, as well as the capacity of native-born citizens to move beyond intolerance, are of critical importance. A world where difference is becoming the norm increasingly selects for the interpersonal competencies needed to work, think, and play with individuals from substantively different backgrounds (Suárez-Orozco & Qin-Hilliard 2004). To adapt education to this new era, educators need to understand how students' development and learning are universal and how they are culture specific. Research in biology, cognitive science, and education are essential to this understanding.

We believe that the emerging field of mind, brain, and education will play an important role in meeting some of the new challenges and needs in education arising from these questions. In particular, a new generation of scholars in MBE is gradually forging connections between cognition, biology (especially neuroscience and genetics), and educational practice, particularly involving learning, teaching, and cognitive and emotional development. This intersection of biology and cognitive science with pedagogy has become a new focus in a growing number of graduate training programs across the world, and promises to connect education and public policy with the major innovations of biology. These graduate programs are strongly interdisciplinary, involving psychology, pedagogy, and biology, as well as philosophy, anthropology, linguistics, computer science, and other disciplines.

Such an interdisciplinary focus is vital to finding answers to the new set of questions that arise from the globalized context. For example, with growing immigration, students from different linguistic backgrounds are increasingly educated together. What will this mean for the students' linguistic and cultural development? Specifically, do different languages (e.g., sign, Latinate, or Semitic) shape the brain differently, and if so, should we then expect different groups of children to take different pathways to learning to read? How does plasticity of brain development affect learning to read, both through typical experience and after brain damage? How can we best accommodate potential differences in learners? Building on the cases of reading and plasticity, how can new findings on brain development inform education reform more broadly? For instance, if a child shows a difference in brain activity after receiving one-on-one tutoring, when does this evidence support the inference that she received appropriate remediation? And how should this inference be shared with the public? What standards for critical consumption of brain research should be disseminated by the media?

To begin to answer some of these questions, we first describe the field of mind, brain, and education—its history and overarching goals as they relate to the era of globalization. The second part of the chapter provides two examples of MBE research. The first reveals contributions to our understanding of reading and literacy development, especially in multilingual contexts. With the second example, we discuss issues related to plasticity in brain development by presenting two exceptional adolescent boys, one Argentine and one American, who have undergone a hemispherectomy, surgery in which half of the brain is removed to control severe seizures. Despite incredible odds against them, both boys are compensating well in mainstream social and educational environments. We conclude with some promises and cautions associated with research and application of this work.

MBE IN HISTORICAL CONTEXT

The fascination that philosophers and scientists have with the human brain historically centered on the questions of mind-brain duality (Descartes 1850); only recently has research on the mind-brain relationship expanded to include questions about cognitive development and learning grounded in cognitive science, neuroscience, and genetics. Neuroscience, the interdisciplinary study of the nervous system, is less than forty years old and has shown explosive growth, so that today there are more than three hundred graduate programs in neuroscience. As a testament to the complexity of the brain and the many methodological barriers to the objective study of its structure and function, the development of the field has resulted in many interdisciplinary neuroscientific activities, including neuropsychology, neurobiology, neuroimaging, and neurophilosophy (Katzir & Paré-Blagoev 2006). In a sense, the field of mind, brain, and education seems a natural next step in these activities in that it represents a sort of "meta-interdisciplinarity," extending the interdisciplinary enterprises to encompass and accommodate the practice of teaching real children and adults.

However, one roadblock to this next step is the persuasive argument that understanding the brain is not necessary for the construction of theoretical models of human cognition (Marr 1982; Neisser 1967). Some have even argued that although neuronal constructs are part of the explanatory vocabulary of biologists, they are not useful in psychology, which employs a different, behavioral level of inquiry (Pylyshyn 1984). Many educators and psychologists similarly feel that differences between the levels of analysis used in biology and psychology and the primary importance of application to practice in education are simply too large to bridge (Blakemore & Frith 2000).

One solution to this problem was proposed by Bruer (1997), who suggested a middle ground in which cognitive psychology could serve as a midpoint between neuroscience and education. But we argue here and elsewhere that the advent of new technologies and approaches in MBE will allow increasing translation across disciplines and levels of analysis and provide new tools grounded firmly in both cognitive science and biology (Fischer 2006; Fischer, Immordino-Yang, & Waber 2006; Katzir & Paré-Blagoev 2006). Thus we move beyond Bruer's view to argue that experimental paradigms designed to capture relations across levels of analysis (genetic, neuronal, cognitive, behavioral) will help build the very bridges that Bruer thought were impossible between these currently distant disciplines. Specifically, we propose that the application of these concepts in real-life educational contexts will provide the level playing field in which to directly compare, and ultimately unite, different disciplinary approaches. Real children, we feel, will provide the ultimate testing ground for our ivory-tower theories. Describing and explaining real learning in diverse populations necessitates bringing a variety of approaches to bear; thus, the field of mind, brain, and education was born.

MBE IN A GLOBALIZED WORLD

Over the past ten years, education scholars around the world have begun aggressively looking to the biological sciences to inform education policy and practice. The advent of powerful new, in vivo brain imaging technologies; burgeoning discoveries in genetics; and public excitement about the possibility of new, biologically based alliances between cognition and education have made possible real strides in understanding relations between brain and behavior in educational contexts (Battro, Fischer 2006). In a few tantalizing cases, researchers and educators can even begin to observe the functional neuropsychological effects of educational interventions.

For these advances to become generalizable to and meaningful in a broader world context, we need a common language—a shared set of criteria for evaluating, critically consuming, and ultimately contributing to the new neuroscience and genetics. Society's focus on the burgeoning knowledge of biology leads to expectations that sometimes upset the balance between scientific knowledge and meaningful practice, raising numerous ethical and educational issues (Battro 2000; Bruer 1997; Illes, Kirschen, & Gabrieli 2003; *Building better brains*, 2003; Sheridan, Zinchenko, & Gardner, in press).

For an example of brain research misapplied, one need look no further than the 1998 decision in Georgia to provide Mozart CDs to all new mothers. In establishing this policy, which cost hundreds of thousands of dollars, the governor of Georgia drew on work in cognitive neuroscience conducted at the University of California at Irvine. The actions were taken in the hopes of "harness[ing] the 'Mozart effect' for Georgia's newborns —that is, playing classical music to spur brain development" ("Random Samples" 1998, p. 663).

However, the media, the main channels for rapid and broad information dissemination, had exaggerated the research findings, and the governor had jumped to inappropriate conclusions. A first study, reported in *Nature* in 1993 (see discussion in Katzir & Paré-Blagoev 2006), found that listening to Mozart raised the abilities of college students on certain spatial tasks for a brief time. Then, another study found that keyboard music lessons boosted the spatial skills of three-year-olds (Schlaug, Jancke, Huang, & Steinmetz 1995). Taken together, these studies were used to justify Georgia's program, although neither involved newborns or showed any long-term effect. Despite what the governor had implied, the research had no relevance to infant intelligence.

Since this debacle, leading scientists have urged caution and care as researchers, educators, and other practitioners proceed down the exciting but pitfall-laden road connecting neuroscience to education (Berninger & Richards 2002; Katzir & Paré-Blagoev 2006; Goswami 2004). To systematically explore the connection between the findings of neuroscience and cognitive science and children's development and learning and thereby to make conservative but confident recommendations requires a forum for rigorous scientific and educational debate and a research language common to researchers and practitioners worldwide. In short, new international forums (journals, books, conferences) dedicated to these topics are needed, both to advance critical examination and formulation of research and to serve as "consumer reporters" on what has been scientifically demonstrated and what remains to be studied.

These regulated forums are essential in a globalized society, as information now travels faster and farther than ever before. Suárez-Orozco

and Qin-Hilliard (2004) argue that one of the four interrelated formations of globalization consists of "information, communication, and media
technologies that facilitate exchange and instantaneously connect people
across vast geographies" (p. 14). This unprecedented accessibility to
information is a double-edged sword because it requires a skilled audience to receive and interpret it. For parents, teachers, and policy makers to find suitable solutions to pressing educational problems, there must
be open dialogue between the scholarly communities of educators and
researchers, particularly since we must be judicious in applying the new
science to clinical and educational settings.

The best research and educational practice require a two-way interaction between scientists and educators working to help children learn.
In an era when travel, communications, and social interactions across physical boundaries are making national borders porous, intellectual bridges
should be built as well to facilitate this cross-disciplinary discussion. Globalization involves a "post-geography" (Bauman 1998) that should facilitate the flow of information across different scientific disciplines as well
as between research and practice in education. In the twenty-first century,
globalization promises to help push research that was once centered in
the ivory tower to application to curricula in schools and communities
across the world.

GOALS OF MBE

Given the global context in which it is operating, the mission of this new
field is to facilitate cross-cultural and cross-disciplinary collaboration in
biology, education, and the cognitive and developmental sciences. Science
and practice in these fields will benefit from rich bidirectional interaction.
Research can contribute usable knowledge to education, while practice
can help define promising research directions and contribute to the ·
refinement of testable hypotheses in diverse populations.

In our view, neuroscientific research can make three major contributions to education:

1. Neuroscientific research methods can provide converging
   lines of evidence for findings and hypothesized processes
   based on traditional educational and psychological methods
   (Kosslyn & Koenig 1992; Posner, Peterson, Fox, & Raichle
   1988; Sejnowski & Churchland 1989). For example, these

methods have confirmed the role of phonological processes in learning to read (Perfetti & Bolger 2004).

2. New findings often help researchers decide among competing rival approaches. For example, are there different subtypes of dyslexia? Is there a genetic component? How might genetic predispositions to dyslexia interact with environmental experiences to produce a range of subtypes?

3. Neuroscience research provides knowledge of the brain that makes possible the generation of new hypotheses. For example, even after achieving reading scores in the average range, some children with dyslexia still process written information differently from their peers. These differences imply that they will also demonstrate differences in learning from written material.

Commensurate with these contributions, the principal goal of MBE is to foster dynamic relationships between neuroscience, genetics, cognitive science, development, and education so that each field benefits from and influences work in the others. The principal objectives of the field are:

- to improve knowledge in and dialogue among education, biology, and the developmental and cognitive sciences
- to create and develop resources for scientists, practitioners, policy makers, and the public that are grounded in research
- to identify and create useful directions for research on education and promising educational practices
- to share ideas, critiques, insights, and issues through a journal and other forums for exchange and dialogue, such as symposia, workshops, and conferences
- to promote collaboration between researchers and practitioners in neuroscience, genetics, cognitive science, and education

To accomplish these objectives, the new generation of MBE scholars can focus on cognitive neuroscience, learning and instruction, cognitive or emotional development, learning disabilities, interventions with children, uses of technology for education, diversity in education, or a combination of these topics. In addition, practitioners can build expertise in hands-on applications of cognitive principles to practical and research problems, thereby promoting a reciprocal integration of research with practice—a kind of engineering that connects research findings and principles to applications in educational settings.

UNIVERSAL VERSUS CULTURE-SPECIFIC PROCESSES: EXAMPLES OF MBE RESEARCH

The educational challenge in a globalized world will be to educate millions of children and adults with diverse needs in different locales (Battro & Fischer 2006). The education of future generations will entail trade-offs not only between quality and quantity of resources but also between global and local management. For example, information and communication technologies may help deliver services to distant communities, but assessment methods will have to be fine-tuned in order to monitor the quality of instruction and provide feedback on the success of the services. MBE research promises to bridge cortex and classroom in the most diverse settings and cultures, because it can help us identify and teach to the needs of particular groups of learners.

In the introduction, we mention that one of the challenges for educating a global society of children is to tease apart which aspects of development are universal to all learners and which are unique to particular learners, either because of their atypical neurological and cognitive development or because of the cultural or linguistic differences between different groups of children. To give a sense of how an interdisciplinary MBE approach can contribute to understanding these issues, we describe two examples from current research. First is the case of reading acquisition, a problem of paramount importance to education in multiethnic contexts worldwide, including atypical reading acquisition, known as dyslexia, in multilingual contexts. Second is cross-cultural research on recovery after a hemispherectomy in two adolescent boys compared to their peers, showing how detailed work with individuals can enhance our knowledge of universal principles of brain plasticity in relation to experience. In each example, we describe how an interdisciplinary approach that incorporates a neuroscientific perspective can contribute novel insights into the education of real children functioning in a globalized classroom.

Example 1. Reading Difficulties

The escalating demands for rapid, accurate reading skills in our increasingly literate and computer-dependent societies make it essential to focus on the factors that influence reading. Reading involves a variety of processes that lead from visual letter identification to comprehension of the content and context of the written word. Most psycholinguistic models of reading distinguish at least three levels of analysis involved in reading: orthographic analysis of the visual forms of words, phonological processes associated with the sounds of the language, and semantic analysis of the meaning of words and phrases (Misra, Katzir, & Poldrack 2005). Many of us take the seemingly simple act of reading for granted. To a significant number of children across the globe, however, learning how to read is tantamount to deciphering a highly enigmatic code.

According to the National Center for Education Statistics (2003), close to 40 percent of U.S. fourth-grade children score below grade level on reading assessments. An estimated 10 to 20 percent of children have been diagnosed with dyslexia, a learning disability signaled by serious difficulty reading, writing, and spelling (Lyon, Shaywitz, & Shaywitz 2003). In the past two decades it has been well established that children with dyslexia often have difficulty with phonological processing. Specifically, dyslexic children often fail to develop an awareness that words, both written and spoken, can be broken down into smaller units of sounds (e.g., Stanovich 2003; Catts 1996). These children experience difficulties with tasks that require the ability to segment the speech stream into phonemes or to blend phonemes to create words. Children with such difficulties in oral language are at risk for having problems learning the alphabetic principle, which involves knowledge of the rules of letter-sound or grapheme-phoneme correspondence (Ehri 1998). These children usually also have difficulty in accurately reading words.

Research in educational psychology has advanced our knowledge of the identification, classification, and treatment of children with reading difficulties (Lyon & Chhabra 2004). Despite this progress, controversy still remains in the field of reading research and practice. A few pivotal issues in the science and practice of reading generate considerable debate. These issues include how reading disabilities should be defined, how to explain the etiology of reading difficulties, and what are the most appropriate reading interventions that should be implemented in schools. Researchers are increasingly demanding the use of multiple research methods in different settings to resolve these research questions (Lyon, Fletcher, Shaywitz, et al. 2001; Stanovich 2003; Vellutino, Fletcher, Snowling, & Scanlon 2004). Lyon and his colleagues (2001) claim that many of the debates in the field can be informed and even resolved with converging scientific evidence. Stanovich (2003) calls for integration of knowledge from qualitative and quantitative research.

A considerable body of evidence indicates that children with reading disabilities exhibit differences in both neural structures and circuitry when compared to nonimpaired readers (Berninger & Richards 2002). Comparative studies of average-achieving and challenged readers contribute to the general understanding of the brain regions and processes involved in normal and impaired reading. Specifically, a growing number of investigations have found regional associations between neurophysiological abnormalities and developmental dyslexia (Richards 2001). The growing consensus seems to be that dyslexic readers exhibit disruption primarily, but not exclusively, in the neural circuitry of the left hemisphere, which in most people serves language (see Lyon, Fletcher, Shaywitz, et al. 2001 for review).

While neuroscientific research is gradually informing educators about the underlying brain markers of dyslexia, the question remains as to how this information will change current reading interventions for different children in diverse classroom contexts. In addition, it is important to acknowledge that dyslexia occurs among all groups, regardless of age, race, or socioeconomic status (Shaywitz 2003), and across different languages, although its manifestations vary as a function of the transparency of the phonetic structure of the written language (Goswami 2006).

In the global context, no orthography appears immune to reading disorders. It is well documented that developmental reading disabilities exist all over the world (Breznitz 1997; Holopainen, Ahonen, & Lyytinen 2001; Tressoldi, Stella, & Faggella 2001). Until the past decade, however, insights about dyslexia based solely on the irregular English orthography were taken as applying to reading in general, even for languages with vastly different orthographies, which naturally require dramatically different diagnoses and interventions (Wimmer 1993). For example, the biological root of dyslexia is widely attributed, based on studies of adult dyslexics who speak Latinate languages such as Spanish, French, and Italian, to the area of the brain called the left temporoparietal region (Paulesu, Démonet, Fazio, McCrory, et al. 2001). But research has focused on letter-based, alphabetic languages and ignored the very different writing systems of many other languages (Katzir, Breznitz, Shaul, & Wolf 2004).

A study of Chinese children, who read in a literacy system based not on letters but on Chinese characters, used neural imaging technology to study the brain activity of sixteen Chinese dyslexics as they performed various language-based tasks (Siok, Perfetti, Jin, & Tan 2004). For these children, the locus of the problem seems to be another area of the brain, the left middle frontal gyrus. With an alphabetic language, reading is done sequentially: letters are recognized and analyzed as a sequence of sounds that are then matched to a known meaning. But with Chinese, the reading is more like parallel processing, in which the brain has to seize the meaning of the pictogram almost simultaneously with producing the sound of the word. The researchers believe their findings suggest that dyslexia may vary depending on the culture in which it is found. They may also suggest the need for different tasks to facilitate learning to read for dyslexics in different languages.

Such findings argue against a simple hypothesis of biological unity for dyslexia. Dyslexia may vary with the language system or the teaching the child has had. For example, in English, children are taught to "break the code" of the alphabet, while the Chinese often encourage children to memorize characters. Dyslexia will manifest differently in different learners, depending on not only individual cognitive differences but also linguistic and cultural considerations.

Understanding how children's developing abilities, including changes in brain areas associated with specific cognitive functions, interact with language systems and teaching strategies will be crucial for teachers working with today's children in globalized classrooms. Two immigrant children in the fourth grade, one from China and one from Latin America, may have reading difficulties for very different reasons. A child from China may have difficulties in understanding the alphabetic code since she is used to memorizing whole words, whereas a child from Brazil who is very familiar with the Latin alphabet may have limited knowledge of English. A thorough assessment informed by findings from both cognitive science and neuroscience can help a teacher understand whether such children have dyslexia or are instead having trouble adjusting to a new language or writing system. Based on this assessment, the teacher can develop more appropriate interventions for each child.

Example 2. Cognitive and Emotional Plasticity: The Case of Having Half a Brain

A cutting-edge issue in MBE is how experience shapes the functional relation of brain and behavior (see Damasio & Damasio, this volume). Neuroscientists see the shaping effects of experience on brain process and organization and emphasize neural plasticity (Gage 2003; Huttenlocher,

2002; Neville et al. 1998; Sur, Angelucci, & Sharma 1999). One area where educators and developmental scientists see the behavioral manifestations of plasticity is the remarkable achievements of some children with major neurological problems or histories of traumatic experiences (Battro 2000; Fischer, Ayoub, Noam, Singh, et al. 1997; Teicher 2002). Analysis of children's evolving skill profiles and neuropsychological abilities in relation to the cognitive experiences created by their cultural and educational environments can help uncover general principles organizing normal learning and brain function.

A good example of this approach comes from the study of two adolescent boys, Nico and Brooke, each of whom suffered severe localized brain seizures during childhood that resulted in the surgical removal of an entire hemisphere of his brain. (Both boys asked that they be identified by their real first names.) Amazingly, despite the poor cognitive prognosis generally associated with removal of a brain hemisphere, both Nico and Brooke are compensating to a previously unexpected extent. Nico lost his right hemisphere at age three, yet at fourteen, he was a charming and sociable young man attending a mainstream school in Spain at grade level. (His family is Argentine, but moved to Spain after testing.) Brooke, an American, lost his left hemisphere at age eleven. Despite predictions that he would never talk again, Brooke graduated from high school and began attending college part-time a few months after testing.

Currently, children like Nico and Brooke are extremely rare, but the two's successful compensation for extensive brain damage raises questions about the broader principles behind their adaptation. How have these boys compensated, and what do their cases imply about how their developing brains made sense of emotional and cognitive experience, given an extreme profile of strengths and weaknesses? (Of course, their successful outcomes may have been possible in part because of specific characteristics in their presurgery neurological profiles.) To address these questions, we analyze one aspect of Nico's and Brooke's development—their use of emotional intonation (affective prosody) in speech (Immordino-Yang 2005).

Based on Nico's brain morphology, neuroscience would predict that he would speak monotonically with little intonational fluctuation or skill, poor emotional expression, and poor comprehension of other people's pitch intonation. Brooke, on the other hand, was expected to produce normal amounts of intonation and emotion in his speech, since the right hemisphere of his brain, which is normally associated with comprehension and production of emotion and pitch, was intact. Contrary to these predictions, both boys were as competent as their peers in discerning tone of voice in sarcasm, a typical use of prosodic intonation in speech. In addition, both used a bit *too much* intonation and emotion in their own spontaneous speech as compared to that of peers. How could this be?

Detailed analysis of their use of speech intonation or contour showed that both boys used strategies atypical of younger and age-matched peers for comprehending and producing emotional intonation in speech. In a series of experiments, Nico, Brooke, and comparison groups of matched boys listened to a series of naturalistic story vignettes involving two characters speaking to each other in either a sarcastic or sincere way. These vignettes were recorded by native speakers of each boy's regional dialect and took one of two forms. In the first form, subjects heard either sarcastic or sincere stories with a report of a speaker's response. For example:

> John and Joe were playing soccer in the park. John kicked the ball toward the goal. The ball bounced off the goal post and hit John in the head, and he slipped and fell in a mud puddle. Joe told John it was a nice shot.

In the second form, subjects heard ambiguous stories that ended with one character making a statement to the other in either a sarcastic or a sincere tone of voice. For example:

> John and Joe were playing soccer in the park. John kicked the ball toward the goal. Joe said, "Nice shot!"

After each story, subjects were asked to decide whether the final statement had been sarcastic or sincere, and to justify their answers and general comprehension of the story via a series of follow-up questions about whether Joe was being serious or funny, what had really happened in the story, and how subjects knew. Subjects' discussion of the test stories was recorded, and several analyses were performed. After discovering the hemispherectomized boys' abilities to recognize sarcasm from both context and tone, investigations of Nico's and Brooke's claim that they discerned a speaker's intent revealed that each was atypical and appeared to rely heavily on a strategy associated with his remaining hemisphere. That is, Nico seemed to categorize, in a pseudogrammatical way, information that is normally emotional. Brooke, on the other hand, engaged in extensive musings about emotion and pitch fluctuation. These strategies left each with a set of strengths and liabilities in relation to his peers.

Additional analyses of the intonation or prosody of the boys' speech led to parallel results. Brooke, with his intact right or "emotional" hemisphere, produced relatively unregulated, unsystematic, and exaggerated intonation. Nico, missing his "emotional" hemisphere, appeared to copy the pitch patterns in his language in rote fashion, almost as if they were song melodies to be memorized and categorized. In this way, both boys appeared to use their remaining strengths based on their surviving hemisphere to solve an otherwise unsolvable problem: imbuing their speech with appropriate pitch and comprehending the sarcastic conversational intent of others. Thus each boy adapted his capacities to solving a fundamental problem in speech intonation, even when this adaptation required processing intonation atypically. An important background factor may be that Nico and Brooke grew up in highly supportive educational and family environments in which family members and teachers made exceptional efforts to help them develop important skills (Battro 2000; Immordino-Yang 2005); exactly how much these supportive environments enabled their recoveries, even though prosody was not explicitly taught, is a question for future investigation.

Even at this point, however, the results demonstrate the flexibility children show in adapting important tasks to their own strengths, even when doing so requires unusual ways of performing the tasks. In very specialized and supportive educational circumstances, a learner's particular neuropsychological strengths may shape his or her approach to learning, enabling the solution of problems in atypical ways that circumvent a basic neuropsychological weakness or deficit. In effect, learners may change processing problems to suit their abilities, so that learners with different sets of neuropsychological strengths approach educational problems in distinct ways. In essence, individual learners transform a "common" developmental or educational experience, at times radically, to create an individualized adaptation based on their neuropsychological profile (Bernstein 2006).

This research has implications for education as well as for neuropsychology. Although we often assume that everyone perceives the same educational problems in the same ways—for example, an arithmetic problem is the same problem for everyone—Nico's and Brooke's cases suggest that, given extreme developmental circumstances, people may approach even relatively low-level, apparently automatic processing in very different ways. In particular, it appears that both boys have compensated for lost abilities by transforming processing tasks that they "should not be able to deal with," based on their neurological profiles, into qualitatively different problems that better suit their remaining strengths. If this approach holds true for children in general, it implies that educators and parents should think seriously about the various neuropsychological ways that tasks can be interpreted and processed. What is presented as a simple arithmetic exercise, for example, may pose a verbal problem to one child and a spatial problem to another. A third child may interpret it as an affective or social problem, just as Brooke interpreted discerning nonspeech melodic pitch as an emotional problem, labeling pitch strings as "sad" or "happy" when he was asked only to judge whether they matched a prototype.

Each child would be approaching the arithmetic problem from a different angle that has repercussions for their performance. A neuropsychological approach to analyzing educational tasks can inform understanding of the possible strategies each child can use (Immordino-Yang 2001). In bringing information about the neuropsychological organization of skills to bear on the design of learning environments, researchers and practitioners can improve education by understanding both the kinds of tasks presented to students and the various possible ways a learner can transform and interpret those tasks. Especially in a global age in which different kinds of learners are lumped together in classroom settings, such insights from neuropsychology about differences in learning and performance can prove valuable for designing curricula and understanding different learners.

CONCLUSION: RESPONSIBLY CONNECTING MIND, BRAIN, AND EDUCATION IN A GLOBALIZED WORLD

Society has great expectations, perhaps unrealistic ones, about the benefits of bringing biology into education. Scientists and educators clamor to make connections, some of which will be productive and others of which may be disastrous (Bailey, Bruer, Symons, & Lichtman 2001; Bruer 1999). One important trap to be avoided is the assumption that laboratory science by itself will provide answers that can then be applied to education. A productive relationship among education, biology, and cognitive science does not start in the laboratory and proceed to direct application of scientific findings to classrooms and students.

What is required instead is a reciprocal process in which education informs biological research as much as biology informs educational research and practice (Battro 2000; Fischer, Immordino-Yang, & Waber 2006; Gardner 1983). The process should be similar to that in medicine whereby medical practice informs biological research as much as biology informs medical practice. In education, reading a textbook is distinct from reading a string of words in a laboratory reaction-time study that measures brain activity with functional magnetic resonance imaging (fMRI). Results from such a different laboratory context seldom apply felicitously to the classroom. That is why so much laboratory research has failed when scientists have attempted to apply it to education.

As a first step toward establishing collaborative teams of researchers and educators, intellectual dissemination of information should be facilitated. As educators, cognitive scientists, and neuroscientists, we have a responsibility to children to establish and maintain dialogue among our respective fields. To be maximally productive, this dialogue must go both ways. New information about the development and functioning of the brain awaits interpretation and judicious application in the classroom, while educational input and practical insights are essential in shaping new brain research. Indeed, the disciplines of education and neuropsychology are growing increasingly interdependent; and scientists cannot carry out useful research, nor can educators carry out good practice, without interweaving these perspectives. Our discussion of how different language systems present different challenges to children with reading problems is an example of the types of information needed to break through geographic and intellectual borders. At the same time, the value of these findings should not be overestimated until they are replicated among and expanded into wider populations.

Educational settings and tasks are essential for useful research in mind, brain, and education, just as medical settings and tasks are essential for useful research in biology and medicine. Laboratory research plays an important role in analyzing fundamental processes, but research in practical settings is key to application—the engineering of scientific findings for practical uses—and it is needed right now! Some scientists believe it is premature to relate biology to education, claiming that education needs to wait for scientific breakthroughs that solve the deep questions of mind and brain. We believe instead that research in education will help to shape the breakthroughs of the future by informing basic biological and cognitive research about human learning and behavior in the educational and home settings where children develop and learn.

REFERENCES

Bailey, D., J. Bruer, F. Symons, and J. Lichtman, eds. (2001). *Critical thinking about critical periods*. Baltimore: Paul H. Brookes.

Battro, A. M. (2000). *Half a brain is enough: The story of Nico*. Cambridge: Cambridge University Press.

Battro, A. M., and K. W. Fischer, eds. (2006). *The educated brain*. Cambridge: Cambridge University Press.

Bauman, Z. (1998). *Globalization: The human consequences*. New York: Columbia University Press.

Berninger, V., and T. Richards (2002). *Brain literacy for educators and psychologists*. San Diego: Academic Press.

Bernstein, J. H. (2006). Finding common ground to promote dialogue and collaboration: Using case material to jointly observe children's behavior. In *Mind, brain, and education in reading disorders*. K. W. Fischer, J. H. Bernstein, and M. H. Immordino-Yang, eds. Cambridge: Cambridge University Press.

Blakemore, S., and U. Frith (2000). *The implications of recent developments in neuroscience for research on teaching and learning*. www.pdkintl.org/kappan/kbru9905.htm.

Breznitz, Z. (1997). Effects of accelerated reading rate on memory for text among dyslexic readers. *Journal of Educational Psychology*: 289–297.

Bruer, J. (1997). Education and the brain: A bridge too far. *Educational Researcher* 26(8): 4–16.

Bruer, J. (1999). In search of brain-based education. *Phi Delta Kappa International* 80(9): 648.

Building better brains (2003). Special issue, *Scientific American* 289(3).

Catts, H. W. (1996). Defining dyslexia as a developmental language disorder: An expanded view. *Topics in Language Disorders* 16: 14–29.

Descartes, R. (1850). *Discourse on the method of rightly conducting the reason, and seeking truth in the sciences*. J. Veitch, trans. and introduction. Edinburgh: Sutherland & Knox.

Ehri, L. (1998). Grapheme-phoneme knowledge is essential for learning to read words in English. In *Word recognition in beginning literacy*. J. Metsala and L. Ehri, eds. Pp. 3–40. Hillsdale, NJ: Lawrence Erlbaum.

Fischer, K. W. (2006). Dynamic cycles of cognitive and brain development: Measuring growth in mind, brain, and education. In *The educated brain*. A. M. Battro and K. W. Fischer, eds. Cambridge: Cambridge University Press.

Fischer, K. W., C. C. Ayoub, G. G. Noam, I. Singh, A. Maraganore, and P. Raya (1997). Psychopathology as adaptive development along distinctive pathways. *Development and Psychopathology* 9: 751–781.

Fischer, K. W., M. H. Immordino-Yang, and D. P. Waber (2006). Toward a grounded synthesis of mind, brain, and education for reading disorders: An introduction to the field and this book. In *Mind, brain, and education in reading disorders*. K. W. Fischer, J. H. Bernstein, and M. H. Immordino-Yang, eds. Cambridge: Cambridge University Press.

Gage, F. H. (2003). Brain, repair yourself. *Scientific American* 289(3): 47–53.

Gardner, H. (1983). *Frames of mind: The theory of multiple intelligences*. New York: Basic Books.

Goswami, U. (2004). Neuroscience, education, and special education. *British Journal of Special Education* 31(4): 175–184.

Holopainen, L., T. Ahonen, and H. Lyytinen (2001). Predicting delay in reading achievement in a highly transparent language. *Journal of Learning Disabilities* 34: 401–413.

Huttenlocher, P. R., ed. (2002). *Neural plasticity: The effects of environment on the development of the cerebral cortex*. Cambridge, MA: Harvard University Press.

Illes, J., M. P. Kirschen, and J. D. E. Gabrieli (2003). From neuroimaging to neuroethics. *Nature Neuroscience* 6: 205.

Immordino-Yang, M. (2001). When 2 + 2 makes kids trip: Making sense of brain research in the classroom. *Basic Education* 45(8): 16–19.

Immordino-Yang, M. (2005). A tale of two cases: Emotion and affective prosody after left and right hemispherectomy. Ph.D. dissertation, Graduate School of Education, Harvard University, Cambridge, MA.

Katzir, T., A. Breznitz, S. Shaul, & M. Wolf (2004). Universal and the unique: A cross-linguistic investigation of reading and reading fluency in Hebrew- and English-speaking children with dyslexia. *Journal of Reading and Writing* 17(7–8): 739–768.

Katzir, T., and E. J. Paré-Blagoev (2006). Bridging neuroscience and education: The case of reading. *Educational Psychologist* 41(6): 53–74.

Kosslyn, S. M., and O. Koenig (1992). *Wet mind: The new cognitive neuroscience.* New York: Free Press.

Lyon, G. R., and V. Chhabra (2004). The science of reading research. *Educational Leadership* 61(6): 12–17.

Lyon, G. R., J. M. Fletcher, S. E. Shaywitz, B. A. Shaywitz, F. B. Wood, A. Schulte, and R. Olson (2001). Rethinking learning disabilities. In *Rethinking special education for a new century.* C. E. Finn, A. J. Rotherham, and C. R. Hokanson, eds. Pp. 259–287. Washington, DC: Thomas B. Fordham Foundation and Progressive Policy Institute.

Lyon, G. R., S. E. Shaywitz, and B. A. Shaywitz (2003). A definition of dyslexia. *Annals of Dyslexia* 53: 1–14.

Marr, D. (1982). *Vision: A computational investigation into the human representation and processing of visual information.* New York: Freeman.

Misra, M., T. Katzir, and R. A. Poldrack (2005). Applying a clinical approach to an fMRI study of component processes in reading: Bridging clinical practice and neuroscience research. Paper presented at the Society for the Scientific Studies of Reading annual meeting, Toronto, Canada, March.

National Center for Education Statistics. (2003). *Reading: The nation's report card.* http://nces.ed.gov/nationsreportcard/reading/results2003/natachieve-g4.asp.

Neisser, U. (1967). *Cognitive psychology.* Englewood Cliffs, NJ: Prentice Hall.

Neville, H., D. Bavelier, D. Corina, J. Rauschecker, A. Karni, A. Lalwani, et al. (1998). Cerebral organization for language in deaf and hearing subjects: Biological constraints and effects of experience. *Proceedings of the National Academy of Sciences* 95(3): 922–929.

Paulesu, E., F. Démonet, F. Fazio, E. McCrory, V. Chanoine, N. Brunswick, S. Cappa, Z. Cossu, M. Habib, C. Frith, and U. Frith (2001). Dyslexia: Cultural diversity and biological unity. *Science* 291: 2165–2167.

Perfetti, C., and D. Bolger (2004). The brain might read that way. *Scientific Studies of Reading* 8(3): 293–304.

Posner, M. I., S. E. Peterson, P. T. Fox, and M. E. Raichle (1988). Localization of cognitive operations in the human brain. *Science* 240: 1627–1631.

Pylyshyn, Z. W. (1984). *Computation and cognition.* Cambridge, MA: MIT Press.

Richards, T. L. (2001). Functional magnetic resonance imaging and spectroscopic imaging of the brain: Application of fMRI to reading disabilities and education. *Learning Disabilities Quarterly* 24: 189–203.

Schlaug, G., L. Jancke, Y. Huang, and H. Steinmetz, (1995). In vivo evidence of structural brain asymmetry in musicians. *Science* 267: 699–701.

Sejnowski, T. J., and P. S. Churchland (1989). Brain and cognition. In *Foundations of cognitive science*. M. I. Posner, ed. Pp. 301–358. Cambridge, MA: MIT Press.

Shaywitz, S. E. (2003). *Overcoming dyslexia: A new and complete science-based program for reading problems at any level*. New York: Knopf.

Sheridan, K., E. Zinchenko, and H. Gardner (in press). Neuroethics in education. In *Neuroethics: Defining the issues in theory, practice, and policy*. J. Illes, ed. Oxford: Oxford University Press.

Siok, W. T., C. A. Perfetti, Z. Jin, and L. H. Tan (2004). Biological abnormality of impaired reading is constrained by culture. *Nature* 431: 71–76.

Stanovich, K. (2003). Understanding the styles of science in the study of reading. *Scientific Studies of Reading* 7(2): 105–126.

Suárez-Orozco, M., and D. Qin-Hilliard, eds. (2004). *Globalization: Culture and education in the new millennium*. Berkeley and Los Angeles: University of California Press; NY, NY: Ross Institute.

Sur, M., A. Angelucci, and J. Sharma (1999). Rewiring cortex: The role of patterned activity in development and plasticity of neocortical circuits. *Journal of Neurobiology* 41(1): 33–43.

Teicher, M. H. (2002). Scars that won't heal: The neurobiology of child abuse. *Scientific American* 286(3): 68–75.

Tressoldi, P. E., G. Stella, and M. Faggella (2001). The development of reading speed in Italians with dyslexia: A longitudinal study. *Journal of Learning Disabilities*, 34: 414–417.

Vellutino, F., J. Fletcher, M. Snowling, and D. Scanlon (2004). Specific reading disability (dyslexia): What have we learned in the past four decades? *Journal of Child Psychology and Psychiatry* 45(1): 2–40.

Wimmer, H. (1993). Characteristics of developmental dyslexia in a regular writing system. *Applied Psycholinguistics* 14(1): 1–33.

FOUR

Hanna Damasio and Antonio Damasio

SOCIAL CONDUCT,
NEUROBIOLOGY, AND EDUCATION

A defining feature of citizenship is the practice of appropriate social conduct, which, stated simply, consists of behaviors consonant with the social conventions, ethical rules, and laws of a given culture. Because creating a citizen, in the most ample sense of the term, is arguably one of the main goals of education, it follows that teaching and learning appropriate social conduct constitute critical aspects of education. It follows also that the conditions under which individuals acquire and use the knowledge contained in social conventions, rules, and laws would be of interest to educators concerned with issues of curriculum content and educational technique. Our purpose in this text is to consider, from a biological perspective, the possible underpinnings of both the learning and deployment processes of such knowledge.

A reasonable position to take at the start of this inquiry is that appropriate social conduct results both from neurobiological factors and from learning sociocultural knowledge and skills and that the interaction of biological and sociocultural factors is needed for appropriate social conduct to emerge. This position is supported by a host of established facts. For example, for appropriate social conduct to occur, the current environment must be compatible with the execution of the behavior (a distorted sociocultural environment can inhibit the practice of the most laudable ethical rules).

Likewise, appropriate social behaviors must not be inhibited by current biological dysfunction, examples of which include depression and psychosis. Also, the neurobiological devices necessary for any complex behavior to occur must have been put in place by the genome, and the individual's biological development must have allowed those neurobiological devices to mature normally. In other words, the brain substrate for the traditional instruments of behavior—attention, perception, learning and memory, language, reasoning—must have been assembled under the control of the genome and must have matured normally. Certainly, specific impairments of such instruments can be caused by neurological conditions with a genetic component (e.g., learning disorders) or by neurological diseases occurring later in development.

This reasonable position, however, does not address, let alone answer, a set of related questions: What portion of the repertoire of appropriate social behaviors is available spontaneously to the developing individual, based on the operation of both the biological devices mentioned above and perhaps other devices, and what portion of that repertoire is either entirely learned or a modification of the spontaneous repertoire? In other words, are there specific neurobiological devices that support social behavior repertoires *and* are available via the genome as outlined for the traditional instruments of normal behavior? And if there are such devices, how do they express themselves—spontaneously or with the help of educational interventions?

Although a definitive answer to these questions is not possible at the moment, it is possible to consider some of the available evidence regarding the biological underpinnings of the process. One approach is to inquire about the presence of comparable social behaviors in nonhuman species in which individuals are not subject to pedagogy and are not immersed in a historical context. Studies of nonhuman primates and other species have shown, unequivocally, by formal experiments and behavioral descriptions, that in the appropriate circumstances, animals can exhibit compassionate behavior toward other living beings (including individuals of other species); can exhibit behaviors denoting an appreciation of the fairness (or lack thereof) of the conduct of others; can produce behaviors resembling those that denote shame; and can exhibit an exquisite observance of social conventions regarding submission or dominance within a hierarchical scheme (see, for example, de Waal 1996; Damasio 2003; and Brosman & de Waal, 2003). We do not suggest that those behaviors are as complex and subtle as the moral behaviors of humans. But the features of those behaviors resemble the more complex human variety in a convincing way. We regard those animal behaviors as evidence that some repertoires of appropriate social conduct are present in nonhuman species early in development, spontaneously or after limited exposures to minimal tutoring. Such repertoires likely depend, then, on a neurobiological facilitation transmitted by the genome. And if that can be true for nonhuman species, we believe it is reasonable to assume that it would be so for humans.

Another approach to the unanswered questions posed above depends on studies of social conduct carried out in humans with neurological disease using techniques of cognitive neuroscience. This approach is the substance of our article. Here we will focus on our findings from an investigation of a large group of neurological patients who sustained damage to a specific region of the brain: the frontal lobe. The investigation used the lesion method. This method permits an unusual dissection of brain-behavior relationships that derives from the possibility of contrasting brain-behavior states before and after naturally occurring focal brain damage.

Although it is now known that damage to almost any sector of the frontal lobe causes abnormalities of cognition and behavior, the sectors on which we concentrate are the ventral and mesial sectors (the ventromesial prefrontal cortex, or VMPFC). Causes of damage to these sectors include head injury, the surgical resection of certain benign brain tumors (e.g., meningeomas), and cerebrovascular disease (which can cause rupture of anterior communicating artery aneurysms, or a stroke in the territory of the anterior cerebral artery).

An important discovery reported in our studies was that the consequences of frontal lobe damage in adulthood were quite different from those early in life. That is why we will review the evidence relating to these groups of patients separately.

FRONTAL LOBE DAMAGE BEGINNING IN ADULTHOOD

We conducted our studies on patients whose development was normal and who exhibited appropriate social conduct prior to the onset of neurological disease. Because by all accounts the patients' behavior was normal before the onset of brain dysfunction, and because the environment did not change in any significant way before the onset of abnormal behaviors, studying these patients allowed us to investigate abnormal behaviors whose appearance cannot be attributed to genomic, biodevelopmental, sociodevelopmental, or cultural factors. We have described these patients in several previous publications and continued to study them through the years; here we will review the salient aspects of their presentations as originally described (Damasio et al. 1991; Damasio 1994).

After the onset of brain damage the patients maintained a normal general intelligence. Sensory and motor skills, conventional memory, and speech and language also remained normal. However, their daily conduct changed radically after the neurological event. The patients no longer kept their commitments, did not show up on time for their jobs, and did not observe the steps necessary to complete a task. They were derailed by irrelevant side issues and could not make plans for their immediate or distant future. They showed a flattening of primary emotions such as fear and anger and, more important, showed a severe compromise of social emotions such as embarrassment, shame, and compassion (Damasio 1994, 2003). The social emotions embody a wide array of moral knowledge. Although these emotions develop and mature in a sociocultural context, they appear in primitive form in complex species other than humans, as noted earlier.

Damage elsewhere in the brain does *not* cause this syndrome. In other words, focal damage to various regions of the temporal lobe or the parietal and occipital cortices causes all manner of specific disturbances of memory, language, perception, and movement, to name but a few, but not the syndrome described above. Even more important, damage elsewhere within the frontal lobe does not cause the syndrome. Damage to the dorsal aspects of the frontal lobe (the dorsolateral prefrontal cortex, or DLPFC), for example, disturbs mind and behavior but not in quite the same way. In brief, the association between disturbed behavior and site of brain dysfunction is specific. (Further investigation of these cases, as well as complementary investigations using functional neuroimaging, is likely to reveal additional specificities regarding age and gender of the subject).

When these patients are studied in the laboratory, they present with normal profiles in the basic neuropsychological tasks (verbal and performance IQ, learning and memory, language, reasoning skills). Even in completing special tasks, whose impairment is associated with frontal lobe dysfunction; tasks measuring the ability to make cognitive estimates and judge recency and frequency; or the Wisconsin Card Sorting Task, these patients tend to be normal. This is also the case for tasks specifically measuring the capacity for social problem solving. These include the Optional Thinking Test, designed to measure the ability to generate alternative solutions to a social dilemma, and the Awareness of Consequences Test, which measures the ability to generate a list of consequences of a particular action (Platt & Spivack 1977; Spivack, Platt, & Shure 1976); and the Means-Ends Problem-Solving Procedure, which measures the ability to conceptualize step-by-step means to achieve a certain goal (Platt and Spivack 1974, 1977). In brief, patients with adult-onset damage to VMPFC perform these tasks in the same way that normal adult subjects do. In the Kohlberg paradigm of the Standard Moral Interview, a task designed to assess the ability to resolve social and moral situations (Colby & Kohlberg 1987), the vast majority of these patients attained the second level, characteristic of most adults, and one patient reached the third level, which is attained by only a minority of adults (Saver and Damasio 1991). Once again, these behaviors are indistinguishable from those of a normal population. Thus the contrast is dramatic: adult-onset VMPFC patients exhibit abnormal social problem solving in real life and real time, but show normal social problem solving when they are tested in a laboratory setting.

The situation changes dramatically, however, when these patients are exposed to emotionally competent stimuli such as familiar human faces or scenes depicting suffering: they show abnormally low skin conductance responses (SCRs), even while they recognize normally the unique faces and correctly describe the situations of suffering—a clear indication that they do not mount normal emotional responses to stimuli competent to cause emotions.

These patients' behavior is equally abnormal in another laboratory task designed to test decision making, the Iowa Gambling Task, or IGT (Bechara, A. R. Damasio, H. Damasio, & Anderson 1994). The complex setting of the IGT resembles real life in that it involves rewards and punishments for card choices made under uncertainty from unidentified card decks, some of which turn out to be "good" and others "bad." The IGT was developed to investigate and measure the disability in decision making that VMPFC patients show in their day-to-day behavior. The results have been described elsewhere (Bechara, A. R. Damasio, H. Damasio, & Anderson 1994; Bechara, Tranel, H. Damasio, & A. R. Damasio 1996, 1997). In brief, unlike the traditional neuropsychological tasks that VMPFC patients pass, the IGT captures the abnormal decision making these patients show in their daily lives. This is probably due to the realistic conflicts between immediate and long-term gains that the task embodies, and to the fairly long period over which the task measures performance, rather than requiring only a simple, one-time response.

The IGT can be played while skin conductance responses (SCRs) are continually monitored so that different stages of the performance can be analyzed separately from the standpoint of the associated psychophysiological responses. For example, the SCRs that occur immediately after a punishment or reward (which we call the "consequent" SCR) and the SCRs that occur in the five-second interval preceding the actual choice of a card (the "anticipatory" SCR) can be measured. Both normal subjects and patients exhibit consequent SCRs, which tend to be of higher amplitude after a punishment than after a reward. (On average, the amplitude of the consequent responses in VMPFC patients is slightly lower than that of normal subjects, but the ranges overlap.) However, with respect to the anticipatory SCRs, the two groups diverge remarkably. Normal subjects show anticipatory SCRs that discriminate among the decks: the responses are of high amplitude for the decks leading to bad outcomes, and of low amplitude for the "good" decks. Furthermore, the amplitude of the anticipatory SCRs to the bad decks starts to increase early in the session, when the subjects are still sampling from all decks.

VMPFC patients behave entirely differently. Their anticipatory SCRs are of uniformly very low amplitude for *all decks*, thus failing to show any discrimination between good and bad outcomes. Because SCRs are an index, albeit incomplete, of the emotional responsivity of the subject, they capture the emotional defect of these patients during a realistic situation of decision making.

Our interpretation of the IGT results draws on the Somatic Marker Hypothesis (Damasio et al. 1991; Damasio 1994, 1996). The hypothesis posits that we normally rely not only on a cold analysis of a situation but also on an emotionally related signal that steers reasoning and choice to the actions that predict good outcomes. This signal is the somatic marker, which can be conscious, as in a gut feeling, or nonconscious. The somatic marker is related to prior experience of comparable situations of conflict that were either rewarded or punished. We believe that the lack of anticipatory SCRs is an index of the absence of somatic markers, and that the absence of somatic markers precludes an advantageous performance.

As noted earlier, patients with dorsolateral prefrontal cortex (DLPFC) damage may also have abnormal social conduct and can fail the IGT. However, they also show overt cognitive impairments. Their social conduct and decision-making defects are part of a larger picture of cognitive defects. The dissociation between general preserved intellect and impaired decision making that characterized the VMPFC patients does not obtain for the DLPFC patients. The emotional impairments are not as distinct.

Another explanation that has been adduced for the patients' behavior in the IGT is that they fail to learn that the contingencies are being reversed—that is, that a high-reward deck suddenly becomes a high-penalty deck. According to that explanation, patients would simply stick to the bad decks. This explanation is not satisfactory. Many patients with prefrontal damage in the ventromedial sector (as opposed to the dorso-lateral or lateral orbital sectors) who show the neuropsychological profile described earlier do exhibit normal performance in tasks measuring the ability to learn contingency reversals. This is also evident in their ability to perform well in the Wisconsin Card Sorting Task (see also Buse-meyer and Stout 2002; Stout et al. 2002). Only a subgroup of patients with VMPFC damage, those whose lesion involves the posterior sector of the mesial orbital region and damages of the basal forebrain area, may show defects in tasks of contingency reversal learning (Bechara, H. Damasio, & A. R. Damasio 2003; Bechara & Damasio 2004). This is seen, for instance, in patients with damage due to rupture of anterior communicating aneurysms. (That is also true in the patients described by Fellows and Farah in 2003. Most of their cases showed damage to the basal forebrain region, as visible in the image of the lesion overlap, and consequently presented with defects in contingency reversal learning.)

FRONTAL LOBE DAMAGE BEGINNING EARLY IN LIFE

We have also studied patients with lesions similar to those described in the adult-onset group but acquired early in life—as early as the first day of life and as late as age seven. In the thirteen cases we have studied so far, we investigated most of these patients as young adults, long after the onset of their lesions. As in the adult-onset group the cause of damage was varied, and damage could be bilateral or unilateral. Also as with the adult-onset group, these patients were of normal intelligence, and their sensory and motor skills, conventional memory, and speech and language were also normal. As young children they exhibited dysfunctional social interactions, both at school and at home. They showed difficulty in controlling their behavior and were insensitive to punishment. In spite of normal intelligence, they usually needed special schooling because of poor work habits. They did not make friends. After high-school graduation, once they lost a relatively structured environment, their social and behavior problems worsened remarkably. They did not make plans for the future, did not seek employment, and could not maintain whatever jobs may have been found for them. They often got into direct conflict with the law (Anderson, Barrash, Bechara, & Tranel 2006).

As indicated for patients with adult-onset damage, the relation between disturbed behavior and site of dysfunction is specific. Early-onset damage elsewhere in the brain does *not* cause this same collection of symptoms.

The neuropsychological profile of these patients is comparable to that of the adult-onset group (see Anderson et al. 1999). They also show hypoemotionality, or a remarkable absence of social emotions, and their performance on IGT is abnormal. The remarkable difference compared to the adult-onset group appears in the results of tasks measuring social interactions. Here the early-onset VMPFC patients perform *abnormally* in the tasks in which the adult-onset patients do so well. In the Kohlberg paradigm they do not advance beyond the first level (the level most normal children reach by age nine). In brief, while adult-onset VMPFC patients have abnormal social conduct but appear to know the rules they violate, early-onset VMPFC patients not only show abnormal social conduct but also seem not to have learned the social rules that govern their social conduct.

That these patients can learn a large body of information taught at home and in schools but fail to learn social conventions, social skills, and the specific rules under which social behavior operates is an intriguing fact that requires explanation. It is not reasonable to suppose that social knowledge poses greater difficulty than other kinds of knowledge. For example, children with neurological conditions leading to mental retardation (e.g., Down syndrome) can engage in social conduct of a far more adaptive quality.

THE NEUROANATOMICAL AND NEUROPSYCHOLOGICAL CORRELATES OF ABNORMAL SOCIAL CONDUCT

Let us begin with the salient neuroanatomical correlates of abnormal social conduct. Damage to VMPFC, bilateral or unilateral, whether acquired in adulthood or in childhood, causes a marked disturbance of social conduct but leaves largely intact the principal cognitive instruments: attention, learning, memory, language, and basic reasoning strategies. The strength of the defect appears to be related to the hemispheric side of the damage and to the gender of the subject. A preliminary study from our laboratory suggests that frontal damage in the right hemisphere is more likely to cause the defect in men than in women, while frontal damage in the left hemisphere has the reverse effect (Tranel, Damasio, Denburg, & Bechara 2005).

Damage to the posterior sectors of the VMPFC, the sector closest to the basal forebrain region, and damage to the dorsolateral prefrontal sector are also associated with abnormal social conduct, but the defects are manifested in significant cognitive impairments such as defective working memory.

As for the most salient neuropsychological trait present in these patients, there is no doubt that a disorder of emotion and feeling, especially in relation to the social emotions, is the obligatory accompaniment of impairments of social conduct.

THE NEUROLOGICAL MECHANISMS
BEHIND ABNORMAL SOCIAL CONDUCT

The VMPFC region appears necessary for triggering several, perhaps most, social emotions, and its function in this regard is comparable to that of the amygdala regarding fear. Following early damage to the VMPFC, neither the spontaneous expression nor the early sociocultural tuning of social emotions would be possible. In the absence of spontaneous social emotions, early-onset VMPFC patients would not react normally and would thus be deprived of normal interactions with others, namely by receiving abnormal reactions from others. Given this two-way disruption of relationships, individuals so affected would likely not acquire a normal view of social interactions. An alternative and complementary mechanism posits that following early damage the individuals would lose the brain substrate best suited to inscribing the learning of the sort of inhibitory responses that curb socially unacceptable survival responses.

The two mechanisms outlined above would not be the only path to developing abnormal social conduct in the early-onset cases, and might not be the critical mechanism in patients with adult-onset frontal damage. The critical mechanism in the adult-onset patients would depend on another function we have long proposed for the VMPFC. We believe this sector of the prefrontal cortex is a repository of the learned linkage between, on one hand, situations calling for a decision and the outcomes of decisions and, on the other, the emotional state associated with the situations or with the outcome of the decisions. We see the VMPFC as housing the record of the situation-and-associated-emotion linkage (or the outcome-and-resulting-emotion linkage). When a situation of the same category as one previously experienced presents itself, the VMPFC generates the emotion previously linked to that situation category and to the outcome of the ensuing decision. This emotion-on-demand is the somatic marker. It can be conscious or unconscious and can be indexed by physiological manifestations such as SCRs (though SCRs are *not* somatic markers, but rather a *consequence* of the deployment of a somatic marker). In this specific role, once again, the VMPFC is a trigger region for emotions, both social and primary (such as fear).

Following both early-onset and adult-onset VMPFC lesions, the learning of new somatic markers *and* the evocation of previously learned somatic markers would be precluded, thus accounting for many of the defects seen in the adult-onset patients and for some of the defects in the early-onset cases.

What is the likely neural mechanism of the VMPFC? The normal VMPFC would operate on other brain structures, namely the DLPFC, where we suspect that signaling from VMPFC plays a role in reasoning and decision making via the intermediary action of subcortical regions such as the amygdala. In other words, the somatic markers evoked by the VMPFC would depend on signaling from subcortical structures and exert their role in guiding behavior via brain regions that participate importantly in the reasoning process, namely the DLPFC.

Conceiving of the role of the frontal lobe in this manner helps explain the role of emotion impairments in the conduct of these patients. First, the social emotions embody the sort of social knowledge with which normal social conduct can be shaped by means of gradual fine-tuning in childhood and adolescence. Without the deployment of social emotions, social fine-tuning is not possible. Second, emotions probably play a major role in the individual's learning of which actions produce good and right outcomes, or bad and wrong outcomes, relative to social norms. This is because positive and negative emotions incorporate, respectively, elements of reward and punishment that automatically qualify the associated actions in terms of normative judgments. In brief, positive and negative emotions would be necessary to construct a personal ethical profile. Therefore, in adults, the acquired emotional knowledge regarding the link between actions and outcomes would play an important role in promoting and facilitating socially adaptive behavior. Emotions, in their many varieties, would be an indispensable tool in both constructing and utilizing "personalized" social knowledge.

Patients with other kinds of pathology provide evidence that does converge with what we posit here. Cleckley (1955) and Hare (1993) have shown that developmental psychopaths whose intelligence can be regarded as normal when evaluated with standard psychometric tests have a profound blunting of emotion, a profile somewhat reminiscent of that seen in patients with VMPFC damage. Moreover, Hare also demonstrated that emotionally competent stimuli fail to evoke SCRs in such individuals, supporting the notion that in these patients the threshold for triggering emotions is abnormally high (Hare & Quinn 1971). More recently, Raine has shown that criminal psychopaths have a significant volumetric reduction of prefrontal lobe structures. Remarkably, neither drug addicts nor nonpsychotic psychiatric patients show a comparable defect (Raine et al. 2000). It is thus conceivable that in some instances, developmental psychopathy is caused by dysfunction in prefrontal cortices, although not necessarily due to overt focal damage. And it seems also plausible that such dysfunction may be related to environmental factors.

CONCLUSIONS

Considered together, the findings discussed above suggest the following: (1) certain neurological conditions in which appropriate social conduct is disrupted in relative isolation can be traced to the failure of specific brain systems and can, in the absence of causative sociocultural factors, be accounted for by neural dysfunction alone. (2) In these conditions the impairment of normal emotion appears to play a critical role in the disruption of social conduct.

IMPLICATIONS FOR EDUCATION

The evidence discussed above supports the notion that the development of appropriate social conduct is the result of interacting biological and educational factors. Children probably do not become socially competent citizens exclusively on the basis of the concepts they are taught at home and in schools, anymore than they become linguistically competent entirely from the language teaching provided by parents, teachers, and peers. On the other hand, children are not innately programmed moral agents.

The impairment of specific brain systems in children (1) precludes the normal development of social emotions, a repertoire of behaviors that is directly linked to the governance of social interactions and that implicitly contains moral knowledge; (2) precludes learning how to inhibit socially unsuitable behaviors; and (3) precludes learning the linkages between outcomes of choices and associated emotions. In adults, in whom the learning referred to in (2) and (3) has already occurred, damage to the same brain systems precludes access to the learned know-how, along with the compromised development of social emotions. In other words, brain damage not only can disrupt the instruments of cognition necessary to learn about the social world and effectively operate in it— perception, attention, memory, language, reasoning—but can also disrupt brain systems that support a specialized repertoire of social knowledge and skills.

The evidence also suggests that emotions play an indispensable role both in the acquisition of social knowledge *and* in the ultimate practice to which the acquisition leads. Emotion is part and parcel of the acquisition and deployment processes and, in effect, forms a part of the very body of social knowledge. This in turn suggests that a detailed investigation of emotional factors in the educational practices related to social conduct would be a valuable area of future inquiry.

NOTE

This work was supported by grants from the National Institutes of Health (PO NINDS NS19632) and the Mathers Foundation.

REFERENCES

Anderson, S. W., A. Bechara, H. Damasio, D. Tranel, and A. R. Damasio (1999). Impairment of social and moral behavior related to early damage in the human prefrontal cortex. *Nature Neuroscience* 2: 1032–1037.

Anderson, S. W., J. Barrash, A. Bechara, and D. Tranel (2006). Impairments of emotion and real-world behavior following childhood- or adult-onset damage to ventromedial prefrontal cortex. *Journal of the International Neuropsychological Society* 12: 224–235.

Bechara, A. (2003). Risky business: Emotion, decision-making and addiction. *Journal of Gambling Studies* 19(1): 23–51.

Bechara, A., and A. Damasio (2004) The somatic marker hypothesis: A neural theory of economic decision. Special issue on neuroscience economics, *Games and Economic Behavior* 1: 1–37.

Bechara, A., A. R. Damasio, H. Damasio, and S. W. Anderson (1994). Insensitivity to future consequences following damage to human prefrontal cortex. *Cognition* 50: 7–15.

Bechara, A., D. Tranel, H. Damasio, and A. R. Damasio (1996). Failure to respond autonomically to anticipated future outcomes following damage to prefrontal cortex. *Cerebral Cortex* 6: 215–225.

Bechara, A., D. Tranel, H. Damasio, and A. R. Damasio (1997). Deciding advantageously before knowing the advantageous strategy. *Science* 275: 1293–1294.

Bechara, A., et al. (1998). Dissociation of working memory from decision making within the human prefrontal cortex. *Journal of Neuroscience* 18: 428–437.

Bechara, A., H. Damasio, and A. R. Damasio (2003). The role of the amygdala in decision-making. *Annals of the New York Academy of Sciences* 985: 356–369.

Brosman, S. F., and F. B. M. de Waal (2003). Monkeys reject unequal pay. *Nature* 425: 297–299.

Busemeyer, J. R., and J. C. Stout (2002). A contribution of cognitive decision models to clinical assessment: Decomposing performance on the Bechara gambling task. *Psychological Assessment* 14: 253–262.

Cleckley, H. (1955). *The mask of sanity*. St. Louis, MO: C. V. Mosby.

Colby, A., and L. Kohlberg (1987). *The measurements of moral judgment*. New York: Cambridge University Press.

Damasio, A. R. (1994). *Descartes' error: Emotion, reason, and the human brain*. New York: Penguin Books.

Damasio, A. R. (1996). The somatic marker hypothesis and the possible functions of the prefrontal cortex. *Philosophical Transactions of the Royal Society of London (Biology)* 351: 1413–1420.

Damasio, A. R. (2003). *Looking for Spinoza: Joy, sorrow, and the feeling brain*. New York: Harcourt.

Damasio, A. R., et al. (1991). Somatic markers and the guidance of behavior: Theory and preliminary testing. In *Frontal lobe function and dysfunction*. H .S. Levin et al., eds. Pp. 217–229. Oxford: Oxford University Press.

de Waal, F. B. M. (1996). *Good natured: The origins of right and wrong in humans and other animals*. Cambridge, MA: Harvard University Press.

Fellows, L. K., and M. J. Farah (2003). Ventromedial frontal cortex mediates affective shifting in humans: Evidence from a reversal learning paradigm. *Brain* 126: 1830–1837.

Hare, R. D. (1993). *Without conscience*. New York: Pocket Books.

Hare, R. D., and M. J. Quinn (1971). Psychopathy and autonomic conditioning. *Journal of Abnormal Psychology* 77: 223–235.

Platt, J., and G. Spivack (1974). Means of solving real-life problems: I. Psychiatric patients versus controls and cross-cultural comparisons of normal females. *Journal of Community Psychology* 2: 45–48.

Platt, J., and G. Spivack (1977). *Measures of interpersonal problem-solving for adults and adolescents*. Philadelphia: Department of Mental Health Sciences, Hahnemann Medical College.

Raine, A., T. Lencz, S. Bihrle, L. LaCasse, and P. Colletti (2000). Reduced prefrontal gray matter volume and reduced autonomic activity in antisocial personality disorder. *Archives of General Psychiatry* 57: 119–127.

Saver, J. L., and A. R. Damasio (1991). Preserved access and processing of social knowledge in a patient with acquired sociopathy due to ventromedial frontal damage. *Neuropsychologia* 29: 1241–1249.

Spivack G., J. Platt, and M. B. Shure (1976). *The problem-solving approach to adjustment*. San Francisco: Jossey-Bass.

Stout, J. *et al* (2002) Cognitive modeling of decision making in a simulated gambling task in frontal or somatosensory cortex damage. *Journal of Cognitive Neuroscience* C27 Suppl.: 75.

Tranel D., H. Damasio, N. L. Denburg, and A. Bechara (2005). Does gender play a role in functional asymmetry of ventromedial prefrontal cortex? *Brain* 128: 2872–2881.

PART TWO

LEARNING AND THE FUNCTIONS OF EDUCATION IN A CHANGING GLOBAL ECONOMY

FIVE

Robert A. LeVine

THE GLOBAL SPREAD OF
WOMEN'S SCHOOLING

Effects on Learning, Literacy, Health, and Children

INTRODUCTION

At the Tensta Gymnasium in Stockholm in March 2005, I found myself conversing with three teenage girls whose families came from Eritrea and Ethiopia. As they were correcting my inadequate knowledge of the linguistic relationships between ethnic groups in their home region, I could not help thinking that, had they grown up in that region, the East Horn of Africa—they probably would not have been attending secondary school or speaking English. They might not have gone to school at all. The adult female literacy rate in 2000 was 45 percent in Eritrea and 31 percent in Ethiopia. The proportion of girls enrolled in secondary school between 1997 and 2000 was 23 percent in Eritrea and 14 percent in Ethiopia (UNICEF 2003). The Tensta students were thus educationally more advantaged than their counterparts "at home"; this disparity has long created a strong incentive for parents in poor countries to improve the life chances of their children by moving to Sweden and other countries where schooling is universal and of relatively high quality.

The focus of this chapter is on the women in poor and developing countries who stayed behind when others emigrated during the second half of the twentieth century. Their access to formal education also improved during this period (though less dramatically than that of the emigrants)—for some through migration from rural villages to urban centers, and for the others through the expansion of rural schools—and the greater inclusion of girls in schooling—throughout the country. There is much to be learned by examining the consequences of their educational experience, partly because so much of it was in schools of low quality and partly because it did not involve the dislocations of international immigration. Low-quality schooling raises the question of whether anything at all is learned, a question my research group has been investigating. Without the associated changes involved in international immigration, it may be easier to identify the effects of schooling per se apart from those of other factors that have also changed. We believe that the findings from our research are relevant to women, children, and families everywhere there is variation in the school attendance levels of girls and women.

In the year 2000, 86 percent of the world's school-aged population (aged six to twenty-three years) lived in less developed countries; by the year 2025, this proportion will rise to 90 percent; for primary school-aged children the figures are 88 and 91 per cent, respectively (United Nations Population Division 2005, p. 10). In other words, most children in the world today, and their parents, live outside Europe, North America, and Japan. The diverse contexts in which their learning takes place should compel the attention of educational policy analysts.

In this chapter I present findings from and reflections on a comparative study of the effects of women's schooling in four countries—Mexico, Nepal, Zambia, and Venezuela—during the second half of the twentieth century. The study was designed to identify the processes by which sending girls to school results in benefits to families and children and to find out the extent to which learning and literacy are involved. By directly assessing the literacy and language skills mothers acquired in school, we have demonstrated in some detail the part such skills might have played in the social transformation and demographic transition of developing countries from 1950 to 2000.

The value of women's schooling for achieving gender equity goals and addressing health, population, and family problems in developing countries is so well established in international discourse (e.g., in United Nations declarations and the publications of UNICEF and the World Bank) that it is easy to overlook our lack of knowledge of how school experience actually influences socially desirable outcomes related to health, fertility, and child development. Furthermore, because Western researchers are predisposed by their ideological heritage to assume that universal education, including that of girls, is socially beneficial,[1] it may seem unnecessary to investigate the matter further. Our research shows, however, that much is to be gained from such investigations conducted in the diverse contexts of the poor and middle-income countries where mass schooling, particularly that of girls, has only recently been introduced. The evidence from our studies concerning the effects of school learning on mothers holds many implications for social policy in the developing world.

EFFECTS OF MATERNAL SCHOOLING: THEORY AND EVIDENCE

Figure 5.1 outlines the pathways through which the micro-level processes of our theoretical model and our findings exert a causal influence, indicating that maternal school attainment in childhood and adolescence (box 1) leads to the acquisition of literacy and language skills (2) that influence a mother's health skills (3) and health behavior (4), on the left side of the chart, and her educational practices (6), on the right, with both having outcomes (5 and 7) beneficial to children.

A large body of evidence from demographic and health research shows that developments represented by the top and bottom of the chart on the left side (boxes 1 and 5) are robustly related. In other words, maternal school attainment is related to reduced child mortality, malnutrition, and fertility even when other socioeconomic factors are controlled (R. A. LeVine, S. E. LeVine, & Schnell 2001). Similarly, a substantial educational research literature shows maternal school attainment to be related to child literacy skills (box 7) in the United States and some other places, when other socioeconomic factors are statistically controlled (Hoff-Ginsburg & Tardif 1995). Our research focused on measuring the intervening variables of the middle boxes—literacy and language skills, health skills, utilization of health services, and maternal tutoring of preschool children—to test the validity of these hypothetical pathways from women's schooling to the outcomes indicated in figure 5.1.

Instead of presenting our findings in detail, I shall outline a history of the developing countries in the half century after World War II as it affected the predicament of mothers striving to provide for their young children. Suffice it to say at this point that the evidence supporting the causal pathways of figure 5.1 comes from the field studies we conducted between 1983 and 1998 in six sites located in Mexico, Nepal, Zambia, and Venezuela.[2] The literacy data were one-time (i.e., cross-sectional) studies of at least 160 mothers in each country.[3] The quantitative data from the studies were analyzed by regression and published in peer-reviewed journals (Dexter, S. E. LeVine, & Velasco 1998; R. A. LeVine, S. E. LeVine, Rowe, &

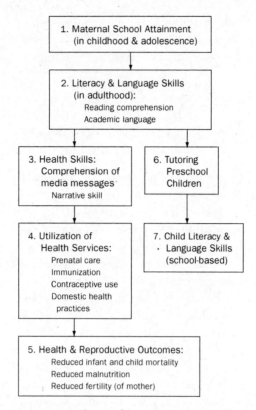

1. Maternal School Attainment
   (in childhood & adolescence)

2. Literacy & Language Skills
   (in adulthood):
   Reading comprehension
   Academic language

3. Health Skills:
   Comprehension of
   media messages
   Narrative skill

6. Tutoring
   Preschool
   Children

4. Utilization of
   Health Services:
   Prenatal care
   Immunization
   Contraceptive use
   Domestic health
   practices

7. Child Literacy &
   Language Skills
   (school-based)

5. Health & Reproductive Outcomes:
   Reduced infant and child mortality
   Reduced malnutrition
   Reduced fertility (of mother)

Figure 5.1 Pathways from maternal schooling and literacy to outcomes related to health, reproduction, and child learning.

Schnell-Anzola 2004; Schnell-Anzola, Rowe, & LeVine 2005; Stuebing 1996). Although the findings largely confirmed the links appearing on figure 5.1, and a large-scale UNICEF–Tribhuvan University survey conducted during 2000 in two other districts of Nepal provided additional support for the literacy–health behavior linkage (Rowe et al. 2005), interesting variations and qualifications are discussed later in this paper. At this point I turn to the history and the processes—political, institutional, and economic—in which these causal pathways were embedded.

HISTORICAL PERSPECTIVE

Over the past 150 years, an educational vision that originated in eighteenth-century Europe has been realized through the spread of mass institu-

Table 5.1 Adult female literacy rates in four
developing countries, 1980 and 1995 (%)

	Venezuela	Mexico	Zambia	Nepal
1980	82	80	43	7
1995	90	87	71	14

NOTE: Females aged fifteen years or over.

tionalized schooling—first for men, then women; first in Western, then
in other countries; and first at the primary, then at the secondary and
postsecondary levels. As late as 1945, it did not seem inevitable that the
countries of Latin America, Africa, Asia, and the Pacific would have
mass schooling on the Western model, especially for females, but by 2000,
virtually all of them did, and many were expanding school attendance
at postprimary levels. The scale and rapidity of this expansion in the developing countries during the second half of the twentieth century was
truly dramatic. In 1970, 56 percent of adults in the less developed regions
had *never* been to school; by 2000, only 34 percent were unschooled,
despite enormous population growth. The adult female literacy rate in
the developing world was only 35 percent in 1970, but 66 percent in
2000. There were great variations across countries, captured by figures
for 1980 and 1995 for the four countries in which we did our research
(table 5.1).

The Latin American countries we studied, Venezuela and Mexico, had
already achieved high levels of female literacy by 1980, but less than half
the women in Zambia and very few in Nepal had attended school for five
years at that time. Fifteen years later, Zambia's adult female literacy
rate exceeded two-thirds, and Nepal's rate had doubled, though the
country was still far behind. Rates at all levels were continuing to grow
at the turn of the century.

But many other features of the environment of families were changing at a similar pace at the same time, often obscuring the impact of
women's schooling on outcomes related to health, reproduction, and child
development. These changes can be divided into three categories: structure, resources, and communications.

Changes in structure include urbanization; the advent of an urban occupational structure with a social hierarchy based on educational credentials for employment, rather than an agrarian social hierarchy based on
age, sex, and participation in domestic agriculture and craft production

(LeVine & White 1986); and the growth of bureaucratic institutions, concentrated in cities or metropolitan areas, for health, education, economic production, government, transportation, and communications.

"Changes in resources" refer to increases in cash incomes and consumer goods at the household level. Despite the simultaneous growth, often massive, of income inequality, most families in the developing world gained in income and basic goods during the second half of the twentieth century. (This does not mean they became more content; on the contrary, they were likely to have become less satisfied with their permanently low positions in the new social hierarchy, but many did acquire some resources that could be used for health care, school fees, and so forth.)

And finally, "changes in communications" refer to the exposure to new kinds of information and symbol systems by means of mass media and also through schooling, which provides training in literacy-based codes of communication, enabling pupils to access a wide range of information and models for behavior through the print and broadcast media. Of particular interest in our research has been the acquisition in school of a speech code based on written texts that can be used (in adulthood) for communicating in other bureaucratic settings such as health clinics.

By the late 1970s, social science research made clear that in spite of all these concomitant changes in Third World countries, women's schooling had a strong and independent effect on reduced child mortality and fertility and increased use of health facilities and contraception, as demonstrated by statistical analyses that controlled other socioeconomic factors such as community size, household income, and husband's occupation and school attainment. Those findings have been replicated many times over in the massive World Fertility Study of the 1970s and the Demographic and Health Surveys since the 1980s (for reviews, see R. A. LeVine, S. E. LeVine, & Schnell 2001; United Nations Population Division 2005).

THE QUESTION OF LITERACY

Literacy, however, was not in the picture, at least for many of the demographers and sociologists who analyzed these bodies of data. Rather, those researchers favored explanations based on the idea that women's schooling changed the status of girls from agrarian backgrounds (through the awarding of credentials for employment and advantageous marriages) or altered their social attitudes (sense of self-worth, aspirations), rather than the notion that the girls acquired any of the skills that schools are officially organized to teach.

There were reasons to imagine that school learning of literacy and other parts of the official curriculum might not be responsible for the powerful impact of women's schooling. The schools were generally of low quality and became worse as enrollments expanded with population growth (Fuller & Heyneman 1989): schools lacked basic physical facilities (chairs, desks, blackboards, textbooks); teachers were unqualified and often absent; classes were large and crowded; truancy was rife. It was plausible that nothing was being learned there. Furthermore, even if students did learn something, women often entered situations at marriage in which they had no chance to practice whatever skills they had acquired in school; thus they would lose their ability to read and write.

As it turned out, these plausible guesses were wrong. Children who have gone to low-quality schools for a few years in childhood do retain some literacy skills years later. This has been shown in longitudinal studies by Wagner (1993) in Morocco and Gorman and Pollitt in Guatemala (2001), the latter study also showing an impact on maternal health care. In our cross-sectional studies, the retention into adulthood of literacy skills learned in school—indicated by performance on reading comprehension and noun definition tasks that correlate highly with school attainment—is consistent across all four countries. Our ethnographic data show that selection bias cannot explain these results. Girls left school not because of poor performance but because they were needed at home or required to marry (S. E. LeVine 2006). Thus it becomes possible to conceive of literacy as mediating the effect of schooling on maternal behavior.

Literacy is not the only mediator of social change. All three of these categories of change contribute to improved child survival. A woman who lives in the city has better access to health care for her children. One with more income can better afford needed medicines, a private doctor, or transportation in an emergency. The woman with more income may also be married to a man of higher status whose position provides her access to higher-quality medical care. The mother who lives in the city and has more income and higher status and who is also sufficiently literate to read the labels on medicine packages, adopt recommended sanitary practices, give clinic personnel a coherent account of her child's illness, and understand the medical advice transmitted by radio and TV is least likely to lose a young child to infectious disease. Thus each of the three categories contributes to lower mortality; together, they minimize the risks to child survival in a particular context. A similar argument can be made for improvement in the child's chances of success in school. Yet while we acknowledge these co-acting factors—particularly the joint influence of urbanization, income, and status on child health and school performance—our research isolates the contribution of literacy so that it is not bundled into a conceptual package like "socioeconomic status" and forgotten. Just as health researchers in the United States have identified the unique contribution of formal education to health (e.g., Mirowsky and Ross 2003), so have we in our studies of maternal health care in developing countries.

BUREAUCRATIC SCHOOLING
AND COMMUNICATION PATTERNS

To explain these changes after 1950, we need to examine more closely the spread of schooling in the developing world. The Western school was a particular historical invention that was socially and culturally constructed in Europe and North America and then diffused to other countries in the nineteenth and twentieth centuries without major changes. John Meyer, Francisco Ramirez, and their colleagues at Stanford have documented how few changes took place in the organization and curriculum of schools as Western school systems were borrowed throughout the world (Meyer 1977; Meyer & Hannan 1979; Meyer, Kamens, & Benavot 1992; Meyer, Ramirez, & Soysal 1992; Chabott & Ramirez 1994).

Japan might seem an exception to this finding, and certainly it was exceptional during the nineteenth century as a noncolonial country outside the West able to refashion some aspects of schooling according to indigenous models of teaching and learning (LeVine & White 1986). Yet even Japanese schools retained the bureaucratic organization and basic curriculum borrowed from the West. Other non-Western countries proved far less independent than Japan in this respect.

By the late nineteenth century, with the rise of nationalism in Europe, school systems with compulsory primary-school attendance were seen as part of national power; any nation that aspired to military power, it was thought, had to have mass schooling on the European or Euro-American model. Thus the borrowing of a school system became less a function of educational vision and ideology than a requisite for building a nation-state, like a standing army, a civil service, and a diplomatic corps.

The bureaucratized mass schooling of Europe and North America, characterized by standardization of structures, roles, and training, lent itself to rapid expansion, which borrowing nations needed. Though it came from Western capitalist countries, the model was adopted with alacrity by the Soviet Union and the People's Republic of China. After the end of World War II, the founding of the United Nations, and the decolonization of Asia and Africa, nation building or "national development" became the highest priority for leaders of the new nations, and mass schooling soon spread throughout the world. The timing and pace of educational expansion varied widely among the diverse countries of the developing world. International debate continued until 1980 about the consequences of mass schooling, but few alterations were made in the model of organization and curriculum that was adopted.

Meyer and his colleagues argue that this historical convergence in mass schooling was due, at least at the beginning, to the lack of clear outcomes indicating which school systems were better. National leaders tended to borrow the most prestigious models for the organization of schooling, namely those found in the most powerful countries. In addition, international organizations and American foundations sponsored conferences from 1950 to 2000 that disseminated "common blueprints" for educational organization to developing countries (Chabott & Ramirez 2000; Chabott 2003); financial assistance for adoption of these blueprints came from rich donor countries and the World Bank. Thus the historical diffusion of models for mass schooling was not haphazard but was directed, first by widespread perceptions of national power and prestige, later by the active promotion of international organizations and development assistance agencies.

Western-style schools are standardized not only in their structural characteristics but also in their communication patterns, in which all children participate. They learn to communicate—that is, to comprehend and produce messages—in forms of discourse derived from written texts. These forms are so different from the local conversational norms the children already know that they constitute a specialized academic speech code or "register," with a number of distinctive features: the use of abstract nouns superordinate to the terms for common objects (as "animal" is to "dog" or "furniture" to "chair"), explicit descriptions that presume no shared background knowledge, and several grammatical characteristics (Snow 1991; Schleppegrell 2001). Catherine Snow and her colleagues have shown that mastery of this speech register is positively correlated with school performance. We believe children become more proficient in this language the longer they stay in school.

We used Snow's Noun Definitions Task to measure proficiency in this academic language, asking our sample mothers to define ten common nouns and counting their use of superordinate terms. We discovered their performance to be highly correlated in all four countries with maternal school attainment. In other words, the further a woman had progressed in school the better her performance on the Noun Definitions Task in adulthood. We also found academic language proficiency to be highly correlated with reading comprehension, confirming Snow's argument that such proficiency is part of the package of literacy and language skills acquired in school.

The academic register is characteristic of communication in bureaucratized schooling, but it is, in our view, characteristic of discourse in other bureaucratic settings as well, such as health clinics, employment offices, and government agencies. Thus schooling provides training for participation in bureaucracies in general, conferring skill in comprehending and producing the messages they use. This is reflected in our results concerning comprehension of public health messages in the print and broadcast media and ability to construct a coherent health (illness) narrative, both of which skills are strongly related to and predicted by academic literacy skills in our samples. The influence of schooling on health is, in other words, mediated in part through the learning of an academic speech code that facilitates communication in settings dedicated to health care. Even when it comes to radio health messages that do not involve reading texts, or medicine labels that have pictures along with words, women with better mastery of academic language and literacy skills better understand health communications and better "navigate" the communication requirements of a bureaucratic health care system (see Nielsen-Bohlman, Panzer, & Kindig 2004). Thus the learning of a bureaucratic language in school that can be used in health settings is a critical contribution of women's schooling to their maternal behavior.

Heath (1986) long ago pointed out that mothers with more schooling were more likely to tutor their preschool children, from infancy and toddlerhood onwards, using the kind of interaction sequences (interrogative-reply-evaluation) that prepares them for classroom discourse (see boxes 2, 6, and 7 in figure 5.1). We found this to be the case in Mexico (LeVine et al. 1991; R. A. LeVine, Miller, & Richman 1996; Richman, Miller, & LeVine 1992). In Nepal we found that the more-schooled mothers engaged in the kind of book reading and word labeling that facilitates learning of the academic speech register (Dexter, Schnell-Anzola, S. E. LeVine, & R. A. LeVine 2007).

SUMMARY AND CONCLUSIONS

In this section I summarize our findings and explore some of their implications for policy.

First, our comparative study of mothers in four geographically and cul-turally diverse countries—Nepal, Mexico, Zambia, and Venezuela—found that women acquire literacy and language skills in low-quality schools and retain them into adulthood. This is confirmed by longitudi-nal studies in Guatemala and Morocco. Thus there is an empirical basis for the claim that *learning*—even in low doses—may be involved in the pathway from school attendance to changes in health, family, and child outcomes in developing countries.

Second, we found that the literacy and language skills learned in school have an impact on mothers' skills in understanding public health messages and giving coherent illness narratives, skills essential to navi-gating the health care system in their local contexts. We also found that mothers with more schooling and literacy and language skills more fre-quently promote literacy skills in their preschool children. Our findings show maternal behavior is also influenced by structural factors such as urban residence and by resource factors such as household income, but that when these are controlled, literacy and language skills remain pre-dictors of maternal behavior. Thus we have evidence that maternal lit-eracy skills broadly defined are critical factors in facilitating health and education outcomes for children in diverse Third World contexts.

Third, a key aspect of literacy as we assessed it is *academic language proficiency,* or mastery of the context-reduced language skills that schools require. This is the standardized and specialized linguistic code or speech register of all bureaucracies. It is learned in school and needed for nav-igating effectively other bureaucratic environments encountered in adult life. For those who have achieved this proficiency in school, it facilitates effectiveness in health care settings and other bureaucratic contexts, but for those who do not have it, inadequate communication becomes an obstacle to effective outcomes.

Fourth, the impact of schooling and literacy on health and educational outcomes is neither automatic nor universal, but rather contingent on local conditions. For example, in Zambia during the 1980s and 1990s infant and child mortality *increased* despite widespread urbanization and women's schooling, mainly because children were dying of diseases (AIDS, hepatitis B and drug-resistant malaria) that medical care could not cure. In such a situation, the maternal health behaviors usually predic-tive of lower mortality—prenatal care, infant immunization, rapid emer-gency care—cannot prevent child death even when they are optimized by a mother's greater access to health care and possession of a higher income and more developed literacy skills. Furthermore, in many parts of the developing world, primary health care services are so inadequate in terms of resources and trained personnel that a mother's access and use of those resources, especially in rural areas, is no guarantee of efficacy. On the education side, it can be—as we found in Nepal (Dexter, Schnell-Anzola, S. E. LeVine, & R. A. LeVine 2007)—that the mother's tutoring of her preschool children does not strongly predict the child's literacy and language skills during the early school years, probably because there are so many other influences on those outcomes operating in the child's environment, including diverse private schools, television, and interaction with more educated members of the extended family. Thus the pathways we have shown in our theoretical model (figure 5.1) and largely confirmed through our research are the products of particular conditions found recurrently in developing countries during the closing decades of the twentieth century. But they will change when the conditions supporting them change.

It is this dependence of school effects (particularly those of women's schooling) on historical conditions that presents the challenge and the hope of women's schooling as we have analyzed it. On one hand, the finding that a relatively small dose of schooling during childhood and adolescence can have positive effects through the retention of literacy and communications skills bodes well for women's adaptation in the new bureaucratic environments they encounter as they migrate in large numbers to the city or to more developed countries.

On the other hand, those who manage the health care systems and other bureaucratized services and employment in these cities and countries face the challenge of accommodating women whose communication skills do not match those systems' prior expectations. The same academic speech register that is the standardized lingua franca of bureaucracy in much of the world is also a barrier excluding those who speak the local vernacular language without having acquired the academic code—those likely to be in greatest need of certain government services. Their difficulty in navigating hospitals and other bureaucratic environments raises the question of how necessary the use of an esoteric language is for bureaucratic institutions to function effectively. It was a high priority in the early days of nation building, when standardizing communication in the face of multiple vernacular languages was an urgent goal for government in every organizational setting. But the established institutions of developing countries now have additional, even more urgent, needs: to reach everyone with information and services in order to prevent the spread of

HIV-AIDS and other infectious diseases and to prepare low-income children for school entry. If these needs are not met, the mass schooling of women will contribute to widening the already great inequalities in health and economic resources within many poor and middle-income countries. There is, in other words, a need to rethink the way bureaucratic organizations communicate with a general public that varies widely in school attainment.

For policy makers and practitioners, the evidence from our project showing a literacy pathway from women's schooling to improved health and learning raises the question of whether the effects of formal education during childhood can be replicated with adult literacy training programs for women who never went to school or who left after a few years. This legitimate question has been asked many times but never effectively answered through research (Wagner & Stites 1999). One of the ironies of educational development in the second half of the twentieth century is that adult illiteracy was an early target for action by UNESCO, and many developing countries institutionalized adult literacy programs, particularly in reaching out to the rural poor. The political value of these programs as symbols of the state's concern for the people has been considerable; their systematic evaluation has seemed unnecessary and even a threat to a popular status quo.

Thus it remains unclear whether adult literacy programs work with mothers who have little or no schooling. We know of many factors that make participation in these programs difficult for low-income women in rural and urban areas and limit the attention and energy they can invest in learning Thus drop-out rates are high, and informal observations of gains in learning are not impressive (Stromquist 1999; Weber 1999). Programs of sufficient duration, however, with well-trained teachers and consistent student attendance could succeed in producing demonstrable literacy gains for adults (Comings 1995). At present, it seems that further expansion of primary and secondary schooling for girls in developing countries represents the best method of realizing the benefits of literacy for them, their children, and their communities.

Another unanswered question, one more critical for future generations of women, is the extent to which school quality, especially the quality of literacy instruction, makes a difference in the impact of women's literacy on their children's health and learning. It seems highly plausible that it would, but this obvious question should be high on the agenda for future research in developing countries.

NOTES

The writing of this article was supported by the Spencer Foundation and a Fellowship from the John Simon Guggenheim Memorial Foundation. The field research mentioned was funded by the William T. Grant Foundation (Nepal), the National Science Foundation (Mexico), the Rockefeller Foundation (Zambia) and USAID and UNFPA (Venezuela). My collaborators on the Project on Maternal Schooling are Sarah E. LeVine, Beatrice Schnell, Meredith Rowe and Emily Dexter; we are currently writing a book presenting our results in detail.

    1. The expectation of social benefit from the mass schooling of girls as well as boys has roots in four centuries of European religious and political thought, particularly that emerging from the Protestant Reformation, the Enlightenment, the French Revolution, and nineteenth-century nationalism. By the 1870s, when schooling became legally compulsory in most Western countries and Japan, its value was rarely questioned, and it was thereafter taken as necessary for all children by policy makers of otherwise differing ideological positions.

    2. Our research strategy was to select low-income local populations varying internally by level of maternal school attainment, within developing countries diverse in geographical location, cultural traditions, and economic development, but in which it had been shown that women's schooling was associated with declining fertility and mortality at the national level. Residents of the four countries who were doctoral students at the Harvard Graduate School of Education led the field research teams, which were coordinated by Sarah LeVine. There were urban and rural sites in Mexico and Nepal and urban ones in Venezuela and Zambia.

    3. In each field study a community-level survey was conducted. A roster of mothers of young children was obtained by canvassing neighborhoods previously known to exhibit variations in adult female school attainment, and a sample was drawn with roughly equal numbers of mothers with incomplete primary, complete primary, and postprimary school attainment. (In Nepal an additional category of mothers had no schooling at all.) Further information on sampling methods is provided in the articles cited.

REFERENCES

Chabott, C. (2003). *Constructing education for development: International Organizations and education for all.* New York: Routledge Falmer.

Chabott, C., and F. Ramirez (2000). Development and education. In *Handbook of the sociology of education.* M. Hallinan, ed. Pp. 163–187. New York: Kluwer Academic.

Comings, J. (1995). Literacy skill retention in adult students in developing countries. *International Journal of Educational Development* 15(1): 37–46.

Dexter, E., S. E. LeVine, and P. Velasco. (1998). Maternal schooling and health-related language and literacy skills in rural Mexico. *Comparative Educational Review* 42: 139–162.

Dexter, E., B. Schnell-Anzola, S. E. LeVine. and R. A. LeVine. (2007). Women's literacy in Nepal: Effects on maternal behavior and child literacy skills. Poster presented at the Biennial Meeting of the Society for Research in Child Development, March 29–April 1, Boston.

Fuller, B., and S. Heyneman. (1989). Third World school quality: Current collapse, future potential. *Educational Researcher* 18: 12–19.

Gorman, K., and E. Pollitt (2001). The contribution of schooling to literacy in Guatemala. *International Review of Education* 43: 283–298.

Hannum, E., and C. Buchmann (2003). *The consequences of global educational expansion: Social science perspectives.* Cambridge, MA: American Academy of Arts and Sciences.

Heath, S. B. (1986). What no bedtime story means: Narrative skills at home and school. In *Language socialization across cultures.* B. Schieffelin and E. Ochs, eds. New York: Cambridge University Press.

LeVine, R. A., S. E. LeVine, A. Richman, F. M. T. Uribe, C. S. Correa, and P. M. Miller. (1991). Women's schooling and child care in the demographic transition: A Mexican case study. *Population and Development Review* 17: 459–496.

LeVine, R. A., P. M. Miller, and A. Richman (1996). Education and mother-infant interaction: A Mexican case study. In *Parents' Cultural Belief Systems.* S. Harkness and C. Super, eds. New York: Guilford Press.

LeVine, R. A., S. E. LeVine, and B. Schnell (2001). "Improve the women": Mass schooling, female literacy, and worldwide social change. *Harvard Educational Review* 71: 1–50.

LeVine, R. A., S. E. LeVine, M. L. Rowe, and B. Schnell-Anzola. (2004). Maternal literacy and health behavior: A Nepalese case study. *Social Science and Medicine* 58: 863–877.

LeVine, R. A., and M. I. White (1986). *Human conditions: The cultural basis of educational development.* London: Routledge.

LeVine, S. E. (2006). Getting in, dropping out, and staying on: Determinants of girls' school attendance in the Katmandu Valley of Nepal. *Anthropology & Education Quarterly* 37(1): 21–41.

Meyer, J. W. (1977). The effects of education as an institution. *American Journal of Sociology* 83: 55–77.

Meyer, J. W., and M. Hannan (1979). *National development and the world system.* Chicago: University of Chicago Press.

Meyer, J. W., D. W. Kamens, and A. Benavot (1992). *School knowledge for the masses: World models and national primary curricular categories in the twentieth century.* London: Falmer Press.

Meyer, J. W., F. O. Ramirez, and Y. Soysal (1992). World expansion of mass education, 1870–1980. *Sociology of Education* 65: 128–149.

Mirowsky, J., and C. E. Ross (2003). *Education, social status, and health.* New York: Aldine.

Nielsen-Bohlman, L., A. M. Panzer, and D. A. Kindig, eds. (2004). *Health literacy: A prescription to end confusion.* Washington, DC: National Academies Press.

Richman, A., P. M. Miller, and R. A. LeVine. (1992). Cultural and educational variations in maternal responsiveness. *Developmental Psychology* 28: 614–621.

Rowe, M. L., B. Thapa, R. A. LeVine, S. E. LeVine, and S. Tuladhar. (2005). How does schooling influence health practices? Evidence from Nepal. *Comparative Education Review* 49: 512–533.

Schleppegrell, M. J. (2001). Linguistic features of the language of schooling. *Linguistics and Education* 12: 431–459.

Schnell-Anzola, B., M. L. Rowe, and R. A. LeVine (2005). Literacy as a pathway between schooling and health-related communication skills: A study of Venezuelan mothers. *International Journal of Educational Development* 25: 19–37.

Snow, C. (1991). The development of definitional skill. *Journal of Child Language* 17: 697–710.

Stromquist, N. P. (1999). Gender and literacy development. In *Literacy: An International Handbook*. D. A. Wagner, R. L. Venezky, and B. V. Street, eds. Boulder, CO: Westview Press.

Stuebing, K. W. (1997). Maternal school and comprehension of child health information in urban Zambia: Is literacy a missing link in the maternal schooling–child health relationship? *Health Transition Review* 7: 151–172.

United Nations Population Division (2005). *World population monitoring 2003: Population, education, and development*. New York: United Nations.

UNICEF (2003). *The state of the world's children 2004: Girls, education, and development*. New York.

Wagner, D. A. (1993). *Literacy, culture, and development: Becoming literate in Morocco*. New York: Cambridge University Press.

Wagner, D. A., and R. Stites (1999). Literacy skill retention. In *Literacy: An International Handbook*. D. A. Wagner, R. L. Venezky, and B. V. Street, eds. Boulder, CO: Westview Press.

Weber, Rose-Marie (1999). Adult education and literacy. In *Literacy: An international handbook*. D. A. Wagner, R. L. Venezky, and B. V. Street, eds. Boulder, CO: Westview Press.

SIX

Bernard Hugonnier

GLOBALIZATION AND EDUCATION

Can the World Meet the Challenge?

By its very nature, education has always been considered a national good, that is, a good that is intrinsically national in origin and can be provided only by national institutions. This is not to say that curricula should be free of influence by foreign cultures or should exclude all foreign elements (geography and history do contain many such elements); neither is it to ignore young people who have studied abroad or scholars who have taught in foreign countries.

The difference today lies, first, in the numbers in higher education. Some 2.2 million students are studying abroad every year, and this number is rising by more than 9 percent annually (OECD 2005a). Second, the number of universities with a campus located in a foreign country is also increasing rapidly. In addition, numerous universities and other higher-education institutions have developed some sort of partnership or cooperative relationship with a foreign institution.

Nevertheless, whatever the importance of these trends, of greater significance are the direct and indirect repercussions that the growth of the knowledge economy, the use of information and communication technologies (ICTs), and globalization can have on education. Indeed, the world has dramatically changed over the past twenty years, and while economies have rapidly adjusted to these changes—in some countries, less rapidly than expected, with all the dramatic consequences that one can expect—our societies have found these changes harder to accept and thus have been slow to adjust to the new realities.

This is particularly true of education. For example, while in many OECD countries the knowledge economy (i.e., the economic sector in which the main production factors are information and knowledge rather than labor or capital) is becoming prevalent, few changes reflecting this major shift have been introduced in curricula to nurture knowledge workers instead of industrial workers. As noted by Cheng (in an earlier draft of his essay for this volume), "With the collapse of the pyramidal social structure, education systems, particularly schools, remain in the industrial mode. Education is not fast enough to catch up."

ICTs are revolutionizing both teaching and learning methods; distance learning is rapidly gaining ground everywhere in the world, and ICT skills (accessing, managing, integrating, evaluating, and reflecting on information using modern technologies) are among the most important competencies today. Yet they are far from being part of the curriculum in many countries.

Even more important for education are the challenges posed by globalization. These challenges are fivefold:

- Globalization is increasing world economic interdependence, which in turn enhances competition among countries and modifies the world distribution of labor. The consequence for education is that, on one hand, people need to acquire or update their knowledge and skills more often than before and, on the other, they must change jobs more frequently (they are required to become lifelong learners).

- Globalization leads to more economic exchanges and, as the case of Tensta makes clear (see Suárez-Orozco and Sattin, this volume), more cultural interchange between countries, and to greater social heterogeneity in terms of culture, ethnicity, language, and religion. Social capital (i.e., values and principles such as tolerance, cooperation, solidarity) needs to be further developed, and individuals are expected to learn more foreign languages and to know more about foreign cultures.

- Globalization increases social and income disparities at the expense of social cohesion, necessitating improvement in equality of access to quality education and equality of educational outcomes.

- With globalization certain issues such as protection of the environment; poverty reduction; trafficking in drugs, arms, and human beings; and terrorism are becoming, and should be, the concern of every individual. This implies that we are no longer citizens of only one country but also citizens of the world. We should all be informed on these issues, and our awareness of our responsibilities should be heightened (see Boix Mansilla & Gardner, this volume).

- Globalization is leading to the internationalization of education, notably higher education, which presents several risks for students and for developing countries in the form of a wider education gap, low-quality or nonrelevant programs, and rogue providers and degree mills. Action at the international level is crucial to maximizing benefits and minimizing risks.

INCREASING WORLD ECONOMIC INTERDEPENDENCE

Global economic interdependence, the main cause of globalization, has rapidly expanded since 1950. The volume of merchandise exports has grown by 6 percent a year on average for the past fifty years, and world trade has consistently grown faster than global GDP (Krueger 2005). One of the most direct effects of globalization is the rapid relocation of the production of many goods and services. This is epitomized by the increasing production of manufactured goods in China and the growth of services provided in India, due notably in India's case to information and communication technologies. Low-skilled tasks are increasingly subcontracted to countries where labor costs are far lower than in developed countries (see Levy & Murnane, this volume). Labor cost differentials are often so large, that several OECD countries have no option but to adjust their economies to the new situation, thereby transforming their labor forces.

If an economy is to adjust rapidly to the changing needs of the world distribution of labor, it is not only the labor market that must be flexible. Enterprises should also have the ability to adjust their workforces as rapidly as possible to the new situation (see Cheng, this volume). Educational systems and workers alike must be flexible: the former should be able to develop new programs or expand existing ones to permit the latter to acquire the qualifications necessary to undertake new tasks or change jobs, possibly in a new city or region. Countries where enterprises, the labor market, and the educational system are highly flexible (e.g., the United States) can expect to have greater and more sustainable growth than countries where flexibility in these areas is low (e.g., France, whose educational system is only minimally flexible).

The challenge of globalization leads developed countries to progressively concentrate on high-value-added production of goods and services. This goal presupposes that the educational systems of these countries can be adjusted as rapidly as required to increase the number of graduates and to distribute them where needed in the various production sectors. These countries have to address three issues: the difficulty of responding fully and in time to the requirements of the job market, the need to train people to enable them to change jobs, and the financing needs of higher education.

The first issue relates to the difficulty of meeting the job market's changing demand for qualifications (Cheng, this volume). This challenge is notable in science and technology, two domains that are crucial for countries willing to reorient their production toward more value-added goods and services. As shown in figure 6.1, between 1998 and 2002 the share of engineering and manufacturing students declined in fourteen of the twenty-three OECD countries for which data are available.

This trend will accelerate as lack of student interest in these subjects results in a lack of teachers for them. Figure 6.2 shows that the subject areas for which OECD countries had the greatest difficulty employing teachers in 2003 were the sciences, mathematics, and technology.

The second issue concerns the fact that, because economies must rapidly adjust to world competition, the goods and services produced by OECD countries must evolve. This imperative implies a paradigm shift in the professional life of individuals who, more then ever before, need to continuously upgrade their skills, but who also have to acquire new knowledge and skills as they change jobs (see Cheng, this volume).

This new situation implies that curriculum, pedagogical practices, and the organization of learning all need to be re-examined. Appropriate linkages and pathways should be developed to enable individuals to transition to and progress through various learning stages. Reallocation of education and training resources will be necessary, and ministries will have to cooperate with one another, as none will have the power to adjust the economy on its own.

In addition, successful reforms must address the need for not only economic but also societal and individual competencies. Development of the following skills and aptitudes will be crucial: flexibility and adaptability, mobility, creative and critical thinking, motivation to learn and relearn,

Figure 6.1 Change in number of engineering graduates as a percentage of all tertiary graduates, 1998–2002. SOURCE: *OECD Education Database*, 2004.

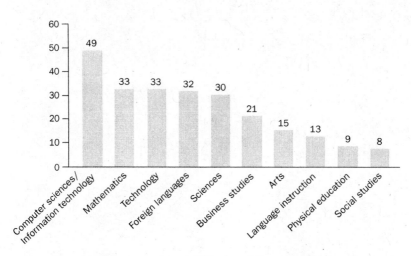

Figure 6.2 Average perceived difficulty of hiring qualified teachers in various study areas, 2001. Cross-country mean percentages of upper-secondary students attending schools where the principal reported that hiring fully qualified teachers is difficult. SOURCE: *OECD International Survey of Upper Secondary Schools (ISUSS) database, 2003.*

capacity to learn independently, digital literacy, ability to develop networking (Suárez-Orozco & Sattin, this volume).

The new situation has implications also for training. In OECD countries, adult access to further education and training often increases with the level of education previously attained. Accordingly, while low-skilled workers and the unemployed may be expected to benefit first from continuing education, exactly the contrary actually prevails. This is in part because employers spend more resources on training their highly-skilled, already well-educated employees than they do on training those with lower skills and less education. Education and training of adults therefore tends to reinforce skill differences. Furthermore, in some countries (France, Greece, Portugal, Spain) training rates decline with age, whereas the reverse is true in the United States and the Nordic countries (except Finland).

Countries must also achieve a better balance among the different education levels and recognize that learning occurs during the whole course of a person's life (lifelong learning). This approach places the learner at the center of educational strategy, shifting the focus from the supply to the demand side of learning. It emphasizes the motivation to learn and the need for self-directed learning and recognizes both formal and informal learning.

The OECD (2003) recently identified four categories of countries that have progressed in lifelong learning (LLL):

1. The Nordic countries' performance stands out.

2. Canada, the Czech Republic, Germany, the Netherlands, and New Zealand also have done well but have certain weaknesses.

3. Australia, Switzerland, the United Kingdom, the United States, and some other countries have shown weak and uneven performances.

4. Ireland, Hungary, Portugal, and Poland performed poorly on most measures.

The OECD noted that a formal education system is not the only platform for further progress. (Some countries, such as Australia and the Netherlands, are doing well by fostering childhood development at home.) It also noted that because not enough attention is given to LLL, there is still a scarcity of information on what works and what does not.

To face the challenges of globalization, countries have to raise educational attainment. Results from the Program for International Student Assessment (PISA) on the percentage of fifteen-year-olds whose performance in reading or in scientific or mathematical literacy is below average evidence a huge untapped economic resource (OECD 2004b). For instance, for mathematics, PISA 2003 revealed percentages of students achieving proficiency as measured on a scale from below 1 to 6. In the majority of countries, at least 10 percent of students perform below level 1, which involves the most basic skills. This percentage, however, ranges from less than 10 percent in Finland and Korea to more than 50 percent in Turkey and 60 percent in Mexico (figure 6.3). Students performing below level 1 will certainly have difficulties in obtaining a job but also in becoming fully integrated in society and fulfilling all the social responsibilities that are expected from citizens in today's society.

The last issue centers on the financing of higher education. In the 1960s, the proportion of the population in OECD countries that was enrolled in tertiary education averaged 16 percent. This percentage climbed to 21 percent in the 1970s, to 24 percent in the 1980s, and to 28 percent in the 1990s. As table 6.1 shows, the situation differs substantially from country to country. Although progress has been significant in all countries, it

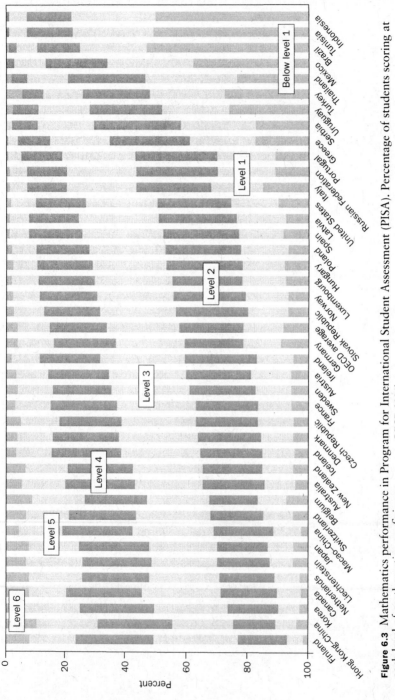

Figure 6.3 Mathematics performance in Program for International Student Assessment (PISA). Percentage of students scoring at each level of mathematics proficiency. SOURCE: *OECD 2004b.*

Table 6.1 Percentage of population attaining tertiary education in selected countries, 1960s and 1990s

	1960s	1990s
Canada	32	51
Finland	23	40
France	15	36
Germany	21	21
Ireland	14	37
Japan	18	50
Korea	9	41
Portugal	5	15
Spain	10	37
United Kingdom	20	31
United States	33	40

SOURCE: OECD 2005, table A3.3.

has been more rapid in the countries least advanced in the 1960s (Korea, Portugal, and Spain), a little less so in the more advanced countries (Finland, France, Ireland, Japan, and the United Kingdom, with Germany showing no change), and even less in the most advanced countries (Canada and the United States).

Financing this increasing participation is quite a challenge. Indeed, expenditures on tertiary education are growing as a result not only of the rising number of students but also of the mounting individual cost of higher education. In the twenty-two OECD countries where the number of students rose between 1995 and 2001, expenditure per student has increased in all but five (OECD 2005a, table B1.5). In countries where higher education is mostly publicly financed, in view of the pressure to reduce budget deficits, governments are almost obligated to raise the student contribution (in some instances accompanied by student loans) if the level of quality is to be maintained. However, for reasons of equal access to educational opportunities, in certain countries (e.g., France), resistance is high to having recourse to this solution.

THE DEVELOPMENT OF MORE MULTICULTURAL SOCIETIES

One of the most visible effects of globalization is the trend toward similar consumption and leisure patterns around the world. Whether there will be a convergence toward a world culture modeled after one country or group of countries' culture (along the lines of the so-called Westernization of the world), or the development of a genuine world culture, is yet unclear. Evidence suggests that the former hypothesis seems the most likely, with the expected inherent difficulties resulting from the rejection of that model by some cultures (see Huntington 1996). In any event, societies worldwide are integrating elements of foreign cultures at an unprecedented speed and are facilitated in this process by satellite and high-speed cable transmission (television, telephone, the Internet) and the expansion of fast and ever cheaper international transportation. Our societies are becoming multicultural. This trend is obviously facilitated by international migration, as Tensta Gymnasium and countless other sites in the world reveal (Suárez-Orozco & Sattin, this volume).

With the increase in migration flows, certain host countries are experiencing enormous and sometimes insurmountable social problems as the proportion of first- and second-generation migrants in their populations grows. Certainly, the situation differs greatly from country to country: 38.1 percent in Luxembourg cannot be compared with 10 percent in France nor with 5.3 percent in Sweden or 1.5 percent in Japan (OECD 2004a). In addition, while Luxembourg and France have histories of immigration, this is quite a new phenomenon for Sweden and Japan, where the difficulties of adaptation are much greater.

There is an implicit social contract in most receiving countries between the country and the immigrants: the latter are expected to make every effort to integrate into the economy and society of their new home, while the host country's responsibility is to facilitate this integration by providing immigrants with the same mandatory education as nationals. This "Republican" school of thought implies that migrants must learn the language, traditions, habits, and culture of the host country, often to the detriment of their own culture. The objective was that over two or three generations the original culture would progressively disappear or would become less prevalent than the culture of the host country; integration was the short-term goal, assimilation the long-term one. This was indeed the case in many countries for many past generations of migrants.

This approach has recently been questioned. In several countries, the integration of migrants did not occur through a mix of different ethnic groups but rather through the development of clusters (communities) of ethnic or religious groups (see Wikan, this volume). This trend facilitated the maintenance of migrants' original culture, and some of the immigrants have expressed strong concern about receiving an education from which their own culture was totally absent or insufficiently represented (Roosens, this volume). They tended either to reject such education or to seriously contest it and objected to being judged on their capacity to adapt to the new culture—to "fit in." In short, if a certain degree of integration can still be accepted, assimilation is often rejected.

This situation is evidently socially dangerous. A society can stay together only if three conditions are met (Putnam 2000): each community lives in peace and prospers (bonding social capital); all communities agree to live together (bridging social capital); and all communities respect the institutions, laws, and regulations of their resident country (linking social capital). The development of separate communities without bridging social capital (called communatarism) is therefore bound to create social disruption.

The difficulty of integrating immigrant populations is highlighted by table 6.2, where the performance of fifteen-year-olds as reported by PISA is classified according to place of birth (see also Süssmuth, this volume). Two groups of countries can be identified. In the first (Australia, Canada, and New Zealand), the difference in performance between the native, first-generation, and foreign-born students is limited. This is mainly due to a selective immigration policy. In all the other countries, native students outperform, in some cases (e.g., Germany and Denmark) by far, the first generation, which in turn generally outperforms the foreign-born students. In these countries, educational systems obviously do not sufficiently contribute to the integration of migrants, and this might intensify communatarism as the population of migrants might decide that not enough effort is being made to provide them with educational opportunities equal or at least similar to those available to the native population. Today, in most OECD countries, and particularly in Europe, unemployment among migrants is higher than that among the native-born. While the foreign-born and native-born unemployment rates were the same in the United States in 2002, the foreign-born jobless rate was 1.5 times the native-born rate in Germany, 1.8 times higher in Sweden, and twice the native-born rate in France (OECD 2005a).

At the same time, a selective immigration policy cannot be considered an appropriate solution in view of the brain-drain consequences such a policy might have for developing countries. It is difficult indeed for these countries to accept the loss of their educational investment in nationals who emigrate permanently or the loss of the value they would have added to the economy and society. Already, more than 400,000 scientists and engineers originating from developing countries are working in the

Table 6.2 Place of birth and
mathematics performance

	Native	First generation	Foreign-born
Australia	527	522	525
Austria	515	459	452
Belgium	545	454	437
Canada	537	543	530
Denmark	520	449	455
France	520	472	448
Germany	525	432	454
Luxembourg	507	476	462
Netherlands	551	492	472
Norway	499	460	438
New Zealand	528	496	523
Sweden	517	483	425
United Kingdom	510	503	n.a.
United States	490	468	453

SOURCE: OECD 2005a.

OECD area, where the demand for them will increase as a result of challenges posed by the aging of populations and could lead to a sort of brain war. The objective of enhanced international cooperation should be to transform this unilateral brain drain, which is presently a zero-sum game, into a multilateral brain gain.

In addition, instead of the Republican school's sterile opposition to communatarism, a new approach should be sought based on the recognition that the introduction of a foreign culture by migrants is not a threat to the host country's culture but, on the contrary, an asset on which the country should capitalize (see Crul, this volume). This reorientation would have two immediate benefits: First, it would lessen the fear among migrants of losing their roots and thus part of their identity, which is certainly not easing their social and economic integration. Second, it would enrich the culture of the host country and that of its residents and facilitate the integration of both in the world.

Even if host countries accomplish the already difficult task of integrating elements of immigrant cultures in their curricula, this will not be sufficient. All groups will have to learn to accept one another's "differences." It is essential that the different communities strive to accept one another, respect one another's culture, and live together in peace and harmony. This spirit of tolerance, cooperation, and solidarity, which constitutes the cement of our societies, is not inherent in each individual; it needs to be taught, and this is where the challenge lies. While teaching cognitive skills is somewhat easy—for instance, to become an accountant one has only to learn the accounting rules and methods—teaching values and attitudes is totally different, even more so in the case of values such as tolerance and solidarity. In addition, as stressed by Süssmuth (this volume), educators themselves also have to possess intercultural skills if they are to pass these on to learners.

More social capital is crucial in our interdependent world, whether at the local, national, or international level. But "more" is extremely difficult to obtain. In addition, educational policy alone will not suffice to ensure the social integration of immigrants. Labor policy would have to address the job discrimination many migrants are facing in certain countries; urban policy would have to respond to the challenge posed by communities segregating people according to ethnic origin or religion; and immigration policy would have to adjust the flows of migrants according to the absorption capacity of the society and economy, and account for the negative potential effect on the sending countries (brain drain).

SOCIAL COHESION THREATENED BY INCREASING SOCIAL DISPARITIES

While it can certainly reduce poverty, economic growth is not decreasing income disparities. On the contrary, in most countries, although the number of poor people is decreasing and income per capita is increasing, the per capita income of the richest 10 percent is increasing even faster. The percentage of poor people is greater in Egypt than in Portugal or the United States, but income disparities are greater in the United States than in Portugal or in Egypt.

Globalization can only accelerate this phenomenon as pressure increases to hold down workers' wages in order to maintain economic competitiveness and as other workers lose their jobs because firms move production facilities to countries where production costs are lower (Levy & Murnane, this volume). Globalization thus poses a threat to social cohesion: more people feel that society provides them with fewer opportunities and that social protection for the less wealthy is diminishing.

Can education provide a solution, even if only a partial one? The answer lies in the capacity of educational systems to be equitable. Equity in education has at least three levels: equal access to education for all; equal

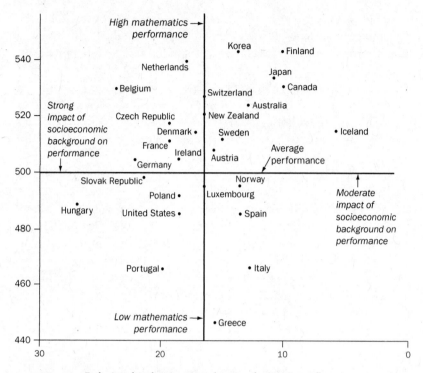

Figure 6.4 Relationship between student performance and socioeconomic background. Mathematics performance is measured by PISA 2003. Values on the x-axis represent the percentage of the variance in student mathematical performance in PISA that is explained by socioeconomic background. A low percentage indicates low impact and hence high equity. A high percentage (maximum 30) indicates high impact, hence a low equity.
SOURCE: *2003 PISA results, in OECD 2004.*

access to *quality* education for all; and equality of education outcomes, so that students' socioeconomic background has minimal impact on their performance. Equity implies that countries should avoid two pitfalls: elitism and mass education. That is, their educational systems should provide a high-quality education to more than just a fortunate few and should not provide educational access to all at the expense of quality. Figure 6.4 shows that differences in students' socioeconomic background pose major challenges for education systems. As a general rule, students whose parents have better-paying jobs, are better educated, or have more cultural possessions in their homes tend to perform better in mathematics. But the performance advantage varies: in Australia, Canada, Finland, Iceland, and Japan the impact of socioeconomic background is smaller than in Belgium, Germany, Hungary, and the Slovak Republic. The former group demonstrates that it is possible to combine educational quality and equity, while the latter reveals large socioeconomic inequalities in the distribution of learning opportunities.

As shown in figure 6.4, the challenge is not the same everywhere: countries with mass education (Italy, Greece, Luxembourg, Norway, and Spain) would have to raise the quality while maintaining the level of equity; countries with an elitist education (Belgium, the Czech Republic, Denmark, France, Germany, and Ireland) would have to raise equity while at least keeping the level of quality unchanged; finally, countries such as Poland, Portugal, the Slovak Republic, and the United States face the much greater challenge of raising quality and equity simultaneously. The situation is particularly difficult in the United States, where children from poor backgrounds are often trapped in the worst schools and less likely to continue their studies, and where the number of students from the poorest 20 percent of society who earn a diploma or degree rose less rapidly than that of the wealthiest 20 percent. As a result, the United States has one of the worst records for social mobility in the developed world, a situation similar to that in the United Kingdom (according to a study by the London School of Economics cited in *The Guardian*, "UK low in social mobility league, says charity" 2005).

ISSUES BECOMING GLOBAL

With globalization, some issues can no longer be solved at the national level. The involvement of the international community is needed for these issues to be correctly addressed. This is notably the case with environmental protection; poverty reduction; trafficking in drugs, arms, and human beings; and terrorism. Indeed, to be satisfactorily solved, these issues have to be considered by all countries concerned. Perhaps the best example is environmental protection: no long-term solution can be reached unless the main stakeholders, especially the largest polluting countries, agree to ratify and implement the Kyoto Protocol.

But not only countries should be accountable; all citizens of the world have a share of the responsibility. Clearly, the more they are aware of the issues, the more they can pressure their governments to take action. This means that we are no longer only the citizens of our respective countries; we are also citizens of the world for which we have social and economic responsibility.

The concepts of sustainable development and good governance are particularly relevant here. We no longer live in a world where the main objectives are economic growth, full employment, and financial stability. These quantitative objectives defined prosperity from the Second World War to the first oil shock in the early 1970s. Since then, OECD countries have progressively realized that the protection of the environment, social cohesion, participative democracy, and improved governance of both private and public institutions also contribute to prosperity. The well-being of today's and tomorrow's populations is now at stake.

The main challenge is how to inform people and raise their awareness about global issues—what Boix Mansilla and Gardner (this volume) call "global consciousness." Education has obviously a major role to play, yet environmental education is barely developed in OECD countries. Similarly, the responsibilities of a world citizen are rarely addressed in the curriculum of these countries. Major progress is necessary in this area before one can claim that every country is aware of the important role its population can play in shaping globalization for the benefit of all.

THE INTERNATIONALIZATION
OF HIGHER EDUCATION

Since the 1980s, cross-border higher education through the mobility of students, academic faculty, programs/institutions, and professionals has grown considerably. Paralleling this development, new delivery modes and cross-border providers have appeared, such as foreign campuses, electronic delivery of higher education, and for-profit providers. This internationalization of higher education, which is directly linked to globalization, is posing major challenges to countries.

There is no doubt that cross-border higher-education services can offer increased opportunities for improving the skills and competencies of individual students and enhance the quality of national higher-education systems. These improvements can prevail, however, only if such services aim at benefiting the human, social, economic, and cultural development of the receiving country and if major risks are mitigated such as the development of rogue providers and degree mills. Action at the international level is called for to maximize the benefits and minimize the risks of the internationalization of higher education. The quality of a country's higher-education sector, and its assessment and monitoring, is increasingly important as the key not only to the country's social and economic well-being but also to the reputation of higher-education systems at the international level. As a consequence, the number of quality-assurance and accreditation bodies for higher education has risen impressively in the past two decades.

However, existing national quality-assurance and accreditation systems often focus exclusively on domestic delivery by domestic institutions, and are still not geared to addressing the challenges of cross-border provision. These systems must develop appropriate procedures and frameworks to cover foreign provision of higher education in order to maximize its benefits and limit its potential drawbacks.

Furthermore, the lack of comprehensive frameworks for coordinating initiatives at the international level, together with the diversity and unevenness of quality-assurance and accreditation systems at the national level, creates gaps in the quality assurance of cross-border higher education, leaving some cross-border higher-education provision outside any framework of quality assurance and accreditation. This leaves students and other stakeholders more vulnerable to low-quality provision and disreputable providers. Consequently, international cooperation and networking need to be strengthened, and information on procedures for and systems of quality assurance, accreditation, and recognition of qualifications needs greater transparency.

These efforts should have a global range, involving countries both receiving and sending higher education students. They should focus on encouraging developing countries to establish robust higher-education systems that

- enhance the protection of students/learners from low-quality provision, including that by degree mills, and from qualifications of limited validity provided by accreditation mills
- ensure that the quality of higher education provided by foreign institutions is comparable to that offered in the country of origin
- increase the international validity and portability of qualifications and ease the work of recognition and credential evaluators
- make procedures for the recognition of qualifications more transparent, coherent, fair, and reliable and impose as little burden as possible on mobile students and professionals
- provide students/learners with adequate and user-friendly information for decision making, and protect them from the risks of misleading guidance and documentation
- encourage international cooperation and mutual understanding among national quality-assurance and accreditation agencies

In this light, UNESCO and the OECD have worked together to develop the Guidelines on Quality Provision in Cross-border Higher Education (OECD 2005b). These guidelines emphasize the shared responsibility for quality assurance and accreditation of countries that import and export cross-border higher education. Two major conditions will have to be met, however, for cross-border higher education to appropriately respond to world needs: First, all stakeholders must be directly involved, including governments, higher-education institutions/providers, student bodies, quality-assurance and accreditation bodies, academic recognition bodies, and professional bodies. Second, developing countries must be supported in elaborating their own quality-assurance and qualifications recognition agencies. These are missing today in more than 120 countries in the world, which offers a fair indication of the challenge ahead.

The internationalization of higher education is a prerequisite for world economic integration and the international mobility of workers. This point is well understood by the more than forty countries that intend through the Bologna Process to harmonize their degree structures and make their respective qualifications systems more compatible. The Bologna Process may serve as the model for other countries; some, including China, are contemplating similar action.

A final but equally important challenge is for higher-education institutions (HEIs) to remain attractive to students while competition for the best scholars and students is increasing throughout the world. The governance of HEIs needs to be adjusted accordingly: without more autonomy in terms of programs, recruitment of scholars, and enrollment of students, these institutions will find it difficult to improve their competitiveness. They also need to have more financial leeway, which can be acquired only by increasing student contribution and funding from such nonpublic sources as consultancy businesses. Finally, HEIs need to be better integrated with nations and localities by incorporating in their governing boards representative of the civil society, notably the private sector.

In many countries where higher education is still considered a public good, giving more autonomy to HEIs, increasing student contribution, and changing the composition of HEIs' governing boards is far from being acceptable. Yet, to meet the challenge of the rapid democratization of higher education and the need to respond quickly to the challenge of globalization, these reforms are indispensable, even if their exact content and design and implementation depend on the institutions and socioeconomic characteristics of each country.

CONCLUSION

Globalization is often seen as an economic phenomenon. Indeed, the sustainability of economic growth, which is the ultimate objective of every country, greatly depends on international trade and investment. This increasing economic interdependence is changing the nature of growth in most countries. In a knowledge economy, human capital is by far the most important of these factors. National educational systems therefore have no other choice but to adjust accordingly.

As we have seen, adjustment is a difficult process. Because human capital is underdeveloped in many countries, including those of the OECD, the distribution of educational opportunities in the world is largely inequitable. As a consequence, not only are the benefits of globalization inferior to what they could be, but with the adjustment process in various countries evolving at different paths, the distribution of these benefits is unequal both between and within countries, a situation that can only enhance tensions at the international and national levels.

Although quality and equity in education have long been considered as two incompatible objectives, recent evidence shows otherwise. Still, even the most developed countries have much to do to achieve both quality and equity. Although developing countries cannot sustain long-term economic development if they are not fully emerged in the world economy, their limited educational endowment and inequality in educational opportunities can only limit their ability to reap the full benefits of globalization.

Can the world, then, meet the challenge of globalization and education? As seen from the analysis above, much action is required both at the national and international levels for this to happen. At the national level, countries should consider the following:

- Changing their curricula to reflect the fact that we are now living in a knowledge economy in which demand is higher for knowledge workers than for industrial workers. Individuals should be equipped with the appropriate competencies, notably intra- and inter-personal skills and ICT skills

- Adjusting educational systems to reflect the fact that working relationships are increasingly based more on networking, partnerships, autonomy, and accountability than on hierarchy, command, and control

- Adjusting the labor force to suit increasing global economic interdependence and the competition posed by emerging economies such as India and China
- Ensuring the financing of tertiary education and adult learning in view of the necessity to increase national education attainment and to help individuals change jobs so as to respond to the requirements of the job market
- Raising the interest of students in areas where there is a shortage of competencies, notably in science and technology
- Facilitating the cooperation of all ministries having a stake in education to ensure the implementation of a genuine lifelong-learning policy
- Ensuring that adult training is benefiting low-skilled workers, immigrants, and the unemployed first
- Adjusting educational systems to the needs of an increasingly multicultural society, notably by ridding curricula of discrimination based on national or ethnic origin, religion, language, or culture
- Ensuring compatibility between education and migration policies
- Improving educational equity by limiting the influence of socio-economic background on student performance
- Enhancing the autonomy of higher-education institutions and improving their governance

At the international level, there are three main objectives:

- Raising public consciousness about issues that are now of global concern and are therefore the responsibility of everyone (e.g., the environment)
- Strengthening international cooperation and networking to ensure high quality in cross-border higher education
- Assisting developing countries in establishing institutions and regulations regarding quality assurance, accreditation, and recognition of qualifications

To help countries make the appropriate decisions, some additional research is essential to provide them with relevant information and evidence. The following issues should notably be addressed:

- How can the use of ICTs help developing countries achieve the Millennium Development Goals for education?
- What are the best practices for teaching soft competencies to satisfy the needs of the globalized knowledge society?
- How should educational systems be modified to better prepare individuals to live in multicultural societies and to act as genuine citizens of the world?

NOTE

I am very grateful to OECD colleagues for their critical comments on parts of this paper and to Patricia Comte for providing editorial assistance.

REFERENCES

Huntington, S. P. (1996). *The clash of civilizations and the remaking of world order.* New York: Simon & Schuster.

International Labour Organisation (2005). *An equitable approach for migrant workers in a globalised economy.* Geneva.

Krueger, A. O. (2005). *Mutual interdependence: Asia and the rest of the world.* Address to the Institute for Global Economics, Seoul, June 30, 2005.

OECD. See Organisation for Economic Co-operation and Development.

Organisation for Economic Co-operation and Development (2002). *Education policy analysis.* Paris.

Organisation for Economic Co-operation and Development (2003). *Education policy analysis.* Paris.

Organisation for Economic Co-operation and Development (2004a). *Trends in international migration.* 2004 Annual Report. Paris.

Organisation for Economic Co-operation and Development (2004b). *Learning for tomorrow's world: First results from PISA 2003.* Paris.

Organisation for Economic Co-operation and Development (2005a). *Education at a Glance.* Paris.

Organisation for Economic Co-operation and Development (2005b). *UNESCO/ OECD guidelines on quality provision in cross-border higher education.* www.oecd.org. Paris.

Putnam, R. D. (2000). *Bowling alone: The collapse and revival of American community.* New York: Simon & Schuster.

"UK low in social mobility league, says charity" (2005). *The Guardian.* April 25.

SEVEN

Frank Levy and Richard J. Murnane

HOW COMPUTERIZED WORK
AND GLOBALIZATION SHAPE
HUMAN SKILL DEMANDS

As this chapter is being written, at the midpoint of the first decade of the twenty-first century, the U.S. labor market continues to recover from the 2000–01 recession. By 2005, for example, seven million more people were working than were employed two years earlier. This employment growth is the net outcome of two competing forces: some occupations expand, while work that can be done at lower cost by computers or by workers in lower-wage countries continues to disappear. The result is a changing mix both of jobs and of tasks within jobs. Our purpose in this chapter is to outline these changes and their educational implications from an economist's perspective. What education and skills are needed to earn a decent living in the labor market created by computers and globalization?

We begin with three caveats. First, whereas most chapters in this volume focus on various aspects of globalization, this chapter focuses on the impact of both globalization and computerized work on the labor market. As we will show, globalization and computerized work currently substitute for workers in similar occupations—they reinforce each other—and this reinforcement occurs in both the United States and other advanced economies. Second, we were invited to write this chapter as economists, but our argument also involves our basic understanding of cognitive psychology. We hope to keep the intellectual violence to a minimum.

A final caveat involves properly distributing credit. Many of the ideas in this paper began in joint work with our colleague David Autor, now associate professor of economics at MIT.[1] The ideas were also anticipated in a remarkably prescient 1960 essay by Herbert Simon that we discovered after we had largely finished our own work. Because Simon was writing for a general audience, he did not present the explanatory theory that we lay out in this chapter. But the theory is implicit in Simon's essay, and his ability to see the future was as remarkable as the rest of his career.

WHAT COMPUTERS DO

We begin by asking the question, How do computers substitute for human work? Consider some examples:

- In U.S. airports, the job of dispensing an airline boarding pass, a moderately skilled job, is increasingly performed by self-service kiosks rather than by desk agents.

- When an outside caller punches in the MIT general telephone number, a software-generated voice asks the caller to speak the first and last names of the person he or she is trying to reach— "Larry Brown," for example. The software then matches the caller's response with data in the MIT telephone directory and says, "Dialing the extension for Larry Brown," which it does. Whereas human operators used to handle all of these tasks, now they handle only calls the software fails to match.

- Recently, two interventional radiologists used computerized imaging to insert a stent into a large arterial aneurysm near the brain of a young man. Fifteen years ago, such imaging did not exist, the operation would not have been attempted, and the young man would have soon died.

Why do we see this particular mix of outcomes? How do we explain the fact that computers have *substituted* for human skills in the first and second tasks, while they have *complemented* human skills in third task? The answer begins with two ideas:

- All human work involves the cognitive processing of information. The financial analyst who reads numbers in a spreadsheet, the farmer who looks to the sky for signs of rain, the chef who tastes a sauce, the carpenter who feels the hammer as it hits a nail—all these people are processing information to decide what to do next or to update their picture of the world.

- Computers execute rules. Some of the rules involve arithmetic ($6 \times 9 = 54$). Other rules involve logical conditions (If [AGE > 35] go to Statement 13). We can think of a properly running computer program as a series of rules that specify an action for each contingency.

These two ideas, combined with common sense, imply that a computer can substitute for a human in processing information when two conditions are present: the information to be processed can be represented in a form suitable for use by a computer; and the processing itself can be expressed in a series of rules. The first condition is common sense, and we return to it below.

The rules to which the second condition refers can be either deductive or inductive. Deductive rules arise from the logical structure of the process. For example, in the case of the airline boarding-pass kiosks, one deductive rule might be "Does this credit card number match a number in the reservation database? If yes, check for seat assignment." Information processing based on deductive rules is often called rules-based logic.

Inductive rules, which are more complicated, typically involve equations of regressions, neural nets, and other statistical models the parameters of which have been estimated on "training samples" of historical cases. The equations with their estimated parameters are then used to process new cases. Information processing based on inductive rules is often called pattern recognition.

An example of pattern recognition is Fannie Mae's Desktop Underwriter software, now widely used by mortgage brokers to assess the risk of a mortgage application. Applying a regression-like technique to a large sample of previously approved mortgages, Fannie Mae statisticians estimated the relative importance of fourteen different application items in predicting whether a mortgage had defaulted in its first four years.[2] The result was a mortgage-scoring model, an estimated equation (an inductive rule) that processed the fourteen application items into an *ex ante* probability of default. The estimated scoring model or rule was built into software that now assesses risk in new mortgage applications.

Other examples of pattern recognition using inductive rules include models estimated on historical credit card purchases to flag the possibility of fraud, and computer security software designed to recognize specific fingerprints. In all of these examples, estimation of the inductive rules is equivalent to discovering a pattern in the historical information.

The ability to articulate rules—deductive or inductive—explains the first two of the three examples that begin this section. The task of issuing a boarding pass can be fully expressed in deductive rules, particularly since any unanticipated situation can trigger the message, "Unable to continue: please see a desk agent."

Similarly, speech recognition software can substitute for the simpler part of an MIT telephone operator's work. When outside callers speak the name they want to contact, the software's inductive rule filters out accents and "uh's" and constructs a digital representation of the name that it can then match against data in the MIT directory.

The third example is obviously different. Here, computers complement, rather than substitute for, the radiologists' ability to insert the stent. We now turn to this example.

THE LIMITS OF COMPUTER SUBSTITUTION

A quick look at existing software is enough to confirm that deductive and inductive rules are sufficient to express an enormous number of information-processing tasks. A number of other tasks, however, including the radiologists' insertion of the stent, cannot be expressed in this way. In other words, computer substitution has its limits. Two of these stand out.

An inability to represent information. In many workplace tasks, the information being processed is hard to represent in a form that computers can use. Consider an internist talking to a patient to make an initial diagnosis. The doctor is listening to the patient's words but also thinking about the patient's history and reading his or her body language—the avoidance of eye contact or the broken-off sentence that indicates he or she is holding something back. Or consider a truck driver making a left turn against traffic: he is processing what he sees and hears from the street and the sidewalk, what he feels from the brake pedal and the steering wheel, and so on. In these and many other workplace tasks, it can be very hard to represent relevant information in a form that computers can analyze.

An inability to articulate rules. The internist's conversation with the patient and the truck driver's left turn point to the second limit of computer substitution: even if we could represent the information being processed, it is unlikely we could determine the rules that describe the processing. The problem is captured in Michael Polanyi's felicitous phrase "We can know more than we can tell" (Polanyi 1966). This is the problem of describing to a child how to ride a two-wheel bicycle. Nothing one can put into words will keep the child from falling at least a few times as he or she learns to ride.

The inability to determine rules is the major reason the task of inserting the stent cannot be computerized. Mentally translating real-time scanned images from a patient's vascular system into the hand movements necessary for manipulating a stent through an artery is an enormously complex process—too complex to articulate in rules. But programmed rules can be used to process the body's absorption of X-rays into an image of the vascular system. By showing where the aneurysm lies, the resulting CAT scan strongly complements the doctor's surgical skills.

We use the term *pure pattern recognition* to describe information-processing tasks that, at least today, cannot be articulated in inductive or deductive rules. Some of these tasks arise in "high skill" work—for example, the insertion of a stent or the process of writing a convincing legal brief. Others of these tasks arise in "low skill" work—for example, a janitor, entering an unfamiliar room, converts a two-dimensional pattern of photons on his retina to a three-dimensional mental image of the physical space before he can begin to clean.

A critical task hard to express in rules is the writing of *new* rules needed to solve a new problem. As a consequence, most software is limited to solving problems that programmers (the rules writers) foresee. Conversely, solving new problems is still human work. In an automobile repair shop, a customer brings in a newly purchased Ford Taurus with a nonfunctioning power seat. A technician uses a computerized diagnostic tool to search for problems engineers have foreseen: a faulty switch, a break in the wire connecting the switch to the seat motor, a faulty seat motor, and so on. But in a new car, the many new electronic components can interact in ways engineers have not foreseen. If the seat problem is caused by one of these unanticipated interactions, the factory-programmed rules will detect no error, and the technician must solve the problem another way, perhaps by drawing an analogy to a previous experience.

Implicit in this discussion is the educational challenge addressed by several other authors in this volume. While everyone agrees that children need problem-solving skills, "problem-solving skills" have often been taught by focusing only on problems with rules-based solutions. Algebra is an example. Solutions using rules are easy to teach and easy to test. But because, as we now know, a problem that can be solved by rules can also be programmed on a computer, rules-based problem solving has little value in the labor market. This leads to the challenge identified in the chapters in this volume by Kai-ming Cheng and Peter Gärdenfors: schools must

Easy	Difficulty in programming	Very difficult
Conscious application of deductive rules (rules-based logic)	Application of inductive rules (pattern recognition)	Rules cannot be articulated (pure recognition)
examples	*examples*	*examples*
Arithmetic; issuing a boarding pass	Predicting mortgage default; recognizing a spoken name	Writing a legal brief; a truck driver making a left turn against traffic

Figure 7.1 Varieties of human information processing.

teach children how to solve new problems for which solution rules are not yet known. This is more subtle work, and we shall return to it at the end of this chapter.

Our argument to this point is summarized in figure 7.1, which lists a representative set of tasks in order of increasing difficulty of computerization. Over the past few decades, many observers have predicted that computers would replace the highest-skill work—work that requires much "thinking." Conversely, other observers have predicted that computers would replace the lowest-skill, "routine" work. While the second prediction is closer to the mark, neither prediction was fully accurate. As the figure shows, and as noted above, computers have difficulty with many skilled cognitive tasks and many "unskilled" physical movements as well.

HUMAN INTERACTION

Return for a moment to the case of the janitor entering an unfamiliar room. One factor that makes this case complex is the fact that we can process information only in context. Based on visual information alone, the janitor cannot know whether he is looking at a four-foot-high chair ten feet away or a forty-foot-high chair one hundred feet away. He resolves this ambiguity on the basis of past experience—information he already possesses.

Similarly, when a salesperson says you look perfect in lime-green pants, you cannot know, based on the verbal information alone, whether the salesperson is being honest. The other things the salesperson does—

reading your body language, quickly correcting misunderstandings, smiling at appropriate times—is designed to establish a context in which you assume you are hearing the truth.

The potential for such ambiguity exists in processing any information. Simon (1960) noted that in some cases the ambiguity can be reduced by routinizing the context. For example, the person calling the MIT general number is instructed to state the person's first and last name; thus the software knows exactly the information to expect. If the software had to process general conversation along the lines of "Oh, hi. I'm looking for a professor in the physics department. Smith, I think her name is," the processing task would be much more complicated.

In many other cases, standardizing the context is not possible, and the resulting ambiguity underlies what might be called the dot.com fallacy regarding human interaction. At the height of the dot.com bubble, some business plans assumed a recipient of information would automatically interpret it just as the author had intended—no face-to-face contact required. To disprove the assumption, you can hand a calculus book to a third-grader and ask him or her to start taking derivatives or, closer to home, try to interpret e-mail from your teenage children ("Dad, I was only joking"). Most business plans that relied on this assumption failed, and human interaction to establish context remains central to many occupations—managing, teaching, selling—and to working in teams in which the task is to exchange not just information but a *particular understanding* of information.

As Süssmuth's chapter in this volume illustrates, a globalized economy complicates this communication problem. Two people from different cultures cannot be assumed to share a common context even if they are in the same line of work. Without a common context, even face-to-face contact may not be enough to create a shared understanding. Mutually beneficial exchanges will be that much harder to attain. Multinational firms have long recognized this problem and have specifically trained managers in such areas as how to do business in Japan. But, as Süssmuth and Gärdenfors argue in this volume, the expansion of globalization means such contacts are likely to occur among people in every walk of life, many of whom have little sense of what to expect.

COMPUTERS AND OFF-SHORING

To this point, we have argued that for a human task to be programmed, we must be able both to construct a representation of the required information suitable for a computer and to express the processing as deductive or inductive rules. To the extent that a task fulfills these conditions, it is also a candidate for being moved offshore. The more a task can be specified in rules—the less it relies on tacit knowledge—the easier it is to explain to someone else without substantial misunderstanding, and the easier it is to monitor.

This overlap suggests that computerization and off-shoring should substitute for many of the same jobs, and that is indeed the case. The call-center work that moves offshore is heavily scripted and rule-like, while other call-center work, as we have seen, is lost to speech recognition software. Assembly-line work is lost to both offshore producers and to robotics. The preparation of basic tax returns is lost to offshore accountants and software programs like TurboTax and TaxCut.

Most of these are what we would call moderate-skill jobs. Most of the few higher-skill jobs that have begun to move offshore are technical jobs in programming, engineering, financial analysis, and the like—jobs that combine tacit analysis with a heavy component of rules and standardized procedures. In sum, in advanced economies, globalization and computerization are eliminating many of the same jobs.

WHICH JOBS WILL BE AVAILABLE?

How are computerization and globalization shaping available work? A rough first answer to this question is contained in figure 7.2, which compares the U.S. adult occupational distributions for 1969 and 1999. Employment between these two years grew by 56 million jobs, or 70 percent. This employment growth is evidence that computers did not cause mass unemployment. The main reason is that, while computerization and international trade eliminated some U.S.-based jobs, they created many others that did not exist thirty years ago, including cell-phone sales representative and Internet installer. But within the aggregate growth, some occupational categories grew faster than others, and this *changing occupational mix* is one place where computers, international trade, and more recently, off-shoring, have had their impact.

In figure 7.2, occupations are listed by increasing average pay. The evolution the graph depicts is best described as a moderate hollowing out of the occupational distribution: some growth in the lowest-paying service occupations,[3] shrinkage in blue-collar and administrative support (clerical) occupations, and growth in all higher-paid occupations, including sales.

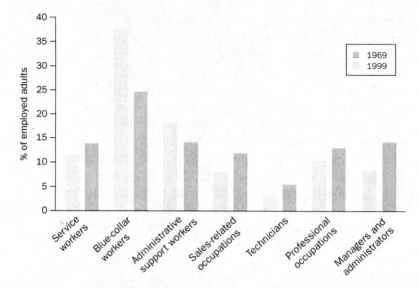

Figure 7.2 Adult occupational distribution, 1969 and 1999. Occupations listed by increasing average pay. SOURCE: *Authors' tabulations of data from Current Population Survey, U.S. Bureau of the Census.*

Multiple forces are at work in figure 7.2—computerization, international trade, and off-shoring but also the rising proportion of employed women and the rising education level of the workforce. Nonetheless, the shifts in the distribution are consistent with the story we have outlined. Specifically:

- The growth in service occupations (e.g., janitors, cafeteria workers, security guards) reflects the inability of rules to capture human optical recognition and many physical movements and the number of tasks that must be performed in this country and so cannot be off-shored.

- The growth in sales occupations (a broad category ranging from fast-food clerks to bond traders) reflects an increased flow of new products—driven in part by computers—that increases the need for selling, and the inability of rules to describe the exchange of complex information that salesmanship requires.[4]

- The growth in professional, managerial, and technical occupations reflects the inability to express high-end cognitive activities in rules, such as formulating and solving new problems, exercis-

ing good judgment in the face of uncertainty, and creating new
products and services.

- In contrast, many blue-collar occupations—particularly assembly-
  line work—and administrative support (clerical) occupations can
  be described by deductive or inductive rules. This accounts in
  large part for the decline in these two categories through both
  direct substitution and computer-assisted outsourcing.

As we have suggested, this hollowing-out is not unique to the United
States. The Japanese word *kudoka* refers to a similar phenomenon in that
country; recent papers demonstrate the pattern in England and Germany (Goos & Manning 2004; Spitz 2004). The process represents a
potential problem because the demand side of the labor market can
change much more rapidly than people can change their skills. Thus, hollowing-out can create a labor market imbalance in which too many
moderately skilled workers are chasing too few moderately skilled jobs
and end up competing for lower-skilled jobs The result is a widening wage
gap between higher- and lower-paid workers.

WHAT SKILLS ARE NOW REQUIRED?

To this point, we have discussed the changing nature of work in terms
of the changing occupational mix. For purposes of education, the question is what these occupational changes mean for the skills workers
need. In work with David Autor, we have categorized human skills into
five broad categories:

- *Expert thinking*, or solving problems for which there are no
  rule-based solutions. Examples include diagnosing the illness of
  a patient whose symptoms seem strange, creating a good-tasting
  dish from the ingredients that are fresh in the market that morning, repairing an auto that does not run well but that the computer diagnostics report says has no problem. These problems
  require what we call pure pattern recognition—information processing that cannot now be programmed on a computer. While
  computers cannot substitute for humans in these tasks, they can
  complement human skill by making information more readily
  available.

- *Complex communication*, or interacting with other humans
  to acquire information, explain it, or persuade them of its

implications for action. Examples include a manager motivating the people whose work she supervises, a salesperson gauging a customer's reaction to an article of clothing, a biology teacher explaining how cells divide, an engineer describing why a new design for a DVD player is superior to previous designs.

- *Routine cognitive tasks*, or mental processes that are well described by deductive or inductive rules. Examples include maintaining expense reports, filing new information provided by insurance customers, and evaluating applications for mortgages. Because these tasks can be accomplished by following a set of rules, they are prime candidates for computerization.

- *Routine manual tasks*, or physical tasks that can be well described using deductive or inductive rules. Examples include installing windshields on new vehicles in automobile assembly plants, and counting pills and packaging them in containers at pharmaceutical firms. Since these tasks can be defined in terms of a set of precise, repetitive movements, they are also candidates for computerization.

- *Nonroutine manual tasks*, or physical tasks that cannot be well described by a set of if-x-then-do-y rules, because they require optical recognition and fine muscle control that have proven extremely difficult to program computers to carry out. Examples include driving a truck, cleaning a building, and setting gems in engagement rings. Computers do not complement human effort in carrying out most such tasks. As a result, computerization should have little effect on the percentage of the workforce engaged in these tasks.

Figure 7.3 displays a conservative picture of how these tasks have evolved since 1969—conservative because available data are limited to skill changes caused by the changing occupational mix. In reality, we know a large or larger source of changing skill demands occurs within occupations. Today's bank teller spends more time selling financial services than he does carrying out the routine cognitive tasks of processing deposits and withdrawals—tasks largely performed by ATM machines. Similarly, twenty-five years ago, auto mechanics did not have to read to learn their jobs—they could learn by watching other mechanics. But the evolution of automobile electronics has transformed many visible, mechanical components into opaque electronic modules. As a result, a mechanic can

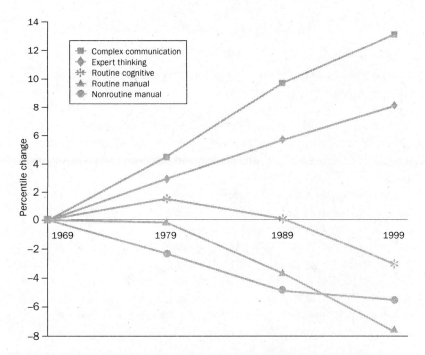

Figure 7.3 Economy-wide measures of routine and nonroutine task input, 1969–1998 (1969 = 0). SOURCE: *Autor, Levy, & Murnane 2003.*

no longer function without the ability to read, to work with computerized testing equipment, and to construct mental models of a problem. If these within-occupation changes were added to figure 7.3, the trends would be sharper.

Going forward, we can expect these trends in skill demands to continue and, if anything, accelerate. Because figure 7.3 is based on 1969–98 data, it reflects the impact of computerization and internationally traded goods. But the impact of traded services—off-shoring—appears only at the end of the period and will continue to eliminate routine cognitive jobs in the future. Similarly, the available measures of complex communication are based on the U.S. economy of roughly two decades ago and so fail to capture how globalization is now raising the bar for communication skills (see, e.g., Süssmuth, this volume).

In summary, the trends in figure 7.3 indicate that demand is shifting toward a higher-skilled, more flexible labor force. The question, at least for the United States, is how such a labor force can be created.

EDUCATIONAL IMPLICATIONS

At various points in its history, the United States has experienced a substantial increase in the educational attainments of the labor force. These episodes suggest that the country's institutions and population will, over the long run, respond to the rising skill demands that the combination of globalization and computerized work creates. Nonetheless, we should not expect an easy transition. Teaching expert thinking and complex communication will require significant adjustments, and the nation's demographics are not on our side.

Let us begin with the demographics. As we have seen (e.g., figure 7.2), skill requirements have been rising for some time. For much of the 1970s and 1980s, the baby boomers' entrance into the labor force permitted the supply of skilled workers to meet demand. The baby boom cohorts represented a large fraction of the labor force of that time and were much better educated than the cohorts that preceded them. These factors together allowed the average educational level of U.S. workers to increase rapidly. While our descriptions of expert thinking and complex communication involve more than just years spent in a classroom, the rapid increases in educational attainment suggests these particular skills are increasing as well.

Neither demographic factor operates today. The baby boom cohorts are now part of the current labor force. The demographic cohorts now entering the labor force are relatively small by comparison, and their educational attainments are no longer substantially higher than the cohorts who immediately preceded them. David Ellwood has estimated that under optimistic projections of existing trends, the proportion of the labor force with college educations will have risen from about 30 percent in the year 2000 to 35 percent in 2020, a percentage that likely lags the shift in employer demand toward more educated workers. In sum, it is likely that significant numbers of jobs—some high skill but most moderate skill—will continue to be lost to computers and foreign workers. Without concerted efforts at retraining, the likely result is the scenario sketched above: growing inequality as significant numbers of moderately skilled workers are displaced and must compete for lower-skill jobs. This competition for lower-wage jobs can occur even as employers continue to push for higher quotas for skilled immigrants.

This brings us to the question of how to teach expert thinking and complex communication. To be clear, we are not suggesting that these skills are additional subjects. Rather, they can be taught by approaching existing subjects in a somewhat different way.

Let us begin with expert thinking—the ability to solve problems that, unlike algebra, lack explicit rules-based solutions and must be solved through some form of pattern recognition. Rules-based solutions must still be part of any curriculum—that is, students still need to know subjects like algebra. But curricula must recognize that a rules-based solution is usually the second part of a two-part problem-solving process. The first part of the process—the part that retains labor market value—is recognizing which rules-based solution applies in a particular case. For example, a mechanical engineer is valued for her ability to formulate a problem as a mathematical model. Once the model is formulated, a computer—not the engineer—will apply rules to calculate the actual solution.

How does the engineer choose the correct mathematical model? As with the earlier case of the auto mechanic, the engineer likely relies on analogies with past experience. In cognitive terms, analogies often involve pure pattern recognition whereby a person recognizes similarities between features of the current problem and features of earlier relevant problems. In this spirit, Peter Gärdenfors (this volume) advances the hypothesis that "understanding consists of seeing patterns." Learning this kind of pattern recognition takes practice. In particular, it requires going beyond traditional assignments in which the student knows that the problems at the end of a chapter on long division can all be solved using long division—no need to think about which rules to apply.

In subjects such as history and literature, the equivalent of rules-based solutions is a focus on narrow facts—dates and names and little more. In this case, going beyond rules-based solutions means teaching the underlying relationships among narrow facts. These relationships form the basis for the analogies needed to solve new problems. An example from a National Research Council Report nicely illustrates the distinction.

STUDENT I

Q: What was the date of the battle of the Spanish Armada?
A: 1588.
Q: How do you know this?
A: It was one of the dates I memorized for the exam.
Q: Why is the event important?
A: I don't know.

STUDENT 2

Q: What was the date of the battle of the Spanish Armada?

A: It must have been around 1590.

Q: How do you know this?

A: I know the English began to settle in Virginia just after 1600, although I'm not sure of the exact date. They wouldn't have dared start overseas explorations if Spain still had control of the seas. It would have taken a little while to get expeditions organized, so England must have gained naval supremacy somewhere in the late 1500s.

Q: Why is the event important?

A: It marks a turning point in the relative importance of England and Spain as European powers and colonizers of the New World.[5]

The skill of complex communication—making effective oral and written arguments and eliciting information from others—can similarly be taught using existing subject matter. But teaching this skill requires both a change in emphasis and additional time—the time needed to review and grade oral presentations and frequent student essays. In practice, computers may be of some help here. Recognizing adequate writing, like recognizing a friend's voice, rests on inductive rules. Researchers have made significant progress in approximating these rules—the general patterns of word use that experts recognize as good writing. These inductive rules now form the basis of software to grade student essays.[6] Although this software cannot distinguish E. B. White's prose from merely adequate writing and consequently will not replace a skilled writing teacher, it can create a better writing experience than many U.S. children now receive.

Perhaps the biggest potential obstacle to increasing students' mastery of expert thinking and complex communication is mandatory state tests that emphasize recall of facts rather than these critical skills. Most states now require all students to complete mandatory assessments as part of programs to increase educational accountability. In many states, these assessments have been designed toward minimizing costs while producing numerical scores that can be compared across districts or over time. In a subject such as history, a multiple-choice test is more likely to meet these criteria than an essay needed to demonstrate complex communication. In an area such as math, a multiple-choice test is much less expensive to grade than an exam with open-ended questions that ask students to describe their thought processes and to demonstrate expert thinking. In the drive for educational accountability, teachers have strong incentives to teach to the test, and thus it is particularly important that we get the tests right.

At this stage, our observations on educational implications can only be preliminary. To say more will require additional research, and not surprisingly, we believe such research is justified. In the first half of the twentieth century, the U.S. labor market was transformed by the mechanization of agriculture. Today, computerization and globalization are driving another significant transformation. It is important to gain a more detailed understanding of how this transformation is changing job requirements and how the required skills can be taught. To do otherwise is to educate our children to compete with either a computer or low-wage workers—a competition our children cannot win.

CONCLUSION

In this chapter, we outline a theory of the way computers and globalization are changing available work. The changing nature of work is not the only result of our increasingly globalized society, but it is clearly an important one. The argument we have presented can be summarized in three points:

- At least for the moment, the jobs threatened by globalization greatly overlap the jobs threatened by computerized work.

- Jobs lost to both forces tend to hollow out the occupational distribution, leaving employment concentrated at the low and high ends of the skill distribution.

- A fair amount may be said about the generic skills required in this evolving economy and the educational challenges involved in teaching these skills.

As in any short summary, there are undoubtedly points we have missed. However, we believe the arguments here presented offer a useful introduction to the future of work in industrial countries and the educational challenges that result.

NOTES

This chapter is adapted from Levy and Murnane 2004.

1. In particular, see Autor, Levy, & Murnane 2003.

2. The technique used was logit, a regression-like model for cases in which the dependent variable is either one or zero (i.e., no default or default). Readers familiar with statistics will recognize that simply analyzing approved mortgages creates a sample selection problem since the estimate cannot incorporate information from rejected applications. When statisticians have access to full samples of applications (including those that have been rejected), they can apply

statistical methods to correct for this problem. But these methods do not seem to make a significant difference in this case.

3. Service *occupations*—for example, janitor or security guard—should not be confused with jobs in the service *sector.* Service-sector employment includes service occupations but also includes jobs such as schoolteacher, brain surgeon, airline mechanic, and financial analyst.

4. But sales occupations may not grow as rapidly in the future. While many sales transactions require actual selling—that is, convincing a customer to buy— others deal with customers who know exactly what they want and so the jobs are more clerical. This second group of transactions can now be handed over to the Internet through websites like Amazon.com.

5. This example is adapted from Pellegrino, Chudowsky, & Glaser 2003.

6. See, for example, Burstein, Chodorow, & Leacock 2003.

REFERENCES

Autor, D., F. Levy, and R. J. Murnane (2003). The skill content of recent technological change: An empirical exploration. *Quarterly Journal of Economics,* 118(4) (November): 1279–1334.

Burstein, J., M. Chodorow, and C. Leacock (2003). *CriterionSM* online essay evaluation: An application for automated evaluation of student essays. http://ftp.ets.org/pub/res/erater_iaaio3_burstein.pdf.

Ellwood, D. (2001). The sputtering labor force of the 21st century: Can social policy help? National Bureau of Economic Research. Working paper 8321, June.

Goos, M., and A. Manning (2004). *Lousy and lovely jobs: The rising polarization of work in Britain.* Centre for Economic Performance, London School of Economics, September.

Levy, F., and R. J. Murnane (2004). *The new division of labor: How computers are creating the next job market.* Princeton: Princeton University Press.

Pellegrino, J., N. Chudowsky, and R. Glaser (2001). *Knowing what students know: The science and design of educational assessment.* Washington, DC: National Academy Press.

Polanyi, M. (1966) *The tacit dimension.* New York: Doubleday.

Simon, H. (1960). The corporation: Will it be managed by machines? In *Management and the corporations.* M. L. Anshen and G. L. Bach, eds. Pp. 17–55. New York: McGraw Hill.

Spitz, A. (2004). *Computer use, job content, and educational attainment.* Manheim, Germany: Center for Economic Research, July.

EIGHT

Kai-ming Cheng

THE POSTINDUSTRIAL WORKPLACE
AND CHALLENGES TO EDUCATION

As a student of education policies, I started feeling uneasy about not looking at the world outside the educational system when the Education Commission was formulating its blueprint for educational reform in Hong
Kong in 2000. This uneasiness was prompted by my daughter, who had
just joined one of the leading investment banks; as a graduate of anthropology and linguistics, she had no prior knowledge of finance and
accounting whatsoever. My curiosity led me to look into the realities of
the contemporary workplace. I was shocked to discover that the kinds
of organizations we were familiar with and used as a backdrop for our
teaching in educational administration were disappearing. Over the past
few years, I have looked into different workplace categories.[1] Not only
have the structures of work changed but human interactions within the
workplace have also taken new forms. I have to conclude that the social
institution of education today belongs to a bygone era and is not preparing our young people for the future (see Suárez-Orozco & Sattin, this
volume).

The thesis of this chapter adds to Levy and Murnane's observations
in this volume. Levy and Murnane vividly describe the disappearance of
certain jobs in the U.S. workplace—specifically, those that are replace-
able by computers or can move to countries where labor costs are lower.
My observation is that jobs are also disappearing as a result of changes
in the organization of the workplace.

I begin this discussion by clarifying two points about the orientation and purpose of this research. First, I am not an economist and do not attempt to conduct a labor market analysis. My primary intention here is not to improve graduates' employability. Instead, I present an anthropological description of the contemporary workplace; it is a reality, I fear, that most educators are unfamiliar with. Second, I am not advocating improvements in education in order to suit or fuel the economy. Rather, my observations lead to the conclusion that vocational preparation even in the broadest sense ("education for jobs") belongs to the fading industrial era and is being challenged in the new global era. The fundamental ideology of education has been distorted by the pragmatic, if not mechanistic, philosophies of industrial society. It is in this context that I identify the challenges to education in the latter part of the chapter. I argue that education should return to its original premise of broadly preparing young people for their future.

WORKPLACE REALITIES

An understanding of fundamental change in the workplace starts with an overview of organizational structures. Workplace organizations are now smaller, flatter, and looser. In September 2006 approximately 304,000 companies were registered in Hong Kong. Of these, over 99 percent were companies known as SMEs (small and medium enterprises) with fewer than one hundred employees. In addition, 68 percent of all people who work in companies in Hong Kong are employed by SMEs. Moreover, 94 percent of these companies have less than twenty employees, and 87 percent of them employ between one and nine people (Census and Statistics Department, 2006). These Hong Kong figures differ from a typical industrial society, in which many more large organizations employ the majority of the working population. Indeed, one may argue that Hong Kong's is largely a service economy with a tiny manufacturing sector,[2] and hence may not be representative of all societies. However, the pattern is also reflected in the United States, a much larger economy. According to the U.S. Census Bureau, in 2003, 97.7 percent of business enterprises had fewer than one hundred employees, and 86.0 percent had fewer than twenty (U.S. Census Bureau 2007, table 738). To varied extents, other urban societies such as Shanghai, Beijing, and Taipei are also moving in the same direction.

This chapter does not purport to explain comprehensively why organizations have decreased in size. It is safe to say, however, that the change in the average company size is related to the general shift away from large-scale production to increasingly customized products and services. In other words, due to customization, the diversity of products has increased and the demand for each product has decreased. Likewise, services are customized and more direct, rendering the large organizations of yesterday unnecessary.

A few examples may help illustrate this new pattern:

Manufacturing. A factory in China run by a Hong Kong investor produces paper-box packaging for electrical appliances. There used to be very few models of rice cookers, for example, and large quantities of each model. This same factory now produces packaging for laptop computers, of which many different models are produced but each in small quantities. The factory has expanded its design department but employs fewer front-line production workers than it did ten years ago. Work is now organized through different project teams.

Food catering. A chain of restaurants in Hong Kong used to be the dominant provider of Cantonese food. It benefited from economies of scale because it was able to mass-produce the same cuisine. It has now developed into an umbrella organization of more than 490 restaurants serving over thirty national and international cuisines and including fast-food, bakery, and coffee shops. Each restaurant now operates with a style of its own, yet is controlled by the same parent group.

Retail banking. Retail banks used to have cashier counters responsible for deposits and withdrawals. Over time, these banks have created and expanded customized services, initially through receptionists, then through individualized tables, and now with private booths for personal consultation. The cashier counters have been relegated to the back office or have been largely replaced by ATM machines.

Insurance. Customers used to buy general insurance policies written by a single company. Agents were salespeople for the standardized policies. Agents now seek to tailor policies to fit individual clients' needs. Insurance brokers further advance the level of customization by searching across companies for the optimal policy for each client.

These examples illustrate a theme common to the changes in traditional production of goods and services. Currently, few organizations maintain the "Fordist" mode of industrial operation in which a top-down management structure divides work among a mass of laborers. In such a mode, workers are coordinated through layers of middle management and separate departments that form the pyramidal structure paradigmatic of industry. Work is done through predesigned procedures and follows strict rules and regulations that connect the entire team in one coordinated effort. This is what Max Weber called bureaucracy in the neutral sense of the term.[3]

Small workplace units such as small firms and nongovernmental organizations (NGOs) cannot support the cost of complex hierarchies and have historically been organized quite differently than large businesses and factories. In these workplaces, maintaining hierarchy, procedures, and rules and regulations have not always been the primary concern. But these more fluid organizational structures are no longer exclusively adopted by smaller businesses. Today even large organizations such as investment banks and consulting firms are shunning traditional departments and middle management and instead are organizing around smaller working groups—known as task forces, production teams, project groups, or deal teams—that are designed to provide tailor-made services to particular clients. In this way, the workplace environment in many large organizations today is not altogether different from small enterprises and NGOs.

Changes in size and structure are among the more visible adjustments to business today. Compared with the workplace in a typical industrial economy, there is much more demand for design and much less demand for production. As a result, the need for designers has increased, and the need for front-line laborers continues to shrink. In the service industries, services have become both customized and direct. Hence, the front-line workers in the service sector also bear the responsibility of design, problem solving, and decision making. There is increasingly less room for traditional blue-collar workers.

The changing requirements for laborers of today have important educational implications in terms of skills, training, and capacity. In a typical small working group, the division of labor is blurred. People no longer work as specialists but are asked to contribute through the integration of different talents, expertise, and experiences. Since people do not work as separate individuals but rather collaborate through teamwork, there is a new premium on communication (see Suárez-Orozco and Sattin; Levy and Murnane, both this volume.) Employees are not mere implementers who abide by strict job descriptions, elaborate procedures, and detailed rules and regulations. They are designers of products and bear responsibility for the deliverables.

Our attention should not be limited to the organization of formal workplaces. We cannot ignore the increasing number of independently employed individuals (freelancers). In Hong Kong, for example, an estimated 220,000 people work as freelancers, compared to the total of 2,200,000 people employed by registered companies.[4] At a diametric extreme from Fordist pyramids, these people work in circumstances that are almost completely devoid of regimented procedures, rules, and regulations (see Weber 1947).

IMPLICATIONS FOR INDIVIDUALS

Changes in workplace structures and dynamics have tremendous implications for individuals. Not only is the entire management structure different from that of the industrial society, but also individuals today are required to work in new modes and face different challenges as compared to those of the industrial era.

- Room for "unskilled workers" is shrinking. New demands are being made of front-line workers, and the capacity for decision making, problem solving, and critical thinking is a basic requirement (see also Levy & Murnane, this volume).
- Teamwork and integration are the common modes of operation in almost all workplace units. People are expected to work beyond any narrow special knowledge and expertise.
- Because of close working relations that are not bound by procedures, rules, or regulations, people have to work with others, demonstrate flexibility in dealing with personal differences and conflicts, and maintain positive relationships with colleagues.
- Workplace activities, including presentations, negotiation, brainstorming, persuasion, debates, and arbitration all entail high competencies in communication skills.
- Due to new structures of work and lack of strict governance in the form of prescriptive rules and regulations, employees are more likely to face dilemmas and decisions regarding ethics, emotions, values, and principles.

- Workplace units have become unstable. They may be changed, restructured, merged, or dismantled over a relatively short time. Organizational loyalty, job security, and guaranteed income are certainly fading away.[5]
- Because of rapidly changing work environments and needs, individuals face constant adjustments in teammates, partners, and social groups at work over time. There is a need for greater capacity for socializing and networking.
- Although tasks are increasingly specialized, people are not. Individuals are expected to move between occupations and across specializations. Occupational identity is also at stake.
- Tasks, jobs, and even careers are frequently shifting; therefore, individuals must be continually engaged in on-the-job, on-demand, and lifelong learning.
- Weakening organizational bonds result in higher expectations of an individual's capacity for self-management, self-confidence, and self-reflection.
- Changes in workplace structure will eventually result in fewer available jobs. At the same time, however, there will be almost limitless space for *freelancing and entrepreneurship*.

Significant adjustments have already occurred in workplace organization, but in fact, the real changes have just started. Globally, these shifts are spreading rapidly from developed to less developed regions, both within and between nations. However, preparation for life is not only limited to the workplace. Individuals must live with family and friends and must engage in other social, political, cultural and/or religious activities. Nevertheless, the workplace serves as a useful window on the scale and direction of the changes.

CHALLENGES TO EDUCATION

It is in the context of the changing workplace that I discern some basic implications for education. The fundamental question is, *If this is the society into which our students are entering upon graduation, are we adequately preparing them for successful integration?* I am at best dubious. Education is being challenged fundamentally; thus, the prevailing paradigms of industrial-era educational systems must also be examined and, indeed, reformed accordingly.

PARADIGM OF SCREENING

Educational systems have long facilitated the classification and ranking of human beings in an industrial society through the reproduction of an educational hierarchy in the workplace. Schools have often served as sieves performing a screening function. People exit the educational system having attained different credentials and training that typically determine and justify their position and status in the social hierarchy.

The pyramidal structure of industrial societies is deeply rooted in the minds of educators. As a result, selection and screening to fit the extant social structure are often seen as legitimate functions of education. Several assumptions operate within this paradigm:

> *Assumption 1:* "There are smart kids and dumb kids." Peter Senge (2000) identified this as one of the fundamental assumptions of education in the industrial era. Under this assumption, not everybody can learn, and those who cannot deserve less education.

> *Assumption 2:* A student's intelligence is measured by knowledge, often in terms of amount of knowledge. Such a measure is often translated into academic performance, which is in turn reduced to a test score.

> *Assumption 3:* The qualification pyramid in education exactly matches the manpower pyramid in society.

These assumptions can be challenged in at least three ways. First, society has progressed and now demands that more people receive postsecondary education and training. There are indeed fewer and fewer work opportunities for those without education beyond secondary school, as evidenced by youth unemployment. In Hong Kong, for example, since the turn of the century, the unemployment rate has stayed at 4.5 to 7 percent, independent of economic cycles (Hong Kong SAR Government, 2006, p.109). A phenomenon of "double disengagement" is apparent among young people in that an estimated 19 percent of youth ages fifteen to twenty are not engaged in either study or work (Commission on Youth 2003). In educational terms, our current school system does not equip students to survive in society. Manufacturing industries, which used to hire the less academically successful students to fill positions as frontline laborers, have shrunk dramatically. The educational system still produces such students, but society can no longer absorb them to the same extent. Indeed, labor forecasts consistently predict a shortage of people with postsecondary education and a surplus of those with only second-ary education. Yet schools continue to perpetuate the shortage and the surplus by failing to adequately serve all students. The crisis is serious. And Hong Kong is not alone.

Second, in Hong Kong, people in their forties and fifties are tending to lose their jobs because their credentials and capacities no longer match the new expectations of the changed workplace. The schooling they had twenty or thirty years ago did not prepare them for the new requirements of today's workplace.[6] What may be called midcareer unemployment is widespread in most major cities in Asia. As an institution, our educational system is increasingly anachronistic. It is supposed to prepare people for life, but it does not. In other words, it is not sufficient for education to give graduates a *job* upon graduation. Education should enable people to sustain their work engagement throughout their lives.

Third, recent expansion of tertiary education has contradicted the pyra-mid assumption (see Hugonnier, this volume). According to OECD fig-ures, one-third of all students of the same cohort were admitted to tertiary education programs in 1996 (OECD 1998). In 1999, 40 percent of students were admitted to Type A tertiary education programs (full-time degree-bearing programs) (OECD 2001). By 2003 Type A enroll-ment had risen to 53 percent (OECD 2005). The same trend is happening in major educational systems in Asia. Korea and Taiwan have an over-supply of higher-education institutions, and Japan is experiencing a sim-ilar phenomenon. In major Chinese cities such as Beijing and Shanghai, the enrollment ratios in tertiary education have exceeded 70 percent. Yet in none of these countries is there any significant decline in the quality of tertiary education. In Hong Kong, enrollment in tertiary education has leaped from 30 percent to 66 percent in the past five years. Community colleges, which contribute most significantly to this expansion, appear to be providing a real alternative route for students who have been failed by conventional school systems. These students have disproved the assumption that only a select group of students can succeed beyond sec-ondary schooling. These data question the purpose of screening in pri-mary and secondary schools.

PARADIGM OF SPECIALIZATION

Education gives people qualifications. Such qualifications specify not only the level of academic achievement but also the individual's unique area of competence. The importance of developing an area of specialization is widely emphasized among educators, particularly in East Asian cultures. Not only are university programs highly specialized, but also specialization affects the design of the school structure and curriculum. In many Asian educational systems, often because of postcolonial influences, students are "streamed" or "tracked" into "science," "arts," or other areas as soon as compulsory education ends, around the time they turn fifteen. A belief in the value of specialization is based on several assumptions:

> *Assumption 4*: Human beings should be classified, and such classification is reflected in people's occupational identity. Individuals living in industrial societies have also self-identified by their occupations. According to this assumption, human beings are no more than manpower that fuels the economy.

> *Assumption 5*: Knowledge is divided, and people who possess such knowledge are divided accordingly. In higher education, disciplines are clearly demarcated such that each works in a unique paradigm. In secondary schools, knowledge is classified in lumps called subjects. There is also the tacit assumption that only these disciplines or subjects constitute knowledge.

> *Assumption 6*: The degree of specialization also indicates a person's intellectual level: the more specialized, the greater the intellect. Accordingly, people who are more educated are expected to be more specialized.

Changes in society are challenging the notion of specialization. First, there is new demand in the workplace for increasingly specialized tasks and jobs, but not specialized people. Division of labor is increasingly blurred. People are asked to contribute to the team by integrating their own knowledge and expertise with other members'. Employees must move across disciplines and knowledge domains. The trend of product and service customization has also created the expectation that they engage in short-term specialization contingent on needs and demand.

Individuals are also increasingly changing jobs and careers over time. They may be required to develop a certain expertise at a specific juncture, then move into another area of specialization at a later point in their working life. Occupational identity does not necessarily have lifelong significance anymore. In most contemporary societies, a person will likely pass through several careers in his or her life. Preparing young people for a particular occupation is not always a positive contribution to their future.

Again, a person's capacities must be versatile and flexible over the course of her or his career.

Currently education is significantly mismatched with work as a result of the focus on specialization in schooling. While certain career paths, such as in medicine, continue to require specialized learning, the majority of students end up in jobs that are not directly related to the qualifications and knowledge they have acquired in school. This holds true in workplaces in the service sector and particularly in NGOs. Increasingly, accounting firms, to take a typical example, hire graduates who have had no experience in accounting. Conversely, law students may not be interested in practicing law. This lack of correspondence between training and profession, which would have been considered irregular in an industrial society, is becoming commonplace today. The dilution of specialization in the workplace is perhaps less a matter of blurring occupational boundaries than of the demand for "generic capacity." When an accounting firm hires a physicist, it is not because its managers do not require accounting expertise (which can be trained on the job) but rather because they are looking for someone who demonstrates flexibility and integrity.[7] When a leading investment bank hires first-year analysts, it looks for a person with a "winning personality" rather than experience in banking. The bank then provides the appropriate training in a matter of a few weeks. Indeed, in one bank in particular, new recruits included graduates of biology, psychology, political science, and comparative literature programs.

Unprecedented changes in higher education have occurred in response to the major shift in what the labor market demands of young people today. Perhaps the most noticeable is the Washington Accord (1999), approved by the Institutes of Engineers, whose signatories moved to dedicate 30 percent of undergraduate coursework to studies outside engineering.[8] Indeed, most North American undergraduate programs in business have reserved half of the required curriculum for nonbusiness studies. Undergraduate journalism curricula have moved to reduce the major component to only 30 percent of the total credits, thus challenging the entire notion of a major.[9]

In addition, many universities around the world have introduced a common core undergraduate curriculum or have delayed specialization to later years of the undergraduate schedule. In Europe, for example, in an effort to achieve mutual recognition of university degrees, the Bologna Declaration (1999),[10] among others, calls on all educational systems within the European community to conform to a three-year generic degree ("first cycle") and allow specialization in the second degree ("second cycle"). In the United Kingdom, where higher education is known for specialization, Minister of Education and Science David Blunkett recently called on institutions to introduce two-year Foundations Degrees. Generic in nature, such degrees leave specialization to the second degree. In mainland China, major universities like Fudan have started a first-year common program followed by a generic core in the second year.

Such changes lead to the question, *If colleges and universities are delaying specialization, and if specialization is blurred in the workplace anyway, what is the point of specialization in schools?*

PARADIGM OF STUDY

Education has always been interpreted as academic *study*. Although there is no shortage of discussion in the literature about student learning and development beyond classrooms and the formal curriculum, people still see books, syllabi, and classrooms as symbols of school-based learning. Moreover, since the 1980s, the bias toward academic study has been exacerbated by the school effectiveness and quality-assurance movements in education. These general trends have tended to reduce both school and student performance to test scores. In many countries, the indicators of school quality all eventually boil down to students' academic performance as measured by scores on standardized tests.

Student activities outside classrooms are often perceived as less valuable "extras" rather than the real forms of learning and development they often can be. In some school systems, teacher unions require their members to confine their activities to classroom teaching. Apart from religious schools and elite private schools, many public school systems lack support for activities beyond classroom learning.

In general, teachers as well as the general public seem to feel comfortable with allowing academic study to dominate students' school lives. This holds true particularly in Asian societies where parents expect schools to provide homework and willingly sacrifice family life for the extension of school activities into students' evenings.

A few additional assumptions in this area go without being questioned:

Assumption 7: The goal of education is to acquire formal qualifications; therefore, education should be about formal learning within school. Other types of learning, such as technical skills or human relations, may be important, but do not enter into the definition of formal education and therefore merit no record or reward.

Assumption 8: Academic performance is the most legitimate representation of human ability. Students who are academically successful are automatically successful in other areas of life. Hence, according to this assumption, academic qualification is a comprehensive representation of the person. Even in scientific academic research, students' test scores are used as the default proxy for "student achievement."

Assumption 9: Examinations are the only trustworthy means of measurement. Although we know that attitudes, interests, confidence, integrity, and other human dimensions are equally important, they are not measurable and hence are not counted.

All these assumptions are currently facing unprecedented challenges. Human interaction has become a much more central element of contemporary workplace dynamics. At one time it was believed that contemporary work environments would become more inhuman due to increased reliance on technology and computers. In reality, teamwork, collaboration, and integration have become the common mode of work. Various forms of human communication have become the most critical workplace activity. Moreover, individuals must face ever-changing partners, teammates, clients, and social networks. An unprecedented level of expectation is now placed on a person's ability to live, work, and learn among different people, as we saw in Tensta's classrooms. But these skills cannot be developed solely through academic study.

Additionally, as a result of the weakened role of procedures, rules, and regulations in the workplace, individual freedom and autonomy have increased, and people are relying more on their own opinions, values, principles, and ethics in decision making. In other words, in lieu of the tight monitoring that was warranted in an industrial setup, the workplace, and indeed the entire society, now depends much more on individual personalities to achieve harmony, integrity, and dignity. There are much higher expectations of individual self-management, self-confidence, self-restraint, self-respect, and self-reflection.

The aforementioned individual characteristics, which have become significantly more important in postindustrial societies, generally develop during the school-age years. Overemphasis on academic study deprives young people of the opportunity to develop these traits. This observation might explain recent urgent calls for tacit knowledge, civic education, character education, and moral education and the emphasis on social competence, emotional intelligence, and "soft skills." It might also justify reforms such as expanding students' learning opportunities, increasing extracurricular or cocurricular activities, and creating after-school programs.[11]

Many school systems are currently restructuring the secondary-school curriculum. As a matter of reform, Singapore has reduced the time spent on formal secondary-school academic curriculum by 30 percent in anticipation of the need for alternative learning experiences. Along the same line of thinking, Japan plans to reduce its formal secondary-school curriculum time by 33 percent. Another approach has been to reduce the content requirements of public examinations in order to shorten the necessary time spent on purely academic materials. In mainland China, for example, students are encouraged to write integrated, rather than subject-specific, papers as part of the national University Entrance Examination. The central question in this regard is, *If a person's character and personality are now major determinants of success in contemporary society, why do schools continue to emphasize academic study almost exclusively?*

PARADIGM OF SCHOOLING

Schools currently resemble typical production lines from the classic industrial model. Schools still understand their primary task as the preparation of students for higher levels of education (i.e., the next stage of production). The practice of teaching and learning in schools seldom goes beyond the target goal of promotion within the educational system. Although the notion of lifelong learning has been on the policy agenda for many years, its influence remains largely confined to the realm of adult learning after formal schooling ends. At the same time, however, it is commonly understood that learning in schools has far-reaching lifelong implications.

Schools are powerful institutions that dictate the learning processes of individual students. A number of additional assumptions contribute to the theories of how schools function:

> *Assumption 10*: Learning takes place only in schools, and schools alone provide legitimate education. A corollary is that all other kinds of learning are illegitimate and should not be formally recognized because they carry little social currency.

Assumption 11: All students learn in the same way. Although there have been discussions about individual needs and special needs, students are seen as "normal" when they follow the mainstream age-grade trajectory, are taught the mainstream curriculum in the conformed mode of learning, and finally, pass the uniform examinations.

Assumption 12: Learning takes place only during structured activities. Students around the world basically live in prestructured environments, with age-determined classes, set-menu curriculum, distinct subjects, prescribed timetables, specialized teachers, and standardized tests.

Schools that operate based on the assumptions listed above often fail to provide young people of today with the personal formation and general capacity they need to survive, let alone thrive, in contemporary society. They are trained to abide by rules and regulations with little room for self-management. They are expected to follow a prescribed path and left with little room for choice or decision making. Asked to provide standard answers, students in such schools are seldom expected to be innovative. They are taught basic, accepted information and rarely expected to explore the unknown. Overall, schooling is largely restrictive rather than broadening, limiting rather than liberating.

Over time, school systems have transformed into bureaucracies with a life, language, and operation all their own, and they often function independently of the larger society. Their focus often shifts from fostering real learning to achieving efficient operation and "production."

Nonetheless, recent breakthroughs are pushing these institutions to change:

- Problem-based learning, which was initiated with medical education, has begun to infiltrate into primary and secondary schools. This type of learning prompts students to develop their own questions, explore their own paths, and arrive at solutions independently or in groups

- Using "key learning areas" or "learning experiences" to enhance learning beyond traditional subjects, and hiring nonteacher experts to facilitate such learning[12]

- The creation of "learning communities," in place of age-grade structures. Students work together in a community based on flexible grouping by learning necessities[13]

- Breakthroughs in student assessment, including "authentic assessment," "student profiles," and emphasis on integration and collaboration
- The creation of the "Credit Unit Bank" (Korea)[14] and "Lifelong Passport" (Taiwan), in which diplomas or degrees are conferred by the state, independent of institutions[15]
- Growth in mentorship and internship programs that provide students with workplace experience during their formal education years.[16]

Many other innovations have been attempted. Separate though they are, they all move in a similar direction. The question to ask, though perhaps prematurely at this stage, is, *If the workplace is moving away from traditional structures and organizations, is there any room for similar change in schooling?*

LOOKING AHEAD

This discussion of the fundamental problems with the current format and ideology of schooling is inspired by my observations of the workplace and its changing structure and demands. Formal school education as it currently exists did not emerge until the mid-nineteenth century. Developed during the height of the industrial revolution, it continues to mirror the methodology and organization of the industrial era. Social transformations and evolution require adaptation and adjustment in education, and the shift to a postindustrial society calls for such changes. While schooling and work go hand in hand, I anticipate a rather dramatic dissociation between the educational system and the workplace. Because occupational identities are becoming increasingly vague in postindustrial societies, I predict that education will likely move away from direct labor market attachment and return to a focus on human development broadly defined—the original purpose of education. I also anticipate that schools will provide young people with the opportunity for personal development in realms that are more pertinent to their future, including developing a passion for nature, a commitment to society (through membership in groups), perseverance, leadership ability, an appreciation of the arts, interpersonal skills, fluency in a second or third language, familiarity with other cultures, a sense of justice, belief in equal rights, and tolerance of diversity and plurality—an education more in sync with the realities of a global era.

NOTES

1. I started with seven major multinational corporations in Hong Kong. Then I looked into a large number of freelancer cases and several cases in the manufacturing and service industries. Hayley Kan joined me in this endeavor when she started her doctoral study in 2001. She has discerned a series of categories of workplace, different in form yet all moving away from the industrial setup.

2. The service sector contributes 90.6 percent of Hong Kong's economic growth (Hong Kong SAR Government 2006, p. 94). Many such services support manufacturing that takes place on the Chinese mainland.

3. See Weber 1947, or for a brief version, see Weber 1996.

4. This is according to a report in *Mingpao*, a local Chinese newspaper (date unidentifiable).

5. Charles Handy's writings may serve as a good reminder. See, for example, the collection in Handy 1996.

6. From an interview with Chan Yuen-ha, who used to lead the union for department store workers and is now a legislator. She vividly described the disappearance of high-status but low-skill jobs in department stores in Hong Kong.

7. Interview with Peter H. Y. Wong, retired senior partner of Deloitte & Touche, Hong Kong.

8. This is among the basic recommendations in the Washington Accord, which represents the consensus of eight major institutes of engineers.

9. This is happening in the Journalism School at Columbia University in the United States, as well as in the undergraduate journalism program at the University of Hong Kong and Shantou University in mainland China.

10. www.coe.int/T/E/Cultural_Co-operation/education/Higher_education/Activities/Bologna_Process/default.asp.

11. For a good summary of the recent developments, see Noam, Biancarosa, & Dechausay 2003.

12. An example is the rather comprehensive curriculum reform in Hong Kong. See Education and Manpower Bureau 2002.

13. As is the case for new schools in Joondalup, Western Australia.

14. See "Credit Unit Bank in South Korea" 1999.

15. Started in 1999, the Lifelong Learning Passport scheme allows learners to customize their learning experience by attending programs in different institutions and be awarded a diploma upon accumulating 150 learning hours. See examples at the Civil Services website http://host.cc.ntu.edu.tw/sec/All_Law/5/5-68.html and at the city of Taipei's site, www.tatung.org.tw/17.htm.

16. A good exposition of the trend may be found in Olson 1997.

REFERENCES

Census and Statistics Department, Hong Kong SAR Government (2006). *Quarterly survey of employment and vacancies*. Hong Kong.

Commission on Youth, Hong Kong Government (2003). *Continuing development and employment opportunities for youth*. Hong Kong.

"Credit Unit Bank in South Korea" (from Chinese translation) (1999). *Review of Foreign Higher Education Teaching and Research* (Beijing) 2(2): 2.

Education and Manpower Bureau, Hong Kong SAR Government (2002). *Learning to learn*. Hong Kong.

Hong Kong SAR Government (2006). *Third quarter economic report*. Hong Kong.

Handy, C. (1996). *Beyond certainty: The changing world of organizations*. Boston: Harvard Business School Press.

Noam, G. G., G. Biancarosa, and N. Dechausay (2003). *After-school education: Approaches to an emerging field*. Cambridge, MA: Harvard Education Press.

OECD. See Organisation for Economic Co-operation and Development.

Organisation for Economic Co-operation and Development (1998). *Education at a glance: OECD Indicators 1998*. Paris.

Organisation for Economic Co-operation and Development (2001). *Education at a glance: OECD Indicators 2001: Education and skills*. Paris.

Organisation for Economic Co-operation and Development (2005). *Education at a glance: OECD Indicators 2005*. Paris.

Olson, L. (1997). *The school to work revolution*. Reading, MA: Perseus.

Senge, P. (2000.) *Schools that learn*. London: Nicholas Brealey.

U.S. Census Bureau (2007). *Statistical abstract of the United States 2007*. Washington, D.C.

Weber, M. (1947). *The theory of social and economic organization*. A. M. Henderson and T. Parsons, trans. New York: Oxford University Press.

Weber, M. (1996). Bureaucracy. In *Classics of organization theory*. 4th ed. J. M. Shafritz and J. S. Ott, eds. Pp. 80–85. Fort Worth: Harcourt Brace. Originally published in 1922.

PART THREE

LEARNING, IMMIGRATION, AND INTEGRATION

NINE

Rita Süssmuth

ON THE NEED FOR TEACHING INTERCULTURAL SKILLS

Challenges for Education in a Globalizing World

The world in which we live is rapidly globalizing. People around the world are developing a common consciousness of the globe as a series of inter-connected components in which changes made in one part of the world have a marked effect elsewhere, despite spatial separation and linguistic, cultural, religious, or ethnic differences. However, local knowledge and the integration of youth into local contexts are still of vital importance in a globalizing world. The greater global context in which young people live plays an ever more important role in the mental, spiritual, and economic development of future generations. Educational systems around the world must adapt traditional teaching strategies to teach cognitive, emotional, digital, and social skills that go beyond the local context. In this essay, I refer to these skills as intercultural. Intercultural skills always go beyond the local context; they can encompass skills other than the four main ones I focus on here.

Modern media expose individuals to people, lifestyles, and events outside their local contexts and known cultural patterns. This experience often challenges an individual and forces him or her to think globally (see Gärdenfors, this volume). The individual faces a new context and often compares his or her identity, abilities, values, culture, lifestyle, and the like to those of persons from different cultural contexts, economic back-grounds, linguistic settings, religious beliefs, or ethnic groups. Modern technology, and the know-how to access and use it, greatly influences a person's ability to seek out opportunities, to learn, and to develop.

Beyond indirect contact with diversity through the media, today's youth, as we witnessed during our instructive visit to Tensta Gymnasium in Sweden, have more direct contact with persons from other cultures and countries than did their counterparts in past generations. Currently, all nation-states are experiencing immigration to varying degrees. Our youth and future generations will not live in a fortress of national isolation. In part, our youth will move and will have to learn to live in new cultural, social, economic, and linguistic contexts. In addition, some youth will stay put, yet will still encounter diverse cultures, a multitude of social perspectives, and foreign languages. Becoming a more close-knit global community means getting to know each other better. It means discovering how different and how similar we are. Most of all, it means recognizing our interdependency and the necessity of mutual respect and tolerance (see Wikan, this volume).

Each of the approximately two hundred countries on this earth is a destination, transit, or source country of international migration, or a combination of all three. According to the Global Commission on International Migration, there are nearly 200 million international migrants worldwide (GCIM 2005, p. 83). Relying on data from the United Nations Population Division, the International Organization for Migration (IOM) has documented a marked rise in the number of migrants worldwide since 1965 (IOM 2003, p. 5). There were 75 million international migrants in 1965. By 1975 the figure had risen to 84 million; it reached 105 million in 1985. In 1990 there were 120 million international migrants, and in 2000, 175 million. In that last year, only one out of every thirty-five people had migrated across international borders. That is, about 2.9 percent of the world's people are living in a country where they are not citizens (IOM 2005, p. 379). The international migrant population, therefore, forms a clear minority of the world's population. However, the portion of the world's population that is on the move is growing faster than the global population as a whole, indicating that the percentage of people on the move will likely increase in the future. One must also consider that the world's migrant population influences both the destination countries and countries of origin far more than the numbers alone would suggest. Virtually every single person on this earth is in contact, in one way or another, with someone who is a nonnative.

Just as we can use recent trends to predict future population growth, we can also sketch a picture of the future of the world's migrant population. According to the U.S. Census Bureau's population projection, by 2050 our current world population of 6.5 billion people will expand to some 9 billion inhabitants.[1] This represents approximately a 50 percent increase in world population. If the international migrant community continues to increase at a constant rate consistent with past trends, which the IOM calculated between 1985 and 1990 to be 2.59 percent annually (IOM 2003, p. 5), then the world's international migrant population would be about 539 million people by 2050. When this forecast immigrant population worldwide is compared with the forecast world population mentioned previously, it would constitute 6 percent of the world population in 2050. Although this calculation is rough, it does demonstrate that we can expect the migrant population to increase relative to the world population. According to this calculation, the international migrant population as a portion of the total world population will more than double by 2050, and the number of international migrants will be three times the current level. A further dimension of globalization and increased international movements of persons is an increase in the number of undocumented persons crossing national borders.

Currently, the majority of educational systems around the world are unprepared for the challenges of globalization and immigration. These systems have a considerable responsibility to prepare youth for the challenges of a globalizing world (see Cheng; Crul; McAndrew, all this volume). Most school curricula do not take into consideration that today's youth—immigrant or native—are learning, interacting, and living in an environment that is connected (with varying degrees of intensity) to different values, cultures, language groups, levels of economic development, and educational systems (see Suárez-Orozco & Sattin, this volume). To meet this challenge, young people need to develop intercultural skills. Educational systems around the planet must therefore adapt and expand their priorities to account for this new context by teaching intercultural skills—cognitive, social, emotional, and digital—that go beyond the local context and teach students to think globally (see Boix Mansilla & Gardner, this volume).

MIGRATION TRENDS IN EUROPE: THE CONTEXT OF EDUCATIONAL POLICIES

Europe is the region with the highest absolute number of immigrants (immigrant or foreign-stock population), according to the Global Commission on International Migration (GCIM 2005, p. 83). Among the countries of the European Union (EU), Germany has the largest immigrant stock with 7.3 million immigrants (IOM 2005, p. 255). In a global comparison, Germany ranks third, after the United States and the Russian Federation, in the size of immigrant stocks (IOM 2005, p. 255). Since this comparative data was published, Germany has updated the figures on its migrant stock population. Currently, 6.7 million migrants live in the Federal Republic of Germany (Bundesministerium des Innern 2005, p. 103).

Although Europe is in the process of harmonizing and unifying its immigration policies (e.g., those for humanitarian migration, integration, and labor migration—see Commission of the European Communities 2005), immigration to the EU varies greatly from country to country and has a variety of historical origins. Despite these differences, some general trends in immigration to the EU have been observed. After the fall of the Soviet Union and also as a result of the Balkan wars came a decade of large flows of immigrants from Eastern to Western Europe. Immigration numbers went down in the mid-1990s, only to increase again at the end of the decade. Current immigration trends in Europe show that the number of labor migrants is increasing, the official number of humanitarian migrants (refugees) is going down, and the number of deportations of unauthorized immigrants is on the rise. Family unification represents the largest category through which immigration is facilitated throughout the EU.

At the same time, the European population is growing older on average, birth rates remain well below the replacement rate, and social security systems are buckling under the pressure of an increasing number of pensioners as compared to the active workforce. The immigration and integration policies in the European Union (currently twenty-five countries) are complicated by a large diversity in economic development, unemployment rates, and GDP.

Based mainly on immediate economic concerns and cultural fears, issues such as investment in education and integration policies often take a backseat to avoid risking political capital in the short run. Long-term solutions for utilizing education as a main motor for driving integration have not yet been realized. The debate about teaching intercultural skills versus demanding immigrant assimilation has not been completely resolved in Germany or in many other countries of the EU, including the Netherlands.

Europe cannot, however, afford to remain passive on integration policies that will help its diverse societies increase their connectivity and cohesion. The best method for increasing social integration is to equip future generations with the intercultural skills they need to become an integral part of our globalizing world. Schools are the most important institutions in which these intercultural skills can be taught and learned. Integration policies implemented in schools should teach new and old members of societies to communicate better with each other (through policies that would address the integration of not only immigrants but also natives), thereby reducing cleavages that often lead to segregation, misunderstanding, and too often, violence.

EDUCATING MILLIONS OF YOUTH
IN TRANSNATIONAL SOCIETIES

The context in which we live has been rapidly changing. Our world is globalizing. Evidence of this can be seen when one compares the speed at which

- ideas can be transferred
- people can move between places
- goods can be transported

The world in which we live is becoming increasingly diverse and complex (Suárez-Orozco & Qin-Hilliard, 2004).

With globalization, we face new threats and dangers. Since September 11, 2001, globalization has occasioned even more skepticism than before, and there is a new awareness that terrorism is an undesired companion to globalization at its current stage of development. Other negative issues connected with globalization are environmental dangers, the threat of a global disease outbreak (e.g., SARS and HIV), and economic concerns (e.g., free trade and protection) (Suárez-Orozco & Qin-Hilliard 2004). Yet globalization also represents many new opportunities, such as an increased ability to travel, interact with diverse cultures, seek out employment, and make a living outside the context into which one was born; pursue a higher standard of living; join family members abroad; or seek protection and humanitarian aid.

This globalizing world, however, demands that the youth of today deal with greater diversity and complexity than the youth of past generations did. These changes are also placing new demands on our educational systems, which should prepare our youth for their future (see Cheng, this volume). In order to educate millions of young people who live in a transnational context—either because they themselves are transnational or because persons in their environment are—we need to make progress in two domains: we need (1) to close the gap in the quality of education provided to young people (see Hugonnier, this volume) and (2) to develop the curricula and learning context in which they optimally learn (see Cheng, this volume).

CLOSING THE EDUCATIONAL
GAP AT THE GLOBAL LEVEL

Recently, methods for organizing and comparing educational input and output interregionally and internationally have been gaining support. Currently, international indicators that provide insights on the comparative quality of education and the foci of school curricula are collected by the UNESCO Institute for Statistics (UIS) and the OECD (see Hugonnier, this volume). Other regional organizations such as the European Institution Eurydice also offer a more in-depth view of what educational systems prioritize and how students behave.

For example, the UIS uses enrollment rates to indicate the capacity of educational systems. The "school life expectancy" indicator used by the UIS "translates current enrollment patterns across education levels into the number of years of schooling that, on average, individuals can expect to receive" (UNESCO Institute for Statistics 2004). Low school life expectancy is a serious problem for many youth in a globalizing world. In countries such as Burkina Faso and Niger, school life expectancy can be as low as four years. On the other end of the spectrum, countries like Norway and New Zealand have a school life expectancy of more than seventeen years. Without first trying to close the educational gap and improve curricula and the learning context in developing and underfinanced educational systems, we cannot prepare youth for the challenges of a diverse, globalizing world. Closing this gap is especially important because a four-year education cannot provide the tools for youth to find nonviolent resolutions to cultural, ethnic, religious, or other conflicts, especially when these conflicts include multiple cleavages.

CLOSING THE EDUCATIONAL GAP
AT THE EUROPEAN LEVEL

In Europe the Program for International Student Assessment (PISA) study raised awareness of how individual educational systems prepare young people for the future. The second PISA study of 2003 assessed over a quarter of a million students in forty-one countries (OECD 2005). This assessment covered the areas of mathematics, reading, science, and problem solving. The PISA study produced several profound conclusions about Europe's educational systems. For one, after analyzing data on student performance based on economic, social, and immigrant status, it concluded that in OECD countries, a significant portion (for example, in mathematics, one-fifth) of all student variation can be accounted for by students' socioeconomic background. Countries with the highest variation were all European: Belgium, Germany, and the Slovak Republic. Furthermore, the 2003 PISA results analyzed performance results based on students' immigration status and the language they speak at home:

> Students whose parents are immigrants show weaker performance than native students in some but not all countries. . . . While circumstances of different immigrant groups vary greatly, and some are disadvantaged by linguistic or socio-economic disadvantage as well as their migrant status itself, two particular findings are worrying for some countries. One is the relative poor performance even among students who have grown up in the country and gone to school there. The other is that after controlling for the socio-economic background and language spoken at home, a substantial performance gap between immigrant students and others remains in many countries—it is above half a proficiency level in Belgium, Germany, the Netherlands, Sweden and Switzerland.

In all other areas assessed by the PISA study, similarly alarming results were revealed, demonstrating that immigrant students in many European countries are not being properly integrated into basic areas of learning. European educational diversity, however, also showed that a few European countries, such as Finland, are top performers at integrating immigrants into the educational system.

Overall, the PISA studies demonstrate the need for educational systems to update their curricula and accommodate a globalizing learning environment. Otherwise, the educational gap in Europe will grow.

DEVELOPING CURRICULA AND LEARNING CONTEXTS IN A GLOBALIZING WORLD

Beyond closing the educational gap, we also need to better define how the time invested by students and teachers can be optimized to equip young people with the tools they need to become active and productive members of our global society. Currently, basic educational goals do not make intercultural skills a priority.

Education policies must raise the value placed on intercultural skills. Our youth must learn that people with values, religions, cultural backgrounds, and ethnicities different from their own do not pose a threat to their identities. They must also learn to learn together, even though the individual learning needs of diverse student bodies require multiple teaching methods. Sometimes youth resort to violence or join right-wing groups that encourage them to reject diversity and identify only with those persons with whom they share a common first language and ethnicity (see Wikan, this volume). Such groups often use violence against other persons who are different from them, because they lack the intercultural skills to communicate and seek solutions to problems.

In wealthier countries with well-funded school systems, the PISA study has revealed that the effectiveness of school curricula depends not only on the best performances of a few students but also on the ability of a learning program to keep all students in the classroom "on board," keeping individuals who face specific learning challenges (such as linguistic or cultural) from falling behind.

In poorer countries, educational policies must be tied to development policies. Here, basic ideas of intercultural understanding must be added to curricula. Along with the abilities to read, write, and do arithmetic, which are essential to a young person's wherewithal to communicate and meet everyday challenges, educational policies must equip youth with the ability to live peacefully with persons from other cultures, religions, ethnicities, and social backgrounds. This ability, which might be included in an expanded educational policy in developing countries, would contribute decisively to development. Development in these countries is often hindered by racial violence and its inhabitants' inability to integrate into a community.

School curricula and additional investment in education must equip schools around the world with the ability to educate youth about the multicultural, globalizing context in which they live. Skills such as showing openness to persons who are different and the ability to confront differences nonviolently must be included in the curriculum of *every* educational system. In this context, youth exchange programs and school partnerships can play a valuable role.

FURTHERING INTERCULTURAL SKILLS THROUGH EDUCATION

We need to push forward innovative educational paradigms at the global level because the fortunes of our children and youth are tied to the processes of global change. Global political, economic, technological, and cultural developments are currently rendering older educational paradigms inadequate (see Cheng, this volume). For example, demographic changes will affect educational challenges in developing countries dramatically. The school-age population is expected to grow by 71 percent by 2030 in developing countries (UNESCO 2004). Demographic changes will also affect education in developed countries in which birth rates have been low. It is expected that immigration in these countries will increase to counterbalance the economic effects of shrinking and aging populations. This increase will not only occur in the total number of immigrants (immigrant stock) but also will represent a significant per capita increase as native populations in developed countries decline in total numbers (due to a mortality rate higher than the birth rate).

As a result, it is of vital importance that young people, beyond acquiring the ability to comprehend, and succeed in, local contexts, learn how to deal with the global influences that penetrate their environment (see Gärdenfors, this volume). The degree of such "global penetration" varies among youth. For example, immigrant youth may be forced to learn a second or third language, whereas nonimmigrant youth might need to learn cross-cultural communication. Regardless of the global penetration involved in a particular learning context, educational curricula should include teaching cognitive, emotional, social, and digital intercultural skills.

COGNITIVE SKILLS

Building on the arguments and analyses of Carola Suárez-Orozco (2004) and Marcelo M. Suárez-Orozco and Desirée Baolian Qin-Hilliard (2004), I claim that globalization places specific responsibilities on educational systems. One major responsibility is to teach young people problem-solving and communication methods "outside of the box," that is, outside the individual's cultural context (see Gärdenfors, this volume). This requires the development of specific cognitive skills (Suárez-Orozco & Qin-Hilliard 2004, p. 6).

In many everyday situations, youth are challenged to compare their own personal perspectives with the perspectives they perceive others to have. This becomes increasingly difficult when the outside perspective that a young person tries to conceptualize and understand is that of someone who may come from a different culture, practice a different religion, belong to a different ethnicity, or speak a different language (or share limited knowledge of the young person's native language). As a result, educational systems must supply young people with the tools to think outside their own familiar context. They must be able to extrapolate based on their experiences and acquired knowledge in order to communicate, cooperate, seek solutions to problems, apply reason, and integrate into a globalizing world.

Educational curricula in elementary schools can provide improved cognitive skills by making youth aware of the challenges they face and teaching them that differences—cultural, religious, ethnic, and linguistic—do not threaten their identities or their ability to live together with others in a community. For example, curricula could include:

- role-playing to solve mock conflicts in diverse settings, so that the youth may learn better to seek solutions to problems and to communicate in multicultural settings (see also Gärdenfors, this volume)

- grounding cultural and social studies curricula in the context of valuing cultural diversity, so that the thinking processes of youth may broaden to better incorporate diverse outside perspectives (see Boix Mansilla & Gardner, this volume)

- offering schoolchildren the option of learning a foreign language earlier (i.e., fifth grade or earlier), so that they might understand the experience of communicating in another language and acquire skills that will help them in a globalizing business world

I fully support the convergence hypothesis articulated by Suárez-Orozco and Qin-Hilliard (2004): "Globalization is deterritorializing the skills and competencies it rewards, thereby generating powerful centripetal forces on what students the world over will need to know" (p. 6). Intercultural cognitive skills will be increasingly required of future generations in our globalizing world.

DIGITAL SKILLS

Digital skills are essential for our youth (Battro 2004). These skills allow youth to communicate and gather information from beyond their immediate environment and help them integrate into globalizing societies. By allowing fast communication through instant messaging, e-mail, SMS (short message service), and the Internet, digital skills can help youth seek out opportunities, forge friendships across vast spaces, and find information essential to their development and learning. Digital skills also go beyond this. Thinking digitally or in terms of the "click option" enables youth to seek solutions to problems by making "the decision to produce a simple change of state in a system" (Battro 2004, p. 79). This improves general problem-solving skills and the ability to create calculated change in one's environment.

Digital skills also allow persons who are not able to physically move (for example, because of visa restrictions or family commitments) to gain access to jobs that may otherwise be inaccessible (see Levy & Murnane, this volume). For example, the dot.com boom brought jobs and income to many computer experts in India. Had these persons not acquired digital skills either as part of their formal education or from their extracurricular learning environment, they would have been less integrated into the global labor market, and the global economy would have experienced lower levels of economic development.

Teaching digital skills must be placed high on the agendas of global educational curricula. For the most part, access to advanced information and communication technologies is available to youth in wealthy regions such as North America and Europe. Here the development of digital skills is a matter of improving and standardizing the learning environment in schools and ensuring the quality of learning. In developing countries, investment in supplying learning institutions with adequate digital equipment must be a higher priority. Investment in this area should not come only from governments and NGOs; global business partners must also be encouraged to increase investment in digital educational equipment.

EMOTIONAL AND SOCIAL SKILLS:
THE IMPORTANCE OF YOUTH IDENTITY

The complexity of our globalizing world requires young people to learn in more diverse ways. It challenges their identities and requires a high degree of emotional maturity. This is the case for both those who are in their home context and those who have left their place of origin and moved to a new context: "Globalization threatens identities of both the original residents of the areas in which newcomers settle and those of the immigrants and their children" (M. Suárez-Orozco & Qin-Hilliard 2004). To increase the benefits of globalization for our youth, schools must increasingly help youth "identity build" and thus reduce their fears of diversity and increase their understanding of the global context in which they live.

NONIMMIGRANT YOUTH IDENTITY: ADAPTING
TO CHANGE IN THE "GLOBAL HOME CONTEXT"

Classrooms in many parts of the world today resemble Tensta's: they are often composed of multireligious, multiethnic, multicultural, and multilingual student bodies. Often youth, especially nonimmigrant or native youth, are not aware of the depth of diversity that surrounds them and are often underprepared to socialize in a diverse environment. As a consequence, miscommunication and social divisions emerge in many global schools. Divisions are drawn along linguistic, ethnic, religious, or cultural lines. Especially where several differences overlap, division between students can escalate into segregation, verbal arguments, or physical violence.

But differences do not have to lead to limited communication or violence. Wherever young people are taught to understand and overcome these differences, learning is facilitated and diversity becomes an asset, not a threat. One example of this is the Europa-Schulen in Germany (Sachverständigenrat für Zuwanderung und Integration 2004, p. 271). In these schools two European languages are given equal status, and students are taught extensively about the language and culture of two countries. Besides German, the (second) languages taught are English, French, Russian, Italian, Spanish, Portuguese, Turkish, Greek, and Polish. At Europa-Schulen, students also learn that monoculture and a single language are not the norm. This builds a bridge and fosters acceptance in other areas such as religious and ethnic diversity.

IMMIGRANT YOUTH IDENTITY:
ADAPTING TO CHANGE IN A NEW CONTEXT

Immigrant youth identity can be very complex. Broad trends can be found in the challenges immigrants face. These trends differ between the first and following generations.

First-Generation Adult Immigrants

First-generation immigrants generally enjoy the advantage of having two points of reference: that of their origin and that of their new home. They often have ties to family members and friends from their places of origin and have a real understanding of why they migrated. Generally, they develop the drive and cognitive flexibility to establish an identity in a new place. In many countries in which jus soli citizenship regulations apply ("law of the soil"—i.e., all those who are born in the country, regardless of origin, automatically become citizens of the country), first-generation immigrants are the only immigrants that count as foreign residents from a statistical point of view.

This group of immigrants faces great challenges. They must learn a vast amount of information that often may conflict with assumptions and ways of interacting deeply rooted in their self-understanding. However, in developing their identities, they face fewer challenges than the generations that follow.

Second- and Third-Generation Immigrant Youth

The second and following generations of immigrants face considerably different challenges than the first, especially in their ability to develop emotionally and socially. With no clear frame of reference, finding an identity represents a considerable hurdle for many non-first-generation immigrants (especially for youth). Often these young people are at risk of adopting an "ascribed identity," one projected on them from the outside based on their ethnic or religious affiliation (C. Suárez-Orozco 2004). Immigrant youth must "achieve" their identities: "Achieved identity is the extent to which an individual achieves a sense of belonging—'I am a member of this group.' An ascribed identity is imposed either by co-ethnics—'You are a member of our group'—or by members of the dominant culture—'You are a member of that group'" (C. Suárez-Orozco 2004). The inner conflict, emotional strain, and social challenges that arise as immigrant youth find a comfortable sense of belonging "on their own terms," not based on outside pressures, are immense. Educational curricula must teach the skills youth need to overcome this challenge. For example, curricula can:

- address identity and emphasize the benefits of individual behavior that may contradict peer expectations
- explore ethnic and social stereotypes and the problems these pose for youth and their identities
- offer career-oriented training for young people who are not familiar with life models beyond their ethnic communities

Second-generation immigrants require a different approach in their educational integration than native students do (see McAndrew; Crul, both this volume). Educational systems should develop a process of evaluation for immigrant children in order to foster their development. This approach must also focus on incorporating the abilities these immigrants bring with them into the learning environment, and on furthering the knowledge they have already acquired. At the same time, the classroom environment must be sensitized to cultural, linguistic, and ethnic diversity so that communication between students is facilitated. Young people have a great capacity to learn from each other. This potential must be harnessed through the classroom environment.

TENSTA GYMNASIUM IN STOCKHOLM: THE AVANT-GARDE OF EDUCATION

Tensta Gymnasium is a multicultural high school in a suburban Stockholm neighborhood dominated by immigrant and refugee-origin families. Low-income housing surrounds Tensta. This part of Stockholm is not frequently visited by persons who live outside the borough. Besides the school, the community has limited infrastructure such as shops or community gathering places.

Prior to making the transition to an avant-garde form of education, the school was failing. Student enrollment was plummeting, and the school was stigmatized due to its location and its mainly immigrant student body. To attract students and to adjust the school's approach to learning to fit not only its community but also the changing features of a globalizing world, the principal of Tensta Gymnasium looked for ways to modernize the school.

After visiting the Ross School, located in East Hampton, New York, and dedicated to educating its students to meet the challenges of a globlalizing world, the Tensta leadership decided to revolutionize education offered at its school. Borrowing forward-looking education models developed by the Ross School and adapting them in collaboration with the teachers, administrators, and community members at Tensta, a new model of education was conceived.

I had the privilege of visiting Tensta Gymnasium in March 2005 and meeting with students and teachers. Tensta teaches according to holistic principles. The "whole student" is considered the pivot around which teaching methods are constructed. The school curriculum is developed in accordance with the skills students will need to achieve their later goals, whether these are the pursuit of higher education or practical training for a specific occupation. The teachers at Tensta see themselves as mentors. Open spaces with natural lighting and comfortable seating corners for small and large groups checker hallways and corridors. Early-morning voluntary assemblies, study halls, and an organic cafeteria that offers students breakfast attract the students to campus outside regular school hours. These services to students increase the interaction, communication, and intensity of relationships between teachers and students, between teachers, and between members of the student body.

Another innovative aspect of Tensta I found relevant is that the school provides each of its students with a laptop computer; the school has a wireless Internet network. Students can take notes, write papers, and research on the Internet with the computers anytime they are on campus. Charging stations allow students to use the computers throughout the school day.

The courses at Tensta are forward-looking and based on the idea that the information we learn has to be connected and put into context with many other things that we know and learn. By exchanging their ideas and discussing the concepts that students need to learn, teachers at Tensta create several integrated multidisciplinary learning blocks for students. Subjects such as art and history or music and drama are taught together. Teams of eight to ten teachers in multiple disciplines come together to plan the semester curriculum. Teachers also ask students to connect the information to their lives by formulating "essential questions" concerning their understanding and by working on answers to these. By connecting the information their students are learning to a personal context, teachers at Tensta aim to create enduring understanding.

Since Tensta has adopted a new approach to learning, it has become a source of pride for and a real asset to the community. It has attracted a growing student body, and very few students end their education prematurely. Tensta is not simply a local success story confined to a Stockholm suburb. It and the Ross School are models of how a school can become an incubator for a future multicultural society, one that is peaceful, well educated, respectful of others, and able to deal with the challenges of our globalizing world.

CONCLUSIONS

By and large, educational systems have taken only small and disconnected steps toward overcoming the challenges that young people face in rapidly globalizing societies. These reactions have been too weak and disjointed to accomplish the necessary results. For example, the majority of global educational curricula simply do not do justice to educating our youth about the challenges of globalization and diversity. Too often, school curricula highlight only linguistic and cultural learning gaps among immigrant youth, without evaluating their abilities or recognizing the capacity and knowledge these young people possess and can contribute to their learning environment (see McAndrew, this volume). Therefore, it is essential that school curricula within the European Union and at the global level develop a common approach to making intercultural education a central part of pre-university education. It is also important that the curricula developed be tested, evaluated, and regularly updated. Such curricula must also be disseminated abroad and compared with similar curricula developed in other regions of the world; good practices should be exchanged regularly. This is one area in which further research is needed.

Only since the mid-1990s has integration become a central political issue. This has not resulted in teaching intercultural skills being made a priority. In Germany, intercultural skills were a foreign concept in the field of education until the last few years. The idea was carried over from the field of business into the educational sciences and educational politics. The newest development in the intercultural teaching agenda is to link intercultural skills of preschool and elementary school teachers. This approach promotes the increased inclusion of immigrant youth in educational systems. In the last few years, universities in Germany have expanded their curricula to include preschool and elementary-school teacher training in the area of intercultural skills. As a result, teachers have begun to include intercultural themes in their curricula. Yet there is a lack of didactic concepts for adequately incorporating intercultural skills in schools. This is a second area that needs further research.

A third area of research that I would like to suggest was identified during a session at the conference in Sweden where this book originated. Participants explored the idea of developing courses for nonimmigrants ("natives") that focus on communication with nonnative speakers, in addition to teaching cultural tolerance and mutual respect. Such courses would include the flip-side of courses such as English as a second language and would instruct students on how to communicate (without conflict or undue stress) in situations in which a common language is shared only partially. Such courses for nonimmigrants would be particularly useful for students who have no background in communicating with nonnative speakers or persons outside their own cultures. We think of integration as a two-way street, but our learning and societal constructs often do not challenge the expectation that "traffic" will flow predominantly in one direction, with nonnatives adapting to the native culture and language.

NOTES

1. The UN Population Division predicts that by 2050 there will be 8.9 billion people on earth, according to the medium variant. See www.un.org/esa/population/publications/longrange2/WorldPop2300final.pdf and www.un.org/esa/population/publications/wpp2002/WPP2002-HIGHLIGHTSrev1.PDF, March 2005, p. 1.

REFERENCES

Battro, A. M. (2004). Digital skills, globalization and education. In *Globalization: culture, and education in the new millennium*. M. Suárez-Orozco and D. Qin-Hilliard, eds. Berkeley and Los Angeles: University of California Press.

Beauftragte der Bundesregierung für Migration, Flüchtlinge und Integration (2003). *Förderung von Migranten und Migrantinnen im Elemetar- und Primarbereich*. Bonn: Bonner Universitätsdruckerei.

Breidstein, L., K. Doron, and J. Walther, eds. (1998). *Migration, Konflikt und Mediation: Zum interkulturellen Diskurs in der Jugendarbeit*. Frankfurt am Main: Haag + Herchen Verlag GmbH.

Bundesamt für Migration und Flüchtlinge (2004). *Migration und Asyl in Zahlen*. Nürnberg: Conrad Nürnberg GmbH.

Bundesministerium des Innern (2005). *Migrationsbericht*. www.bmi.bund.de.

Bundeszentrale für politische Bildung, ed. (1998). *Interkulturelles Lernen*. Bonn

Commission of the European Communities (2005). *EU green paper on an EU approach to managing economic migration*. www.eu.int.

Demandewitz, H., et al. (2002). *Der Vielfalt Raum geben: Interkulturelle Erziehung in Tageseinrichtungen für Kinder*. Münster: Votum Verlag.

GCIM. See Global Commission on Immigrant Migration.

Global Commission on International Migration (2005). *Migration in an interconnected world: New directions for action*. www.gcim.org/en/finalreport.html. October.

Hornstein, W. (2001). Erziehung und Bildung in Zeitalter der Globalisierung: Themen und Fragestellungen erziehungswissenschaftlicher Reflexion. *Zeitschrift für Pädagogik* 4 (July–August): 517–537.

Information Network on Education in Europe (2005). *Indicators and statistics*. www.eurydice.org/Doc_intermediaires/indicators/en/frameset_key_data.html.

International Organization for Migration (2005). *Facts and figures on international migration*. www.iom.int.

International Organization for Migration. (2005). *World migration report*. www.iom.int/iomwebsite/Publication/ServletSearchPublication?event=detail&id=4171.

International Organization for Migration. (2003). *World migration report*. Geneva: IOM.

IOM. See International Organization for Migration.

Koppen, J. K., and I. Lunt, eds. (2002). *Education in Europe: Cultures, values, and institutions in transition*. Münster: Waxmann Verlag GmbH.

Mecheril, P. (2002). Pädagogiken natio-kultureller Mehrfachzugehörigkeit: Vom 'Kulturkonflikt' zur 'Hybrididität.' *Diskurs Zeitschrift* 2: 41–48.

Migration Policy Institute. (2005). *Managing international migration better: Principles and perspectives for gaining more from migration.* Washington, D.C. www.bamf.de.

OECD. See Organisation for Economic Co-operation and Development.

Organisation for Economic Co-operation and Development (2005). *First results from PISA 2003: Executive Summary.* Paris. www.pisa.oecd.org/dataoecd/1/63/34002454.pdf.

Organisation for Economic Co-operation and Development (2004). *Trends in international migration. Annual report, 2003 edition.* Paris. www.oecd.org.

Ostertag, M. (2001). *Kommunikative Pädagogik und multikulturelle Gesellschaft.* Hemsbach, Germany: Leske + Budrich, Opladen.

Sachverständigenrat für Zuwanderung und Integration. (2004). *Migration und Integration: Erfahrungen nutzen, Neues wagen.* Paderborn, Germany: Bonifatius GmbH.

Suárez-Orozco, C. (2004). Formulating identity in a globalized world. In *Globalization: Culture and education in the new millennium.* M. Suárez-Orozco and D. Qin-Hilliard, eds. Berkeley and Los Angeles: University of California Press.

Suárez-Orozco, M., C. Suárez-Orozco, and D. Qin-Hilliard (2004). Minding the global: Education, culture, and globalization in the new millennium. In *Globalization: Culture and education in the new millennium.* M. Suárez-Orozco and D. Qin-Hilliard, eds. Berkeley and Los Angeles: University of California Press.

United Nations Population Division (2005) *Press release: world population to increase by 2.6 billion over the next 45 years.* www.un.org/News/Press/docs/2005/pop918.doc.htm.

United Nations Population Division (2004). *World population to 2300.* New York: United Nations.

United Nations Population Division (2003). *World population prospects: The 2002 revision highlights.* New York: United Nations.

UNESCO Institute for Statistics (2004). *Global education digest 2004: Comparing education statistics across the world.* Montreal: UNESCO Institute for Statistics.

TEN

Maurice Crul

THE INTEGRATION OF
IMMIGRANT YOUTH

The integration of immigrants and their offspring into the receiving society is a primary challenge of globalization (C. Suárez-Orozco 2004, p. 173). The oldest children born to postwar immigrants to west central Europe have recently finished their educational careers and entered the labor market. This group comprising children of immigrants in Europe is very diverse. The largest subgroup consists of children of labor migrants, followed by children of immigrants from former European colonies. The group of children of refugees is growing very rapidly and is also highly diverse. Marcelo Suárez-Orozco and Desirée Baolian Qin-Hilliard (2004) argue that educators should develop an agenda that incorporates the new-comers (p. 16). This chapter responds to the call for a new educational agenda designed to facilitate immigrant children's integration into their new communities.

Immigrant youth's life chances and future careers are shaped not only by family and community resources but also by the opportunities offered by the educational institutions they attend. While immigration is a global phenomenon, responses to it have largely occurred within individual nations. In this chapter I look for globally relevant responses. I begin by examining optimal institutional arrangements for incorporating children of immigrants into educational systems across countries. The structure of educational institutions is the product of a long history of national policies. By looking at the integration patterns of the same immigrant group in different countries, I identify and describe the best institutional practices. I also discuss best practices in mobilizing ethnic resources in different European countries. Integration without community empowerment is doomed to fail. The use of existing knowledge, expertise, and networks of immigrants and their children is vital in bridging the gap with various native populations. Specifically, I will advocate that the capital (knowledge and experience) of successful immigrant-origin students be put to use more effectively.

This chapter focuses on one part of a larger educational response to the effects of globalization. The question of intercultural education, for example, is another important aspect of the discussion that I briefly address here but that is dealt with in greater depth in other chapters in this volume (see McAndrew; Roosens; Süssmuth, all this volume). The debate about globalization and education has largely focused on the need for curricular reforms and their effects on student-teacher interactions. The conversation has generally avoided how our educational systems hinder or stimulate the integration of children of immigrants. In this chapter, I seek to bring these issues to the forefront.

BACKGROUND: THE CHILDREN
OF IMMIGRANTS IN EUROPE

The children of immigrants are now a prominent force in many European school districts. In Amsterdam and Rotterdam they constitute the majority of schoolchildren; in Brussels they make up over 40 percent of the school-age population; in London, English is a second language for a third of schoolchildren. Unfortunately, these children's academic performance generally lags in all school success indicators: they drop out at higher rates, repeat grades more frequently, and are concentrated in the least-challenging educational tracks (Crul & Vermeulen 2003, see also Hugonnier, this volume). The educational gap between these students and the children of native-born parents is of great concern to local and national governments. There is an ongoing debate about whether the "new second generation," mostly children of guest workers from the 1970s, will move up the educational ladder or will form a new underclass in Europe's largest cities (Crul & Vermeulen 2003; Heckmann, Lederer, & Worbs 2001).

Based on the record of earlier waves of migration, some researchers (mostly historians) have been optimistic about the prospects of integration. Other scholars sketch a less optimistic scenario, pointing to the minimal human and cultural capital with which almost all guest workers have arrived and the negative consequences of this deficiency for their children's chances in school. This argument is echoed in public debate when politicians and the media declare that the integration of these immigrants and their children has failed.

Without being fatalistic, we must acknowledge that a fairly large group of immigrant-origin youth is lagging behind their native-born peers. The actual size of this group differs both by country and according to the background and characteristics of the immigrants themselves. In general, children of immigrants who bring low levels of human capital into the country are most disadvantaged. On the European continent this description mainly includes immigrants from North Africa and Turkey; in Britain it includes children of lower-class former-colonial families. The performance of children of refugees also demonstrates the importance of class in determining outcomes. Most of the children from upper-class families from Iran or Iraq do well academically, while children from rural Somalia and Ethiopia experience greater difficulties in school.

IMPORTANCE OF THE INSTITUTIONAL EDUCATIONAL SETTING

Apart from differences between immigrant groups, we can also see differences between countries (see also Süssmuth, this volume). This is most clearly observed when we compare migrants of the same ethnic group in different countries. I compare the educational outcomes of Turkish immigrants across Europe because they form the single-largest immigrant group in Europe, numbering up to four million.

Turkish labor migration has followed similar patterns everywhere in Europe. Beginning with Germany in 1961 and ending with Sweden in 1967, a number of European countries signed official labor agreements with Turkey. Spontaneous migration through family and village networks later ensued, increasing the numbers arriving in Europe. Labor migration peaked between 1971 and 1973, during which time more than half a million Turkish workers came to Western Europe, 90 percent of them recruited by German industry (Özüekren & Kempen 1997, p. 5). European industry needed low-skilled labor at the time, and the majority of the first-generation Turkish guest workers were recruited from the lowest socioeconomic strata in their home country. Typically, these migrants had very little formal education. In the rural areas where most of them had grown up, educational opportunities were limited to the primary-school level.

Table 10.1 Population of Turkish descent in Germany, the Netherlands, France, Austria, and Belgium

Germany (2002)	2,470,000[a]
Netherlands (2002)	299,662[b]
France (1999)	218,360[c]
Austria (2001)	182,000[d]
Belgium (2001)	109,000[e]
Total	3,279,022

[a]Includes estimate of naturalized citizens based on naturalization registers (Worbs 2003).
[b]Includes naturalized and nonnaturalized Turks (Crul & Doomernik 2003).
[c]Includes those born in France to at least one Turkish-born parent, and those with Turkish nationality (Simon 2003).
[d]Excludes those born in Austria to at least one Turkish-born parent (Herzog-Punzensberger 2003).
[e]Includes both nonnaturalized citizens and an estimated number of naturalized citizens (Crul & Vermeulen 2003).

Most first-generation men had finished primary school only, and most women had just a few years of schooling. The first generation made few advances in the European labor market—in fact, the opposite occurred (Crul & Vermeulen 2003).

Most second-generation Turkish children—those born in Northern Europe or, more broadly, those who arrived before the age of primary school—grew up in unfavorable circumstances. With often very low incomes by European standards, most families lived in substandard, cramped conditions. In many neighborhood schools, children from a mix of immigrant backgrounds made up the majority, making segregation by immigration status a growing European reality.

A comparison of second-generation "Turks" in different countries does not necessarily mean one is comparing the same group. An adequate comparison must also account for the differences *within* the Turkish immigrant population based on characteristics such as ethnicity, first-generation education levels, and religion. The biggest difference between the countries' Turkish populations is found in parents' educational levels. Germany sticks out especially, where the educational level of first-generation labor migrants was a bit higher than in the other countries (Crul & Vermeulen 2003); that is, more parents had a diploma from primary school and had had lower vocational education. We would therefore expect the children of Turkish parents in Germany to do a bit better than in other countries. Countries also differ in the numbers of Kurdish and political refugees from

Turkey. For this reason I restrict the comparison to the second generation and look only to those who are fifteen years old or older. This segment of the Turkish youth is comparatively homogeneous in terms of background characteristics. These young adolescents are almost all children of labor migrants recruited in the seventies. Children of political refugees and of refugees of the Kurdish-Turkish conflict tend to be younger (see Crul & Vermeulen 2003).

The educational experiences and outcomes of second-generation Turks in different European countries (Germany, the Netherlands, Belgium, France, and Austria) show startling differences. The greatest distinctions can be seen in the percentages of young Turkish people in vocational tracks—the lowest secondary-school type in all countries (see the appendix to this chapter). In France, about a quarter, and in Belgium and the Netherlands, about a third of the second-generation Turks fall into a vocational track, whereas in Germany and Austria the figure is between two-thirds and three-fourths (Crul & Doomernik 2003; Herzog-Punzensberger 2003; Simon 2003; Timmerman, Vanderwaeren, & Crul 2003; Worbs 2003).

Opportunities available to second-generation Turks vary widely by national context. Although one may be tempted to conclude from the data cited above that France and, to a lesser extent, the Netherlands and Belgium provide the best institutional contexts for migrants, a look at the whole story is necessary to understand the implications of the data. Dropout rates paint a very different picture (see appendix). Although enrollment of second-generation Turks in vocational programs is lower in France, Belgium, and the Netherlands, this group's dropout rates are considerably higher in those countries than in Germany and Austria (Crul & Doomernik 2003; Herzog-Punzensberger 2003; Simon 2003; Timmerman, Vanderwaeren, & Crul 2003; Worbs 2003). It is difficult to single out one country where these youth are doing better than in others. We can only tentatively identify good versus bad practices in a particular country as compared to others. On closer inspection, however, the disparities can be attributed to different institutional contexts and practices in each country.

The age at which education begins is an important factor in determining academic success. In France and Belgium, second-generation Turkish children, like other children, start school at age two or three. In Germany and Austria, most second-generation Turkish children start school only at age six. Thus, immigrant children in France and Belgium receive between three and four more years of schooling during the crucial developmental phase when they begin learning the majority language. In

France and Belgium, very young Turkish children are required to speak French (or Flemish) with their peers on a daily basis, and on top of that, they are learning these languages in an educational environment.

Striking differences also result from the number of hours of face-to-face contact students have with teachers during the compulsory schooling years. Once again, these numbers are below average for Turkish pupils in Germany and Austria, especially during the first part of their educational careers. Since children in Germany and Austria attend school for only a half day, nine-year-olds in German schools have a total of 661 face-to-face-contact hours per year, as compared to 1,019 hours in the Netherlands. Turkish children in Germany thus receive about ten hours less instruction per week than those in the Netherlands (Crul & Vermeulen 2003). Although children in Germany and Austria are typically assigned more homework, help with homework is a scant resource in Turkish families. This may also be a serious disadvantage.

A third distinction, which in combination with the first two can result in serious disparities, lies in school selection mechanisms. School selection occurs for children in Germany and Austria at the age of ten. In Germany children are channeled into three school levels; in Austria, two. Coupled with the late start and the below-average contact hours, Turkish second-generation pupils in Germany and Austria are thus given little time to overcome their disadvantaged starting position. In this respect, Turkish children in Germany and Austria are in the worst possible situation. Selection in the Netherlands occurs two to four years later, and in France at age fifteen. Due to early selection in Germany and Austria, most Turkish-origin pupils end up in a short vocational stream called *Hauptschule*.

Given these factors, it is not surprising that second-generation Turks in France enter preparatory schools for higher education at higher rates than elsewhere in Europe. Children start going to school early in France, have more hours of face-to-face instruction, and do not face educational selection until a comparatively late age.

Dropout rates, measuring the number of children who leave school without a secondary-school diploma, are another important indicator. In this area, France, the Netherlands, and Belgium have considerably worse statistics than Germany and Austria (see appendix). In Germany and Austria, only a very small percentage of second-generation Turks fail to earn a *Hauptschule* diploma (lower secondary vocational education) or another secondary-education diploma (Herzog-Punzensberger 2003; Worbs 2003). In the Netherlands the percentage of children who do not earn a diploma, including one from a vocational school (*Vbo*), is much higher (Crul & Doomernik 2003). In France the situation is the most dramatic (Simon 2003). As previously mentioned, not until age fifteen are children split up into different tracks. They attend *collège* together, and a diploma from their *collège* provides access to different types of *lycée*. If a student does not earn a diploma from her *collège*, she automatically enters a vocational school. Due to children's early start and the late selection in France, most second-generation Turkish children enter the more prestigious *lycée*. More second-generation Turkish students are represented in a preparatory track for higher education in France than in any other country. But this also has a flip-side. Because the stakes are higher in a *lycée*, those students who cannot meet the academic demands often end up with no diploma at all.

In the Netherlands a sizable group of second-generation Turkish children move into a vocational track at age twelve. Their situation resembles that of second-generation Turkish children in Germany who move into vocational education at age ten. The dropout rate in the Netherlands, however, is significantly higher. A number of factors related to differences between the vocational tracks in Germany and the Netherlands explain this disparity. In the Netherlands the dropout rate is especially high among youth sixteen years and older. By age fourteen or fifteen, most second-generation Turks in Germany already possess a *Hauptschule* diploma. At age sixteen in the Netherlands, however, they are still required to be at school full-time. Additionally, in the Netherlands the apprenticeship period, which is often an attractive feature of the vocational track, is limited. Half of the classes that students must take are general theoretical subjects, and the other half are devoted to the vocation for which they are training. This alone may explain why many students have negative feelings toward their school experiences, as they would prefer to have more practical, on-the-job training. But other factors are also involved.

The vocational stream in the Netherlands is considered a marginal track. Lower vocational education (Vbo) has often been described as the "garbage can" of the educational system. Students with learning disabilities and those who were unsuccessful in more advanced tracks, often due to behavioral problems, are automatically placed in vocational education. This stream also absorbs newly arrived immigrant children. Pels (2001, p. 6) has researched and described teacher-pupil interaction in a Vbo school. She counted about eighty reprimands during just one mathematics class. Crul (2000, p. 139) reported on the prisonlike climate of Vbo schools and the regular fights that break out there, sometimes between pupils and teachers. The resulting school climate is hardly conducive to positive school performance, and thus, dropout rates in Vbo are high.

The German *Hauptschule* is on the opposite end of the spectrum. Viewed as a mainstream option, this vocational track attracts many children of native-born parents. The educational climate in *Hauptschule* is not considered problematic. These factors help to explain why more second-generation Turkish children complete their academic program in the school system in Germany than in the Netherlands.

In Germany and Austria, most second-generation Turkish pupils enter a dual track at age fourteen. They start to work as an apprentice in a firm three to four days a week. The apprenticeship track facilitates their transition to the labor market. Countries with robust apprenticeship systems have lower unemployment among second-generation Turks than countries without an apprenticeship system.[1] Some second-generation Turks in Germany and Austria continue to work at the company where they started as apprentices (Böcker & Thränhardt 2003, p. 42). Those who do not continue at their original placement can demonstrate two to three years' work experience to potential new employers. In France and the Netherlands, second-generation Turks must enter the labor market on their own.

Discrimination seems to play a more significant role in the labor market in France and the Netherlands than it does in Germany or Austria, where the transition to employment is formalized through the apprenticeship system. There are two explanations for the greater discrimination found in France and the Netherlands. The starting position when second-generation Turks enter the labor market differs significantly across the four countries. In Germany and Austria, second-generation Turks can show a diploma and their employment records as apprentices, while many second-generation Turks in France and the Netherlands have neither a diploma nor any meaningful work experience. The decision to employ someone in Germany and Austria is based largely on the individual employment potential a job applicant can show. The decision in France and the Netherlands is based solely on school qualifications. Research in France and the Netherlands shows that given a choice between an immigrant youth and a native youth with the same qualifications, employers tend not to choose immigrant applicants (Crul & Doomernik 2003, p. 1057; Simon 2003). Another difference between the countries is that youth unemployment rates in France and the Netherlands are much higher than in Germany and Austria. Research shows that discrimination is more prevalent when competition in the labor market is tough. Employers cannot afford to discriminate when there are labor shortages.

The foregoing comparison between the countries illustrates the critical role that institutional arrangements and educational policies play in shaping second-generation students' integration. Specifically, the starting age for compulsory schooling, number of hours of face-to-face contact in primary school, early or late selection in secondary education, and the existence of an effective apprenticeship system significantly affect the likelihood that children of Turkish immigrants will experience success or failure in earning a diploma and obtaining employment.

BEST PRACTICES

It is tempting to design an ideal educational setting for children of immigrants based on the examples from the four countries described above. Any such attempt, however, would not do justice to the unique developments in each country's social and economic history that shaped the formation of its educational systems. Our ambition must be more modest. Based on the research previously discussed, I now consider a number of options for improving the experiences of children of immigrants in education: early start; late selection or second chance; and dual tracks.

Early Start

The early start of compulsory schooling is extremely important in a number of countries for acquiring the second language. Evidence from across Europe shows that starting school at the age of two or three is essential. Lowering the age of compulsory schooling would be a major policy shift, but countries have instituted a number of possible alternatives. Preschool facilities that focus specifically on second-language acquisition have been created in a number of countries (for example, Frühstart in Germany and Piramide and Kaleidoscoop in the Netherlands). The preschool programs developed in Europe have often been inspired by such programs as Head Start and Follow Through in the United States. Evaluations in the United States show that early-childhood programs produce both short-term (after one or two years) and long-term effects on school achievement and retention (Barnett 1995). The programs seem to be effective only if preschool methods and pedagogy are correlated with those used in primary school (Driessen 2004; Veen, Roeleveld & Leseman 2000). Preferably, preschool is incorporated into primary school.

Second Chance

Children of immigrants often start school with disadvantages. It often takes time for them to overcome these challenges. In countries where children receive the support, resources, and time they need to bridge the gap, they are more likely to enter preparatory tracks for higher education than their counterparts in other countries. Late selection also has its downsides. More advanced tracks may be too challenging for some students, which often leads to failure or dropout. Second-chance education offers a viable alternative to a pattern of late selection. A second chance can come in a variety of forms:

- *Top-class primary school.* In many countries the last year of primary school is decisive in determining future schooling. Some motivated children may have a better chance to ultimately succeed by having an extra year of primary school to prepare for the entrance exam for the more advanced tracks. Results in this area so far have proved promising (Bongers, Hoogeveen, & Vaessen 2002).

- *Intermediary classes.* Delaying the transition to secondary school is helpful in some cases. Intermediary classes provide children a transitional environment for two years between primary and secondary school. Research shows that many children of immigrants can gain acceptance to more prestigious tracks after these two intermediary years (Crul 2000).

- *The long route.* Research on children of immigrants who have achieved educational success shows that for many of them, the road to that success is often bumpy (Crul 2000). These students start at a low educational level and gain access to higher education step by step. This reflects the traditional course of social mobility for native working-class children. The structure of the vocational track is essential in this respect. Moving up step-by-step from lower to middle to higher vocational education should be made as smooth and free of obstacles as possible.

Dual Tracks

The apprenticeship system stems from a long tradition of involving companies in the education of youngsters. Apprenticeship experience seems to improve the transition to the labor market, especially for groups whose entrance to work is often difficult. The apprenticeship system can serve as a strong weapon against youth unemployment and school desertion. The trainee posts provided by some firms and the early start (at age fourteen in Germany and Austria) of the dual track have proven essential. For a substantial group of children of immigrants with learning difficulties, an apprenticeship is an appealing alternative to full-time school.

Several countries with no such system have recently developed programs that draw elements from traditional apprenticeship programs (Crul 2004), putting pupils to work in firms earlier and for longer periods. The challenge is to find companies willing to provide apprenticeships.

An important characteristic of the aforementioned options is that because they do not target children of immigrants, they avoid stigmatizing immigrant groups and generating resentment among the native population.

USING THE POTENTIAL IN ETHNIC COMMUNITIES

School Contact Persons and School Assistants

In many countries, schools encounter difficulties in communicating with immigrant parents. Language is one of a number of barriers that can make contact with immigrant families quite challenging. Until recently, language teachers who acted as translators were often asked to bridge the cultural gap between parents and teachers. In the countries where this is still a common practice, language teachers are neither trained nor paid for this work.

The role of intermediary is gradually being taken over by school contact people such as parent or community liaisons and school assistants who themselves may come from migrant backgrounds (Crul 2004). They are trained not as teachers but specifically as intermediaries, a job that requires fewer skills and thus makes it easier to recruit candidates. Intermediaries play an especially important role in communicating with newly arrived immigrants parents, who often face difficulties in supporting their children. In most countries, school contact people and school assistants play a vital role during the transition period, since there are still very few teachers with immigrant backgrounds in European schools (Crul 2004).

Student Mentors as Role Models

The majority of first-generation parents went to school for only a few years or did not attend school at all. This, in conjunction with the difficulty they have speaking the native language, makes them ill prepared for helping their children in school in a new country. Over the past decade, the number of immigrant children pursuing university-level studies has grown significantly. These students are among the best and brightest of their respective communities, of which they will form the future elite. They have succeeded against all odds, overcoming obstacles one by one. Keenly aware of what is needed to succeed in school, they also understand how an immigrant family typically functions. This background and experience make them ideal mentors for children of immigrants in secondary schools. Indeed, a growing number of students with immigrant backgrounds are working as volunteers in student mentor projects or homework-support classes in the United Kingdom, Germany, the Netherlands, Sweden, Belgium, and other countries.

Student mentoring provides direct assistance with career and professional development, emotional and psychological support, and role modeling (see Crul 2002; Crul & Kraal 2004; Jacobi 1991). Mentoring relationships can also bolster students' self-esteem (see the metastudy of Cohen, Kulik, & Kulik 1982). Evaluations of mentoring programs clearly indicate that student mentoring can be a highly effective instrument in immigrant education. The projects evaluated have been reported to have positive cognitive and noncognitive effects for student participants (Crul 2002; Crul & Kraal 2004; Crul & Akdeniz 1997; Groen 2000; Hulst 2000; Meijer & Reuling 1998; Paulides 2000; Vaessen, Walraven, & van Wissen 1998; Veugelers 2000; see also Topping & Hill 1995).

In the Netherlands a nationwide program has been developed to provide mentoring and guidance to children of immigrants, including both "at risk" pupils and "high potential" pupils. Training and project manuals have been developed and tested. One of the oldest mentoring projects is the Moroccan Coaching Project in The Hague. Moroccan higher-education students coach Moroccan secondary-school students one-to-one. The emphasis is on at-risk pupils—those mainly in the lowest educational track (lower vocational education or a form of special education). Crul and Kraal (2004) found that, during a five-year period, of 118 pupils supported by mentor students for one year on a weekly basis, only five of them (4 percent) dropped out of school. This result is even more impressive if we take a closer look at the pupils involved. Before being mentored, many of them had skipped classes on a regular basis and had been known to verbally and physically abuse other pupils and sometimes even teachers. On top of this, many of them had severe learning problems. Girls in the project tended to be extremely shy and have low self-esteem; boys, on the other hand, were often extremely verbal and on their way to becoming gang leaders.[2] In many cases, teachers and even parents had given up on the youth entering the mentorship program. The mentor and pupil work together to prioritize what the pupil wants to change. Generally the focus is on improving their behavior toward teachers and friends. Both the mentor and the contact person at school monitor the student's progress toward reaching her or his goals. One student revealed in an interview (Crul 2007) the influence a mentor can have:

> *What did you learn from your mentor?*
> Actually, almost everything. How you behave with people.
> *Did you change because of her?*
> I can keep my big mouth shut now, no more fights. I always had fights with classmates, not any more. If someone says something to me, I keep quiet, I do not start an argument.
> *How did this change come about?*
> Because of Toeria [the mentor]. She has taught me to keep my big mouth shut. She has taught me a lot. She has already been in University for three years; she already went through a lot. She has more experiences than me. She has taught me how to deal with things. She also had difficulty at school before.

Relationships with friends are important for teenagers and can be a factor in failing grades. Students' friends can distract them during instruction in class, and spending time with friends outside school can compete with homework. Peer pressure from friends at this age can be a strong influence because teenagers may be insecure about their own desires. The mentor recognizes the importance to the pupil-mentee of belonging to a group of his or her own age, but simultaneously makes it clear that one should not let oneself be led solely by what one's friends do. Parents often take no action beyond forbidding their children to hang out with certain friends.

The central idea of mentoring is that it uses existing knowledge within immigrant communities rather than trying to intervene from the outside. The rising number of migrant students in higher education provides a unique form of capital that should not be overlooked.

REFLECTIONS ON THE FUTURE RESEARCH AGENDA

Before focusing on specific areas of research that in my opinion address the most important issues regarding globalization and learning, I make a more general plea for international comparative research. Europe in particular represents a gigantic laboratory for experimentation. Although faced with similar issues of diversity and integration, European countries have created their own individual integration and diversity policies, often without taking any note of programs set up in neighboring countries. Some of the programs are strikingly similar (especially in second-language learning), yet there are also vast differences. This natural laboratory could serve as an enormous reservoir of research. Researchers could study the effects of different forms of intervention in early learning, bilingual learning, remedial teaching, and second-chance learning in a comparative perspective (see McAndrew, this volume). As my research suggests, both institutional arrangements and targeted policies can have a great impact on the educational success of children of immigrants. We often take for granted the structure, organization, and policies of our school systems. International comparisons can make the specific effects of these policies, procedures, and structures on children of immigrants clearer.

In this chapter I have briefly described some of the programs that use the social and cultural capital of immigrants and their children. We need to take advantage of this capital to bridge the gap between educational institutions and immigrant families. The greatest challenge lies in professionalizing and institutionalizing these programs. Research can be helpful in achieving this goal. Most of these projects have not been evaluated or rely on self-evaluation. This lack of adequate evaluation results in missed opportunities for improving existing programs. Project assessment would help to promote further program development and alert policy makers to the programs' potential contribution to immigrant youth's school success. It is a way to build best practices in cities and countries and potentially across countries.

The Tensta Gymnasium in Stockholm could be such an example of best practices for Europe. All over the continent, secondary schools in neighborhoods with high concentrations of immigrant youth face issues similar to those we witnessed at Tensta. The schools can become stigmatized as "immigrant schools," known for their pupils' low performance and for violence and a generally unattractive school climate. As happened in Tensta before reforms were implemented, children of native-born parents start to leave the school, followed by the higher-performing children of immigrant parents. School resources dry up and the school deteriorates further. At a certain point, school closure may even be considered. The experience of the Tensta Gymnasium shows that additional resources alone will not stop this downward spiral. To turn the tide, a whole new concept of learning must be considered and carefully implemented. To an outsider, Tensta's technological innovations and the new interior learning spaces may seem the most striking changes. I would stress a different aspect, however. The school's transformation has resulted in increased contact between teachers and pupils. Both the number of hours of one-on-one contact and the intensity of that contact has increased. Teachers inevitably get to know their students better and therefore notice when a child is not participating, is falling behind, or is regularly absent. Teachers have more time and opportunity to intervene. My hypothesis is that school systems that, like Tensta, create more opportunities for one-on-one contact and give teachers freedom to make individual interventions are more effective in addressing the needs of a diverse school population.

HIGHEST COMPLETED LEVEL OF EDUCATION OF SECOND-GENERATION TURKS IN FIVE COUNTRIES

Table 10.2 Highest completed level of education of Turkish second-generation youth aged 16–25, Germany, 1999

	No degree or degree from a special-needs school	Hauptschule	Realschule	Gymnasium
% of Turkish second generation (N = 239)	6.7	64.4	15.9	13.0

SOURCE: EFFNATIS (Effectiveness of National Integration Strategies towards Second Generation Migrant Youth in a Comparative European Perspective) field study data, author's calculations (Worbs 2003).

NOTE: The academic degree that pupils can earn in the *Realschule* is called a *Mittlere Reife*; a degree from a *Gymnasium* is called an *Abitur (Hochschulreife)*. All degrees may also be obtained in night schools or certain special schools such as *Fachoberschulen*, which are subsumed here under the respective "normal" school type.

Table 10.3 Highest completed level of
education of Turkish second-generation
youth aged 15–35, Netherlands, 1998

	% of Turkish second generation
Primary school	34[a]
Lower vocational (Vbo), lower general secondary (Mavo)	37
Senior secondary vocational (Mbo), senior general secondary (Havo), preparatory university (Vwo)	23
Higher professional (Hbo), university (WO)	5

SOURCE: SPVA 1998, ISEO/EUR (Institute for Social and Economic Research, Erasmus University, Rotterdam).
NOTES: Youth who ended their educational careers by end of 1998. Top row represents individuals who finished primary school only (normally, age twelve). Mbo is equivalent to Havo because both diplomas provide access to higher vocational school (Hbo).
[a]Percentages are rounded.

Table 10.4 Highest completed level of education of Turkish
second-generation youth aged 18–40, France, 1999 (%)

	Drop out	Vocational school	Baccalaureate	University
Males	40.1	27.8	19.1	13.1
Females	51.6	15.3	23.3	7.7
Total	46.4	22.1	21.3	10.1

SOURCE: INSEE, EHF 1999; author's calculations (Simon 2003).
NOTE: "Drop out" means leaving school with no diploma, mainly after the *collège*.

Table 10.5 Highest completed level of
education of Turkish second-generation men
aged 18 years and older, Belgium, 1996

	% of Turkish second generation (N = 272)
Primary	9
Lower secondary (BSO)	37
Higher secondary (ASO, TSO)	50
Higher education	4

SOURCE: HMSM (Survey on Migration History and Social Mobility) survey data, 1994–1996.

Table 10.6 Highest completed level of education
of Austrian residents born in Turkey or
having Turkish citizenship, aged 15–35, 2001

	No diploma	Compulsory	Apprenticeship	Middle secondary	Higher secondary	University
% of second generation (N = 590)	3	62	26	4	4	0

SOURCE: Author's computations based on Microcensus 2001 (Herzog-Punzensberger 2003).
NOTE: Table excludes children (of Turkish immigrant parents) born in Austria who were either Austrian citizens from birth or were later naturalized (but before this count).

NOTES

1. Although the apprenticeship system in Germany and Austria gives second-generation Turks better opportunities than second-generation Turks have in the Netherlands and France, the apprenticeship system does not work perfectly. To the contrary, evidence is mounting that Turkish youngsters especially profit less from the apprenticeship system. They have more difficulty gaining apprenticeship positions with good prospects for future work and more often drop out of the dual track (Worbs 2003, p. 1029; von Below 2003, pp. 44, 45). But compared to their counterparts in the Netherlands and France, where there is no apprenticeship system, second-generation Turks in Germany and Austria are better off (Crul & Vermeulen 2003).

2. Interestingly, the majority of mentors in the Netherlands are girls, leading some to call mentoring a "girls' project." Not only does mentoring attract more girls, but also relationships among participants are more intense among girls.

REFERENCES

Barnett, S. W. (1995). Long-term effects of early childhood programs on cognitive and school outcomes. *The Future of Children* 5(3): 25–50.

Below, S. von (2003). *Schulische Bildung: Berufliche Ausbliding und Erwerbstätigkeit junger Migranten.* Ergebnissen des Integrationssurveys des BiB (Heft 105b). Wiesbaden: BiB.

Böcker, A. and, D. Thränhardt (2003). Is het Duitse integratiebeleid succesvoller, en zo ja, waarom? *Migrantenstudies* 19(1): 33–44.

Bongers, C., K. Hoogeveen, and K. Vaessen. (2002). *Kop—en voetklassen: Ei van Columbus? Inventarisatie en analyse.* Utrecht, The Netherlands: Sardes.

Cohen, P. A., J. A. Kulik, and C. C. Kulik (1982). Educational outcomes of tutoring: A meta-analysis of findings. *American Educational Research Journal* 19: 237–248.

Cooper, B. (2004). *Promising integration practices in member states of the European Union.* Report prepared for the Ministerial Conference on Integration "Turning Principles into Actions," Groningen, November 9–11. Washington, DC: MPI.

Crul, M. (2000). *De sleutel tot succes: Over hulp, keuzes en kansen in de schoolloopbanen van Turkse en Marokkaanse jongeren van de tweede generatie.* Amsterdam: Het Spinhuis.

Crul, M. (2002). Success breeds success: Moroccan and Turkish student mentors in the Netherlands. *International Journal for the Advancement of Counselling* 24: 275–287.

Crul, M. (2004). *Immigrant parents, children, and education: Bridging the gap between home and host countries.* Paper prepared for the Ministerial Conference on Integration "Turning Principles into Actions," Groningen, 9–11 November. Washington, DC: MPI.

Crul, M. (2007). Student mentoring among migrant youth. A promising instrument. Paper presented at Education, Diversity and Excellence conference, January 26–28, 2007, Vilunda Gymnasium, Upplands Väsby, Sweden.

Crul, M., and A. Akdeniz (1997). *Het huiswerkbegeleidingsproject van SOEBA.* Amsterdam: SOEBA.

Crul, M., and H. Vermeulen (2003). The second generation in Europe: Introduction. *International Migration Review* 37(4): 965–986.

Crul, M., and J. Doomernik (2003). The Turkish and the Moroccan second generation in the Netherlands: Divergent trends between and polarization within the two groups. *International Migration Review* 37(4): 1039–1065.

Crul, M., and K. Kraal (2004). *Evaluatie landelijk ondersteuningsprogramma mentoring.* Amsterdam: IMES, Universiteit van Amsterdam.

Driessen, G. (2004). A large-scale longitudinal study of the utilization and effects of early childhood education and care in the Netherlands. *Early Child Development and Care* 174(7–8): 667–689.

Goodlad, S. (1995). *Students as tutors and mentors.* London: Kogan Page.

Goodlad, S. (1998). *Mentoring and tutoring by students.* London: Kogan Page.

Groen, H. (2000). *Mentorprojecten allochtone jongeren Haarlem.* Amsterdam: Bureau toegepast jeugdonderzoek.

Heckmann, F., H. W. Lederer, and S. Worbs (in cooperation with the EFFNATIS research team). (2001). *Effectiveness of national integration strategies towards second generation migrant youth in a comparative European perspective.* Final Report to the European Commission. Bamberg, Germany: EfSM.

Herzog-Punzensberger, B. (2003). Ethnic segmentation in school and labor market: 40 year legacy of Austrian "Guestworker" Policy. *International Migration Review* 37(4): 1120–1144.

Hulst, P. (2000). *Project "Allochtone mentoren in het V.O."* Deventer, The Netherlands: GAO.

Jacobi, M. (1991). Mentoring and undergraduate academic success: A literature review. *Review of Educational Research* 61(4): 505–532.

Lesthaeghe, R. (ed). (1997). *Diversiteit in sociale verandering: Turkse en Marokkaanse vrouwen in België.* Brussels: VUB-Press.

Meijer, F., and M. Reuling. (1998). *Bijvoorbeeld bekeken. Mentorprogramma's in Zuid Holland*. Provincie Zuid, Holland: Den Haag.

Özüekren, S., and R. van Kempen, eds. (1997). Turks in European cities: Housing and urban segregation. In *Research in migration ethnic relations*. Aldershot, UK: Ashgate.

Paulides, H. (2000). *Toveren met aandacht. Evaluatie coaching Marokkaanse rolmodellen*. Amsterdam: Radar.

Pels, T. (2001). Student disengagement and pedagogical climate. Paper presented to the Sixth International Metropolis Conference, November, Rotterdam.

Simon, P. (2003). France and the unknown second generation: Preliminary results on social mobility. *International Migration Review* 37(4): 1091–1119.

Suárez-Orozco, C. (2004). Formulating identity in a globalized world. In *Globalization: Culture and education in the new millennium*. M. Suárez-Orozco and D. Qin-Hilliard, eds. Berkeley and Los Angeles: University of California Press; NY, NY: The Ross Institute.

Suárez-Orozco, M., and D. Qin-Hilliard, eds. (2004). *Globalization: Culture and education in the new millennium*. In *Globalization: Culture and education in the new millennium*, M. Suárez-Orozco and D. Qin-Hilliard, eds. Berkeley and Los Angeles: University of California Press; NY, NY: The Ross Institute.

Timmerman, C., E. Vanderwaeren, and M. Crul (2003). The second generation in Belgium. *International Migration Review* 37(4): 1091–1119.

Topping, K. J., and S. Hill (1995). University and college students as tutors for schoolchildren: A typology and review of evaluation research. In *Mentoring and tutoring by students*. S. Goodlad, ed. London: Kogan Page.

Vaessen, K., G. Walraven, and M. van Wissen (1998). *Tutoring en mentoring. Een klassieke methodiek in een moderne context*. Een inventarisatie van de mogelijkheden. Utrecht: Sardes.

Veen, A., J. Roeleveld, and P. Leseman (2000). *Evaluatie van Kaleidoscoop en Piramide. Eindrapportage*. Amsterdam: SCO-Kohnstamm Instituut.

Veugelers, W. (2000) *De waarde van een mentor-mentee relatie*. Amsterdam: De pedagogische demensie, ILO.

Worbs, S. (2003). The second generation in Germany: Between school and labor market. *International Migration Review* 37(4): 1011–1038.

ELEVEN

Marie McAndrew

THE EDUCATION OF IMMIGRANT
STUDENTS IN A GLOBALIZED WORLD

Policy Debates in Comparative Perspective

INTRODUCTION

Since the beginning of humankind, population movements have been at the heart of the creation and evolution of civilizations and cultures. More recently, at least from a historical perspective, a whole continent, North America, was radically transformed by an influx of colonizers, slaves, and voluntary migrants. The magnitude of this influx in relation to the receiving native population has never been equaled. Moreover, since the nineteenth century, with the spread of the nation-state model in the Western world, newcomers have generally been received in immigration societies with a mix of openness and rejection, as well as with the expectations and fears echoed in today's debates concerning the so-called "new" immigration (Morelli 1992; Palmer 1984; C. Suárez-Orozco & M. Suárez-Orozco 2001).

As a scholar working on integration issues from a historical and comparative perspective, especially as they relate to education, I find the whole concept of globalization quite elusive. I am nevertheless fully aware of the pitfalls of the other perspective—that is, the "nothing under the sun has changed since people have always migrated" paradigm. One of the central tasks that informed and socially responsible academics have to perform for an amnesic or short-term-minded policy community and public opinion is to ascertain the extent to which the challenges we face today are unique and whether we can be enlightened by the lessons of past experiences, positive or negative.

My aim in this chapter is thus to critically examine three policy debates regarding the education of immigrant students: the role of common schooling versus that of ethnocultural institutions in the integration of newcomers; the place that majority versus immigrant minority languages should have in the curriculum; and the extent to which public schools should adapt their norms and regulations to religious and cultural diversity. These issues share two common features. They have generated heated debates and a relatively impressive body of research in most Western immigration countries, and they have been recurrent, though intermittent, preoccupations for over a century. So they serve the aim of this paper well, which is, on one hand, to ascertain to what extent globalization influences the current framing of these old debates and affects the policy options available to us and, on the other, to identify, based on a comparative analysis of policy-relevant research, the minimum consensus about how best to successfully integrate immigrant students. At the end of each of the following sections, I also identify research topics that should be pursued in light of the current transformations taking place in the world.

COMMON SCHOOLING VERSUS ETHNOSPECIFIC INSTITUTIONS

Without doubt, the establishment of common compulsory schooling, which occurred in Europe and North America from the nineteenth century onward, has been a powerful instrument of nation building and homogenization of diverse populations (Holmes 1981; Lê Than K. 1981). Moreover, although the degree of educational autonomy granted to regional subcomponents or national minorities varied greatly according to history and geography, the normative consensus regarding the desirability for immigrant students to attend schools, reflecting the ethos of the receiving society, has always been strong. The arguments expressed as early as 1830 by Horace Mann in the United States and by Jules Ferry in 1885 in France were not radically different from those voiced today by the opponents of community-controlled education or by ordinary citizens concerned with the current fragmentation of the educational market (Gautherin 2000; Parsons & Bales 1955). Common schools were seen as playing a double role in the integration of newcomers: on one hand, they propagated an explicit curriculum, which consisted of shared values and the minimal knowledge needed to be a productive member of society; on the other, they were vehicles for intergroup contact and friendships among children at an early age when identities and attitudes are developed.

Nevertheless, two centrifugal tendencies limited the political impact of common schooling. On the ground, common but de facto majority-dominated institutions were not always receptive to newcomers. In the most lenient cases, resistance to their presence amounted to benign neglect and relegation to "the back of the classroom." In other circumstances, state or local authorities practiced active segregation, creating de facto immigrant schools (Glenn & De Jong 1996; Laferrière 1983). Immigrant parents also often resisted common schooling and established their own schools, as supplementary or parallel institutions, to ensure the retention of their language, their culture, and especially their religion when the last was different from that of the majority community (Anderson & Boyer 1970; Swann 1985). These institutions were rarely supported by public money, even in societies that did not offer the alternative of a genuine secular school system. In some instances, they were seen as political threats; in the United States, for example, Irish Catholic schools and German-language schools after World War I were actively opposed. But most of the time they were simply ignored, since immigrant groups, unlike national minorities, generally do not manifest strong autonomous tendencies.

Research on academic and social outcomes for those attending ethnospecific institutions was also almost nonexistent. But this absence of interest was generalized to all immigrant students, who were not defined as social, and thus research, problems, until the democratization of education in the second half of the twentieth century, when equality of access and of results for different groups became normative ideals (Ballantyne 1989; Samuda, Berry, & Laferrière 1983). The availability of state support for ethnocultural institutions—still a hotly debated issue—became part of the public agenda during roughly the same period. Given the emerging consensus (still strong today) that "public schools were failing minorities," partisans of ethnospecific institutions began to champion them not so much for the sake of cultural maintenance but as alternative vehicles of educational and social mobility for immigrant students (Homan 1992; Smith 1981).

To what extent has the current policy debate on the relevance of common schools versus ethnospecific institutions been reshaped by twenty-first-century globalization? Many previous trends certainly endure, as revealed by international research (McAndrew 1996a; McAndrew

& Ledoux 1998; Orfield & Eaton 1996; Payet 1999). First, it is clear, as it was formerly, that school segregation is as much the product of various forms of exclusion as it is a voluntary alternative actively pursued by parents and communities. In many European countries, as well as in Canada and the United States, de facto concentration of immigrants in specific public schools is on the rise, under the combined effects of the flight of affluent majority and minority groups to private schools, and the concentration of poorer immigrants in some neighborhoods. Some have also equated the specialization of public schools, which serve different interests and lifestyles, to de facto privatization. Globalization—which has weakened the nation-state, heightened the importance of individual choice, and encouraged a tendency to look at education as a global market commodity —has certainly played a role in school segregation (Ball 1993; Van Haecht 1998). But it would be simplistic to contrast the Golden Age of common schooling, which never existed, to the era of fragmented schooling in which we now live.

Second, there is no evidence that voluntary segregation, that is, attending a community-controlled institution, would be more popular today than before among immigrant groups. Although this may be the case in some countries or among specific groups, it is far from a general trend. Numerous contradictory factors, some of which are the product of globalization, probably balance each other out in this regard. On one hand, the generalization of pluralistic, child-centered, and human rights ideologies has certainly made public schools, if not neutral and bias-free, at least more receptive to the needs of immigrant students (Banks & McGee-Banks 1995; Glenn & De Jong 1996). Moreover, contrary to patently racist discourses that stress the greater cultural incompatibility of the "new" immigrants with the receiving society,[1] globalization, especially but not exclusively in countries with a selective immigration policy, has likely helped to close the gap in this regard. More and more immigrants share, for better or worse, the individualistic materialism characteristic of Western society, as well as a belief in shared citizenship and equality. These values make immigrants who uphold them more inclined to fight for the transformation of public schools than for the establishment of parallel institutions (C. Suárez-Orozco & Todorova 2003; Waugh, Abu-Laban, & Burckhardt Qureshi 1991). On the other hand, the intensification of supranational loyalties is a reality, both for religious militant groups and for more discreet immigrant groups that can benefit in this regard from the assets of globalized communications (Shahid & Van Koningsveld 1996; Walford 1996). Thus, choosing an ethnospecific school no longer means attending a second-rate institution or being cut off from various opportunities for social mobility. In fact, the reverse may be true, given the international funding some of these institutions receive.

Finally, as in the past, arguments on both sides are based mostly on normative models of what constitutes "genuine" integration and of the schooling most likely to achieve it, not on research findings that would weight various claims (McAndrew 2001, 2003b). The socialization benefits that the partisans of common schooling stress have rarely been ascertained, much less compared with the identity profile and cultural attitudes prevalent among students attending ethnospecific institutions. The opposite claim (Halstead 1986), that subsequent social integration can occur when a positive group identity has been cultivated during youth, has not been substantiated, nor have the results of ethnospecific institutions in this regard been monitored consistently. Even in the area of academic results, which has generated a bit more research,[2] results are either inconclusive, though slightly in favor of public schools, or limited to a few self-evident truths, such as the fact that institutions controlled by socioeconomically advantaged groups fare better than those attended by poorer immigrants (Driessen & Bezemer 1999; Schwartz 1996).

Research on the impact of immigrant concentration in public schools is not very enlightening, either. In the European context and, in the case of poorer groups, in the United States, such concentration is usually considered and sometimes proven to be negatively correlated with school success (Mahieu 1999; Payet 1999; C. Suárez-Orozco, M. Suárez-Orozco, & Doucet 2003). In other North American cases, especially in Canada, selection produces a more class-balanced immigration. Schools with a high concentration of immigrant students have often been found to outperform others in academic results, especially when their socioeconomic composition is taken into account (Anisef et al. 2004). Although these conclusions seem contradictory at first sight, they point in the same direction: the dominance of social class over ethnic factors in explaining school performance and mobility, even if class does not account for all discrepancies between majority and minority students.[3]

So where does this leave us in terms of desirable strategies? I would dare put forth three minimal tendencies in this regard.

First, it is obvious that multiple fragmented school spaces are here to stay and that, in the current globalized context, they may even hold some benefits—for example, allowing easier mobility for students enrolled in schools belonging to an international network, whether religious or elitist. Nevertheless, if we believe, based perhaps more on common sense than on research, that a lack of common schooling of future citizens at an early age will undermine social cohesion, some of the action taken in various countries regarding voluntary segregation can be inspiring (Commission for Racial Equality 1990; McAndrew 2002; U.S. Department of Education 1999). Such action is basically of two kinds: one, at the level of explicit curriculum, ensures that minimal knowledge and values are transmitted to all students, especially but not exclusively when parallel institutions receive some kind of public funding; the other compensates for the lack of informal socialization by providing other meaningful venues—such as twinning programs, sports, or other extracurricular activities—in which youth attending various school networks can meet.

Second, whenever explicit or implicit school norms regarding student recruitment or placement in schools are at the root of involuntary segregation, it would seem a rather obvious requirement in any democratic society that school authorities actively support immigrant parents who want their children to attend public common schools because they believe such institutions are better vehicles for social mobility and increased contact with the host society. In this area, comparative research (Katz 1992; Leman 1999) points in two directions. For one, we should not strive toward a statistically perfect distribution of the immigrant clientele in the school system. It is more realistic and educationally sound to aim at preserving "medium density" schools, which combine the twin advantages of a sizable presence of the host society's students with a critical mass of immigrant students. For the other direction, although the fight against institutional discrimination in the recruitment and placement of immigrant students should mostly adopt soft, voluntary sensitization mechanisms, a more proactive or explicitly normative legal or administrative framework, such as the Anti-Discrimination School Pact devised by the Flemish government, can be an advantage.

Finally, whenever involuntary segregation is mostly the creation of socioeconomic factors and residential segregation, the literature (Astor Stave 1995; Orfield & Eaton 1996; Willis & Alves 1996) clearly points toward the inefficiency of major "social engineering" endeavors aimed at a better distribution of school clienteles. Small-scale voluntary programs can have a certain impact. But above all, we must ensure that if immigrant students are concentrated in high-density schools, they do not receive a second-class education, especially if ethnic concentration coincides with socioeconomic deprivation. Such instances call for both compensatory and intercultural programs.[4] The former tackles students' various educational deficits, while the latter ensures that school personnel and norms are sensitive to their needs and experiences.

In this area, one research priority is clearly revealed: a systematic assessment of the consequences for social cohesion of the currently accelerating fragmentation of the educational market. Without falling into the pessimistic or alarmist traps identified above, we should better understand how and to what extent identity formation, among immigrant or host society students, is influenced by the potential lack of common socialization associated with such a trend. If instead of normative statements, we gather reliable comparative data in this regard, we can discuss policy options, especially regarding attendance and funding of ethnospecific institutions, in a much more informed manner.

THE PLACE OF IMMIGRANT LANGUAGES

Since most Western states adopted one or more official languages in the nineteenth century,[5] a broad consensus has existed regarding the necessity for school systems to ensure mastery of that language or those languages by all students. Language mastery represents both an essential vehicle of educational and social mobility for immigrant students and a necessary tool for intergroup exchanges and common citizenship. The debate has thus focused not on the role of official or majority languages (which was questioned only by some national minorities), but rather on the legitimacy of making immigrant or "heritage" languages[6] part of the curriculum (Berque 1985; Krashen 1996; McAndrew & Cicéri 1998).

In addition to teaching in or of targeted languages conducted by ethnospecific institutions, we know that bilingual programs—or more often, some teaching of immigrant languages—were implemented in some public schools in Canada and the United States as early as the late nineteenth century (Anderson & Boyer 1970; Samuda et al., 1983). Although the European situation is slightly less documented, there is, at least some evidence of similar trends in this regard. When they were known to the general public, these initiatives generated far from universal support. The concerns voiced at that time are largely the same echoed today: the dangers of a "babelization" of society, the "refusal" to integrate that language retention revealed, the power that "ethnic elites" were, thus, preserving (Crawford 1999; Galindo 1997).

Nevertheless, since the mid-twentieth century, the framing of the immigrant language controversy in public schools has undergone major shifts. The first, which has little to do with globalization, concerns the relationship between mastering the host language and learning heritage languages. Before the 1960s, many decision makers and educators in Europe and North America shared a belief in the "subtractive bilingualism" hypothesis developed by psychologists and linguists at the beginning of the twentieth century (Grosjean 1982; Hakuta 1986). According to this hypothesis, within the brain, learning one language was usually done at the expense of the other. Some experts even argued that bilinguals must be less intelligent than monolinguals.[7] Such beliefs were obviously not shared by people who engaged in multilingual activities, but they certainly prevented them from "selling" such initiatives to the majority community as assets for furthering linguistic integration. This situation changed radically when a new hypothesis, "additive bilingualism," was introduced in the 1960s and soon became the dominant view. It asserts that metalinguistic and metacognitive abilities developed in the first language are transferred to the second and that if basic concepts and skills are not strengthened in the mother tongue, full mastery of other languages will be impeded (resulting in semilingualism) (Cummins 1979; Mackey 1970). Since then, proponents and opponents of a greater role for immigrant languages in public schools have focused their arguments on the impact of various formulas on host-language acquisition.

This debate has been especially heated in the United States, but it has also touched other societies.[8] Research regarding the issue is inconclusive. Fundamental psycholinguistic studies targeting individual learners, as well as the bulk of research on "immersion programs" aimed at national minorities, support the additive bilingualism hypothesis (Artigal 1991; Cummins, 1989; Painchaud, d'Anglejan, Armand, & Jesak 1993). But evaluation studies of actual bilingual programs that target immigrant students have yielded more mixed results, partially due to the methodological complexity of proving that, other things being equal, it is better for immigrant students to continue mastering their heritage languages while learning host languages[9] (Greene 1998; Dolson & Mayer 1992). Thus, while specialists and opinion makers continue to quarrel, school authorities in most countries make decisions based on a mix of personal assumptions, community pressures, and short-term costs-benefit analyses. This is why monolingual mainstream education for immigrant students, complemented by some teaching of heritage languages offered mostly after school hours, largely continues as the norm, even though innovative breakthroughs in multilingual education are reported everywhere (Glenn & De Jong 1996).

The second shift, which can certainly be linked to globalization, is the new importance placed on the potential benefits for majority students of a greater recognition of immigrant languages in public schools. Gradually over the past fifty years, teaching in or of heritage languages has been advocated less as an ethnospecific program aimed at cultural maintenance than as a mainstream initiative that fosters multilingualism and cultural awareness among the full student body (Fishman 1976; McAndrew & Cicéri 1998; Paulston 1980). Primarily in North America and Canada, majority parents have started lobbying to have their children admitted to heritage language or bilingual programs, with a preference for languages considered important on the world scene over obscure ones.[10]

The eruption of the global linguistic market has sometimes created tension between the two competing objectives of heritage language teaching: linguistic maintenance, which is better achieved within a linguistically homogenous group, and linguistic and cultural enrichment, which by its nature requires the presence of nonspeakers of the target language. It has also generated a pecking order regarding the value of various languages, which is incompatible with the conception of bilingual education and heritage language teaching as tools to help immigrant students of any mother tongue master the host language. However, immigrant parents themselves often make linguistic choices based on instrumental motivations when they prefer enrolling their children in prestigious world languages (such as Chinese for Cambodians, or Spanish for Haitians) to having them learn their own mother tongue.

Up to now, research on this new recognition of immigrant languages in the promotion of multilingualism has been limited in magnitude and, even more, in its impact. This neglect is in line with the general lack of interest among researchers studying heritage language teaching in topics other than its impact on mastery of the host language. Indeed, we know very little about the extent to which minority speakers enrolled in such programs master the target language or use it later as an asset for international business or exchange. Everywhere, lip service is paid to the benefits of multilingualism in a globalized world, but the link between this emerging normative ideal and the actual presence of speakers of multiple languages among the immigrant population has not been fully exploited.

Let us now weigh various policy options. I first take a normative position not necessarily shared by everyone. In the current debate about the place of immigrant languages in the curriculum, our main point of reference should be the impact of our choices on immigrant students. If these choices also benefit the multilingual skills of majority students, the maintenance of multilingualism and ethnic communities in the entire society, or the economic competitiveness of the country in the global market, so be it—let's rejoice. But whenever these objectives come into conflict, we must go back to our most immediate responsibilities to the most vulnerable.

The basic needs of immigrant students are pretty obvious, as is the order of priority of those needs. First and foremost, they must master the host language(s) without losing their sense of self-worth or accumulating academic deficits that would hinder their educational mobility. Depending on the age at which students enter the new school system, their academic profiles, and their migration histories, host-language mastery may or may not imply intensive instruction in their mother tongue or access to full bilingual programs. But as the National Research Council found in its meta-analysis of thirty years of American research on the most effective means of teaching English to newcomers (1997), for many students, especially younger ones, the openness of schools to linguistic diversity, along with a minimal presence of their mother tongue in teaching materials and activities (such as the popular European "Language Awareness Program"), is sufficient to generate the sense of security necessary for learning a new language.[11] Given the complex logistics of bilingual programs in countries whose migration influx is not as homogeneous as that in the United States, and considering the generalized lack of resources everywhere, these conclusions give a little more room for maneuvering to policy makers than the usual militant stance of "No salvation without full multilingual programs."

Should we, however, assume that good instruction in the host language in linguistically open settings will answer all immigrant students' needs, especially in a globalized world? Certainly not, but in this regard, they are not fundamentally different from other students (all should master more than one language), except for the special advantage they enjoy of already knowing another one. Thus, the main challenge lies in helping immigrant students fully exploit their multilingual potential and, if possible, to transform it into an opportunity for majority students. Various initiatives have been implemented in different countries with greater or less success; for example, the accreditation of heritage language classes offered by community organizations; the opening of school-based heritage language or bilingual programs to majority students; the inclusion of a wider variety of immigrant languages among the international languages taught in high school; and the opportunity for immigrant students to choose their mother tongue when they take second- or third-language exams, even if the latter is not part of the formal curriculum (McAndrew 2001). Research on the strengths and weaknesses of these programs is needed to foster the exchange of best practices while respecting the specificity of each context.

In a wider perspective, further studies are also needed to better assess the impact of globalization on the need for multilingualism. This need is likely not as obvious and univocal as some oft-voiced amiable banalities would have us believe. It is quite possible that globalization will actually contribute, in the middle run, to a decrease in the need for multilingualism, or at least in a narrowing of the spectrum of useful languages. In this scenario, immigration countries with English as their main language would preserve more room for the learning of immigrant languages, whereas in countries with another official language, immigrant students might choose English as a second language rather than their mother tongue. It is a reality we have to better understand and face if we are to maximize the potential benefits to all of the presence of a multilingual immigrant population, without forcing those immigrants into cultural and linguistic maintenance they may not desire.

CULTURAL AND RELIGIOUS DIVERSITY

Of all the debates discussed here, cultural and religious diversity has been the most controversial and heated over the past ten years in many European and North American contexts. Moreover, even though cultural and religious conflicts in schools or over schooling were not unknown in the past (Holmes 1981; Samuda, Berry, & Laferrière 1983), they have become much more obvious and also more complex. Meanwhile, the normative models that decision makers, principals, teachers, parents, and even students can invoke to legitimize different stands have multiplied. For example, the conception of citizenship that schools traditionally preferred and that immigrant parents or students accepted, or at least did not contest, followed either the republican model popular in France and in many Southern European countries (Gautherin 2000; Kepel 1989), or the liberal model dominant in the United States and in most Northern European countries (Galston 1991; Rawls 1993). Although the two models differ in the degree to which they view schooling as promoting a substantive versus a procedural set of values (thick versus thin culture), they both favor the neutrality of the public space and relegation of diversity to the private sphere. This stance largely inhibited recognition of cultural and religious differences in school norms and practices, even if ad hoc accommodations were not unknown. Also, the dominant epistemological paradigm was realism, which contends that objective, neutral, and universal knowledge exists and that it is possible to define a school curriculum whose mastery would generate consensus among all social groups (Nagel 1994). Finally, in matters of ethical positions regarding pluralism, the field was largely dominated by assimilationists who argued that the historical majority should keep its capacity to control the agenda of curricular change and its right to protect identity-linked elements that it wanted to remain unchanged. Immigrant parents and students were thus much less likely to get involved in contestations regarding the school curriculum and its cultural components (Samuda, Berry, & Laferrière 1983; Glazer 1997).

Today, under the influence of decolonization, which undermined the power base of many of these positions, and of globalization, which has heightened the normative value of a common culture of human rights, other competing paradigms have emerged (Kymlicka 1995; Taylor 1992; Touraine 1994). Both communatarians and renewed liberals, whether they are philosophers, policy makers, or ordinary schoolteachers or parents, have come into the arena defending the recognition of diversity in the public sphere as a condition of equity and an asset for a better integration of immigrant students. They disagree, nevertheless, about the respective weight to be granted the individual or her or his community of origin in the final say regarding cultural and religious conformity, and they take different ethical positions on value conflicts. Communatarians tend to advocate cultural relativism, that is, total respect for those elements perceived as requirements of immigrant cultures or religions, while renewed liberals point to democratic values and laws as necessary limits to institutional adaptation.[12] Curricular issues have also become much more contested, especially under the assault of antiracist educators who, highlighting the social construction of knowledge and of its selection for school purposes, have advocated that the current Eurocentrism be replaced by a multiplicity of perspectives and voices (Dei 1996; Gillborn 1995; Grinter 1992).

At a time when globalized religious movements are on the rise, faith-based claims of immigrant parents and students have proved especially difficult to accommodate on a consensual basis (Bernatchez & Bourgeault 1999; McAndrew 2003a, 2005; McDonnell 1992). On one hand, the requirement of state neutrality in this regard is, with a few historical exceptions, generally more absolute. And compared to cultural tradition, the absolutism of religious belief is far less amenable to either the necessarily critical review of facts associated with schooling or to the practical need to sometimes limit expression of diversity in schools. On the other hand, international conventions and several national constitutions and bills of rights attach more weight to religious freedom than to the mere right to further one's cultural life. This complex set of counteracting factors can lead only to deeper conflicts of legitimacy between educational institutions attempting to produce common practices and identities, and parents or students defending their right to develop their faith. The perfect formula to balance rights, especially religious freedom with gender equity, has not yet been found, as shown, for example, by the wave of criticism that both tolerance and interdiction of the wearing of Islamic veils has generated in many European countries and in some Canadian provinces (Cicéri 1999; McAndrew 2005; Renaerts 1999; Stasi 2003).

Nevertheless, the high visibility of some controversies regarding diversity in schools should not be the tree that hides the forest from view. A comparative analysis of various policies, programs, and evaluative studies of their implementation indicates that many harmonious adaptations happen ad hoc, or at least generate little resistance from the school staff or majority parents (First Amendment Center 1999a, 1999b; Lorcerie 1996; McAndrew, Cicèri, & Jacquet 1997). These findings reflect the coexistence of various ideological positions among principals, teachers, and parents of immigrant and nonimmigrant backgrounds in the same country,[13] even though, at the political level, decision makers favor a more coherent and univocal paradigm. Practice on the ground does seem to be more multiform and to consist of a greater blend of approaches than do official discourses. This hybridization of daily routine is also influenced by the intensive aspects of schooling and the personal nature of relationships it breeds, which often inhibits, for better or worse, a consistent institutional response toward diversity.

Nevertheless, it is possible to distinguish five groups of practices on a continuum from least to most actively committed to diversity and to establish some links in this regard to various models of citizenship, epistemological paradigms, and ethical positions (Banks 1988; Gillborn 1995; McAndrew, Cicèri, & Jacquet 1997; OECD 1987; Pagé 1993).

- Selective incorporation of elements pertaining to immigrant cultures and religions in school activities in order to foster the integration of immigrant students.[14] This type of practice is found everywhere at various degrees and gives rise to little debate, even in countries that prefer a republican model of citizenship.

- Implementation of activities specially tailored to the needs and characteristics of immigrant minorities from an equalization-of-opportunity perspective.[15] These practices are also widespread. However, in countries with a strong republican tradition, they are most often implemented based on socioeconomic disadvantage (e.g., priority education zones in France and French-speaking Belgium), rather than justified explicitly by the presence of immigrant groups (Van Zanten 1997).

- Integration of specific immigrant-oriented content or perspective into the regular school curriculum so that differences and even conflicts over interpretation are acknowledged.[16] These practices are more common in national communities with long-standing divisions or in those dealing with specific conflicting cultural and religious issues concerning some immigrant groups. Although they sometimes appear under the pressure of the discipline itself in countries with a republican ideology (Lantheaume 2002), they are more popular in societies that embrace the communatarian or the renewed liberal models of citizenship and where espousal of a constructivist vision of knowledge is more prevalent.

- In response to religious claims made by certain immigrant groups, adaptation of norms and regulations governing school life.[17] As pointed out earlier, numerous adaptations are made every day, even in systems in which secularism is a fundamental principle. However, such demands meet with far greater resistance when they appear to encroach on mandates that lie at the heart of educational activity. Namely, the critical transmission of knowledge, the promotion of fundamental democratic values (e.g., gender equality), and the preservation of a public space where common identity outweighs differences.

- Tailoring or transforming various elements of the curriculum in response to the demands of the "organized" community.[18] Although they meet with various forms of resistance, these non-consensual and sometimes questionable practices do exist and have on occasion received normative support from public authorities in contexts where the communatarian ideology is popular.

If one takes a dispassionate distance from both normative controversies and specific practices, is it possible to identify optimal policy options regarding the extent to which schools should adapt to cultural diversity? Probably not, if we try to find a "one model fits all" solution or rely exclusively on direct research evidence to do so. Indeed, on one hand, the mere idea of an efficient strategy that runs against the deeply felt ideological beliefs of school decision makers or personnel is an oxymoron. Normative models, whether enunciated by the state or experienced by social actors (or both), must be taken into account when defining the right balance between common norms and respect for diversity (Holmes 1981; Lê Thanh 1981).[19] Moreover, until recently, comparative research on the outcomes of systems more or less open to adaptation to diversity has been limited (Lorcerie & McAndrew 1993; McAndrew 2001). But it would, in any case, also be extremely complex. "All things being equal" is almost an impossible goal in such circumstances. What one might attribute to national choices or specific practices in matters of religious or cultural recognition (or nonrecognition) might well be actually linked to numerous other variables.[20]

However, if we cannot rigorously prescribe "what to do," we certainly can identify consensual guidelines on "what not to do," based on fundamental research in social psychology regarding identity development (Camilleri et al. 1990; De Vos & Suárez-Orozco 1990; Phinney 1990) and on legal guidelines (Guttman 1987; McLaughlin 1992; Thornberry & Gibbons 1997) concerning the state's obligation to all its citizens in a democratic country. Although these safeguards have been developed in much more depth in other publications (Bourgeault, Gagnon, McAndrew, & Pagé 2002; Hohl & Normand 1996; McAndrew 2003a, 2005), I present them here under two general ideas.

First, whenever family and school hold different norms, values, or codes of conduct, which is unavoidable in the context of migration, the aim should not necessarily be harmonization but respect for or at least avoidance of detrimental judgments about the other party. Children are extraordinarily flexible human beings: they can live in two different worlds as long as they are not forced to choose one over the other or made to feel that some cultural or religious characteristics are linked to socially devalued individuals (especially if the latter are their parents). Teenagers will eventually have to devise their own "cultural formula." Here again, at a minimum, schools should avoid pressuring them to take a stand and instead support the development of complex identity strategies more suitable both to the reality of the second generation and to a globalized world. Whether this can be done under any model of diversity recognition (or nonrecognition) is open to debate. It would seem, nevertheless, that both an extreme republican rigidity, which would keep the expression of any differences outside the school space, and an uncritical communatarian approach, which would not recognize the moral independence of students vis-à-vis their community, would not appear conducive.

Second, although religious and cultural accommodation in school is often framed as a socialization issue, weighing our choices in this regard according to their consequences on equal educational opportunities provided to immigrant students might be useful. Or to put it in a negative, less daring manner, one clear limit to adaptation is the obligation not to engage in any practice detrimental to the equality of students or subgroups of students (such as boys and girls). This duty points to the inadequacy of some communatarian practices. But given that democratic societies also have a commitment to ensure equality of results (i.e., equity), not merely formal equality of treatment, many accommodations to immigrant cultures and religions may prove to be long-term assets for the realization of these goals, even though, in the short term, we might not spontaneously consider them desirable. This is especially true of any practice that enhances parent-school communication and collaboration, given the overwhelming research evidence regarding its positive impact on school success (McMillan 2001). But this relationship between the recognition of pluralism and equality could also be an argument in favor of curricular adaptation, although we do not know with the same degree of certainty what difference a culturally and socially relevant curriculum makes in the educational performance and mobility of immigrant students.[21] So any "school as a fortress" model that would refuse any link with the community would also be inadvisable.

In terms of research, what is lacking is neither conceptual work on citizenship and pluralism nor ethnographic studies of ad hoc adaptations, both of which have thrived recently. We really need to understand why so little of the current sophisticated academic knowledge regarding the accommodation of diversity in schools is actually reflected in public debate and professional practices. In both instances, assimilation, often disguised by the now more acceptable term *integration*, and multiculturalism, often associated with the ghetto and undemocratic practices, are usually considered the only two competing alternatives. Moreover, even in countries where intercultural training is compulsory, numerous studies show that it is rarely invoked by teachers when they describe or reflect on their teaching practices. In some instances, this weakness can be linked to the lack of implementation of official commitments in grassroots programs. In other cases, the approach put forward may be either too theoretical or too remote from classroom preoccupations to really produce an impact. Thus, more action-research aimed at fostering a more critical and deeper appropriation by media analysts, school professionals, and even ordinary citizens, who are often also parents, of some of the theoretical work or research data on the accommodation of diversity in schools is greatly needed, as well as some comparative work on best practices.

NOTES

1. Both Eugene Roosens's and Unni Wikan's chapters in this volume offer vivid examples of these increasing trends in Europe, to which North America, although less affected, is not immune.

2. This is notwithstanding the mountain of research on the impact of integrated versus community-controlled education for African Americans, which I do not discuss here, since they do not constitute a voluntary migrant group (Gibson & Ogbu 1991).

3. This is exemplified by the PISA data presented in Rita Süssmuth's chapter in this volume. Maurice Crul's enlightening chapter also points to the impact of the general structural features of the school system in this regard, a dimension not covered in my discussion here.

4. Rita Süssmuth's chapter (this volume) proposes a global and balanced strategy in this regard.

5. With the noteworthy exception of the United States, which, given the overwhelming status of English, probably did not feel the need to make it the official language until recently, when some states enacted legislation to that effect.

6. *Heritage languages* is the term used to refer to children born in the new country, as their maternal language cannot be considered something foreign.

7. The fact that this school of thought was developed almost exclusively in regard to immigrant or colonial languages, while elite bilingualism in classical or foreign languages continued unchallenged, is clear testimony, if any is necessary, of the socially constructed nature of "scientific" knowledge.

8. See Eugene Roosens's chapter in this volume for a deeper and fascinating · analysis of the Flemish case in this regard.

9. For example, are we comparing equivalent groups of students when contrasting formulas? What educational practices lie behind the label *bilingual education*? Are all "bilingual programs" alike? Should we expect all academic problems of immigrant students to be solved by adopting one language formula, especially when they belong to socioeconomically deprived groups?

10. This tendency has been less pronounced in Europe for a variety of reasons. First, the socioeconomic status of immigrants is generally lower, as is the desire of majority parents to see their children mingling with immigrant students. Second, the popularity of multilingualism is heavily influenced by the process of

the construction of Europe, and a clear hierarchy exists there between community (i.e., members of the European community) and extracommunity languages.

11. Research (Johnson & Acera 1999; Sammons, Hillman, & Mortimore 1995) also shows that other conditions are needed, such as a high-quality program, dedication of teachers, and their belief in the capacity of students to succeed, as well as effective leadership from the school principal. But these factors are not related to the presence or absence of immigrant languages in the curriculum.

12. A good example of the contrast between these two positions in reference to a specific issue such as honor killing is found in Unni Wikan's chapter in this volume.

13. As for the issue of common schooling, it is also likely that the impact of globalization on the lesser or greater cultural gap between native-born and immigrant parents is ambiguous, as shown, for example, by the fact that across different countries, opponents and proponents of tolerance for the Muslim veil in public schools includes parents of all origins and religious backgrounds (McAndrew 2005).

14. For instance, persons of all origins or various cultural events found in learning material and in school; presence of individuals of various origins among the teaching staff; intercultural or interreligious aspects of the events celebrated and special activities conducted throughout the year. Mentor programs, as described in Maurice Crul's chapter in this volume, would also fall into this category.

15. For example, multilingual or culturally adapted information documents on the school system; implementation of special school outreach activities directed towards the community; intercultural training of teachers so as to provide them with a better understanding of student characteristics or enable them to vary their teaching strategies.

16. Generally in the social sciences, history, geography, and civic and moral education, in which case, these disciplines abandon their claim to universality and neutrality.

17. For example, adaptation of school cafeteria menus; tolerance of certain nonrecurring absences during major religious holidays; adaptation of the school uniform.

18. For instance, nonpresentation of elements deemed offensive in sexual education; setting up segregated male and female classes for physical education or for the teaching of all subject matters; warning teachers about any value judgment on matters deemed racist or sexist within the minority culture.

19. Actually, globalization might well enhance the necessity to do so, as comparative studies (McAndrew 1996b) have shown that, as borders become more porous, decision makers and public opinion seem to cling more than ever to their specificity regarding the preferred model of immigrant integration.

20. Such as those explored in Maurice Crul's chapter in this book between community (i.e., members of the European community) and extracommunity languages.

21. Although it certainly makes schooling a more enjoyable and a less alienating experience, as contributors to this volume all witnessed when we visited Tensta Gymnasium.

REFERENCES

Anderson, T., and M. Boyer, (1970). *Bilingual schooling in the United States.* Austin, TX: Southwest Educational Development Laboratory.

Anisef, P., J.-G. Blais, M. McAndrew, C. Ungerleider, and R. Sweet (2004). *Academic performance and educational mobility of youth of immigrant origin in Canada: What can we learn from provincial data banks?* Rapport de recherche. Ottawa: CIC (Citizenship and Immigration Canada).

Artigal, J. P. (1991). *The Catalan Immersion Program: A European point of view.* Norwood, NJ: Ablex.

Astor Stave, S. (1995). *Achieving racial balance: Case studies of contemporary school desegregation.* Westport, CT: Greenwood.

Ball, S. (1993). Education market choice and social class: The market as a class strategy in the UK and the US. *British Journal of Sociologic Education* 14(1): 3–17.

Ballantyne, J. H. (1989). *The sociology of education: A systematic analysis.* Englewood Cliffs, NJ: Prentice Hall.

Banks, J. A. (1988). *Multiethnic education: Theory and practice.* 2nd ed. Boston: Allyn & Bacon.

Banks, J. A., and C. A. McGee-Banks (1995). *Handbook of research on multicultural education.* New York: Macmillan.

Bernatchez, S., and G. Bourgeault (1999). La prise en compte de la diversité culturelle et religieuse à l'école publique et l'obligation d'accommodement—Aperçu des législations et des jurisprudences au Canada, aux États-Unis, en France et en Grande-Bretagne. *Canadian Ethnic Studies/Études ethniques au Canada* 31(1): 159–171.

Berque, J. (1985). *L'immigration à l'école de la République.* Rapport d'un groupe de réflexion remis au ministre de l'Éducation Nationale, Centre national de documentation pédagogique. Paris: La Documentation française.

Bourgeault, G., F. Gagnon, M. McAndrew, and M. Pagé (2002). Recognition of cultural and religious diversity in the educational systems of liberal democracies. In *Citizenship in transformation.* Y. Hébert, ed. Pp. 81–92. Toronto: University of Toronto Press.

Camilleri, C., J. Kastersztein, E. M. Lipansky, H. Malewska-Peyre, I. Taboada-Leonetti, and A. Vasquez (1990). *Stratégies identitaires.* Paris: Presses Universitaires de France.

Cicéri, C. (1999). *Le foulard islamique à l'école publique: Analyse comparée du débat dans la presse française et québécoise francophone (1994–1995).* Working paper. Montréal: Immigration et métropoles.

Crawford, J. (1999). *Bilingual education: History, politics, theory, and practice.* Los Angeles: Bilingual Education Services.

Commission for Racial Equality (1990). *Schools of faith: Religious schools in a multicultural society.* London: CRE.

Cummins, J. (1979). The language and culture issue on the education of minority language children. *Interchange* 10(4): 72–88.

Cummins, J. (1989). *Empowering minority students.* Sacramento: California Association for Bilingual Education.

Dei, G. (1996). *Antiracist education: Theory and practice.* Halifax, Nova Scotia: Fernwood.

De Vos, G., and M. Suárez-Orozco (1990). *Status inequality: The self in culture.* Cross-cultural research and methodology series, no. 15. Newbury Park, CA: Sage.

Driessen, G. W. J. M., and J. J. Bezemer (1999). Background and achievement levels of Islamic schools in the Netherlands: Are the reservations justified? *Race, Ethnicity and Education* 2(2): 235–256.

Dolson, D. P., and J. Mayer (1992). Longitudinal study of three program models for language minority students: A critical examination of reported findings. *Bilingual Research Journal* 16(1–2): 105–157.

First Amendment Center (1999a). *Teacher guide to religion in the public school.* Washington, DC.

First Amendment Center (1999b). *Public school and religious communities.* Washington, DC.

Fishman, J. (1976). *Bilingual education: An international sociological perspective.* Rowley, MA: Newbury House.

Galindo, R. (1997). Language wars: The ideological dimensions of the debates on bilingual education. *Bilingual Research Journal* 21(2–3) (Spring–Summer): 103–141.

Galston, W. (1991). *Liberal purposes.* New York: Cambridge University Press.

Gautherin, J. (2000). Au nom de la laïcité, Pénélope et Jules Ferry. In *L'école dans plusieurs mondes.* J.-L. Derouet, ed. Bruxelles: De Boecke.

Gibson, M., and J. Ogbu (1991). *Minority status and schooling: A comparative study of immigrants and involuntary minorities.* New York: Garland.

Gillborn, D. (1995). *Racism and antiracism in real schools: Theory, policy, practices.* Buckingham, UK: Open University Press.

Glazer, N. (1997). *We are all multiculturalists now.* Cambridge, MA: Harvard University Press.

Glenn, J. U., and E. De Jong (1996). *Educating immigrant children: Schools and language minorities in twelve nations.* New York: Garland.

Greene, J. (1998). *A Meta-analysis of the effectiveness of bilingual education.* Claremont, CA: Thomas Rivera Policy Center.

Grinter, R. (1992). Multicultural or antiracist education? The need to choose. In *Cultural diversity and the schools, Volume one: Education for cultural diversity: Convergence and divergence.* J. Lynch, C. Modgil, and S. Modgil eds. London: Falmer Press.

Grosjean, F. (1982). *Life with two languages.* Cambridge, MA: Harvard University Press.

Guttman, A. (1987). *Democratic education.* Princeton, NJ: Princeton University Press.

Hakuta, K. (1986). *Mirror of language. The debate on bilingualism.* New York: Basic Books.

Halstead, J. M. (1986). *The case for Muslim voluntary aided schools: Some philosophical reflections.* London: Islamic Academy.

Hohl, J., and M. Normand (1996). La prise en compte de la diversité culturelle et religieuse dans les normes et pratiques de gestion des établissements scolaires:

balises psychopédagogiques. *Revue française de pédagogie* (October–December): 39–52.

Holmes, B. (1981). *Comparative education: Some considerations of method.* London: George Allen & Unwin.

Homan, R. (1992). Separate schools. In *Cultural diversity and the schools, Volume one: Education for cultural diversity: convergence and divergence* J. Lynch, C. Modgil, and S. Modgil, eds. Pp. 59–72. London: Falmer Press.

Johnson, J., and R. Acera (1999). *Hope for urban education: A study of nine high performing, high poverty urban elementary schools.* Report on method to the U.S. Department of Education Planning and Evaluation Services. Houston: Charles A. Donna Center, University of Texas.

Katz, J. Y. (1992). Educational interventions for prejudice reduction and integration in elementary schools. In *Cultural diversity and the schools, volume two: Prejudice, polemics, or progress?* J. Lynch, C. Modgil, and S. Modgil, eds. Pp. 257–271. London: Falmer Press.

Kepel, G. (1989). L'intégration suppose que soit brisée la logique communautaire. In *École et intégration des immigrés.* Problèmes politiques et sociaux, no. 693. C. Wihtol de Wenden and A. M. Chartier, eds. Paris: La Documentation française.

Krashen, S. (1996). *Under attack: The case against bilingual education.* Culver City, CA: Language Education Associates.

Kymlicka, W. (1995). *Multicultural citizenship.* Oxford: Clarendon Press.

Laferrière, M. (1983). L'éducation des enfants des groupes minoritaires au Québec: De la définition des problèmes par les groupes eux-mêmes à l'intervention de l'État. *Sociologie et société* 15(2): 117–132.

Lantheaume, F. (2002) *L'enseignement de l'histoire de la colonisation et de la decolonisation de l'Algérie depuis les années trente: État-nation, identité nationale, critique et valeurs. Essai de sociologie du curriculum.* Paris: EHESS, INRP.

Lê Thanh K. (1981). *L'éducation comparée.* Paris: Armand Colin.

Leman, J. (1999). School as a structuring force in interethnic hybridism. *International Journal of Educational Research* 31: chapter 8, 341–353.

Lorcerie, F. (1996). À propos de la crise de la laïcité en France: dissonnance normative. In *Pluralisme, citoyenneté et éducation,* F. Gagnon, M. McAndrew, and M. Pagé, eds. Pp. 121–136. Montréal: L'Harmattan.

Lorcerie, F., and M. McAndrew (1993) Modèles, transferts et échanges d'expériences en éducation: le cas de l'éducation interculturelle en France et au Québec. In *Modèles, transferts et échanges d'expériences en éducation: Nécessité d'une analyse conceptuelle et d'une réflexion méthodologique.* R. Toussaint and O. Galatanu, eds. Pp. 203–219. Actes du 21e colloque annuel de l'Association Francophone d'Éducation Comparée, 1995. Trois-Rivières: Publications de l'Université du Québec à Trois-Rivières.

Mackey, W. (1970). A typology of bilingual education. In *Bilingual schooling in the United States.* T. Anderson and M. Boyer, eds. Austin, TX: Southwest Educational Development Laboratory.

Mahieu, P. (1999). Minorities, policies and strategies in Europe: A Belgian (Flemish) view. In *Cultural identities and ethnic minorities in Europe.* D. Turton and J. Gonzalez, eds. Pp. 35–42. Bilbao, Spain: University of Deusto.

McAndrew, M. (1996a). "Diversité culturelle et religieuse: divergences des rhétoriques, convergences des pratiques?" In *Pluralisme, citoyenneté et éducation*. F. Gagnon, M. McAndrew, and M. Pagé, eds. Pp. 287–317. Montréal: Éditions l'Harmattan.

McAndrew, M. (1996b). Model of common schooling and interethnic relations: A comparative analysis of policies and practices in the United States, Israel, and Northern Ireland. *Compare* 26(3): 333–345.

McAndrew, M. (2001). *Immigration et diversité à l'école. Le débat québécois dans une perspective comparative*. Montréal: Presses de l'Université de Montréal.

McAndrew, M. (2002). Ethnic relations and education in divided societies: Belgium, Catalonia, Northern Ireland, Quebec. *Kolor, Journal on Moving Communities* 1: 5–19.

McAndrew, M. (2003a). School spaces and the construction of ethnic relations: Conceptual and policy debates. *Canadian Ethnic Studies/Études ethniques au Canada* 35(2): 14–29.

McAndrew, M. (2003b). Should national minorities/majorities share common institutions or control their own schools? A comparison of policies and debates in Quebec, Northern Ireland, and Catalonia. In *The social construction of diversity: Recasting the master narrative of industrial nations*. D. Juteau and C. Harzig, eds. Pp. 369–424. New York: Berghahn Press.

McAndrew, M. (2005). The hijab controversies in Western public schools: Contrasting conceptions of ethnicity and ethnic relations. In *The making of the Islamic diaspora*. S. Rahnema and H. Moghissi, eds. Toronto: University of Toronto Press.

McAndrew, M., and C. Cicéri (1998). Immigration, diversity, and multilingual education: The Canadian example. *Zeitschrift für internationale erziehungs- und socialwissenschaftliche Forschung* 15(2): 295–322.

McAndrew, M., and M. Ledoux (1998). Identification et evaluation de l'impact relative des facteurs influençant la dynamique de concentration ethnique dans les écoles de langue française de l'île de Montréal. *Revue canadienne des sciences régionales* 20(1–2): 195–216.

McAndrew, M., C. Cicéri, and M. Jacquet (1997). La prise en compte de la diversité culturelle et religieuse dans les normes et pratiques de gestion des établissements scolaires: Une étude exploratoire dans cinq provinces canadiennes. *Revue des sciences de l'éducation* 23(1): 209–232.

McDonnell, M. W. (1992). Accommodation of religions: An update and a response to the critics. *George Washington Review* 60: 685–687.

McLaughlin, T. H. (1992). Citizenship, diversity and education: A philosophical perspective. *Journal of Moral Education* 21(3): 235–250.

McMillan, Robert. (2001). Competition, parental involvement, and public school performance. In *Proceedings of the Annual Meeting of the National Tax Association* (93rd, Santa Fe, NM, November 9–11, 2000). Washington, DC: National Tax Association.

Morelli, A. (ed.) (1992). *Histoire des étrangers et de l'immigration en Belgique de la préhistoire à nos jours*. Bruxelles: Éditions EVO et CBAI, collection EVO-Histoire.

Nagel, T. (1994). *Égalité et partialité.* C. Beauvillard, trans. Paris: PUF.

Nash, G. B. (1996). Multiculturalism and history: Historical perspectives and present prospects. In *Public education in a multicultural society. Policy, theory, critique.* R. K. Fullinwider, ed. Pp. 183–202. New York: Cambridge University Press.

National Research Council (1997). *Improving schooling for language minority children: A research agenda.* Washington, DC: Commission on Behavioral and Social Sciences and Education, Committee on Developing a Research Agenda on the Education of Limited English Proficiency and Bilingual Students.

OECD. See Organisation for Economic Co-operation and Development.

Organisation for Economic Co-operation and Development (1987). *L'éducation multiculturelle.* Paris: Centre pour l'innovation et la recherche en éducation.

Orfield, G., and S. E. Eaton (1996). *Dismantling desegregation: The quiet reversal of* Brown vs. Board of Education. Harvard Project on School Desegregation. New York: New Press.

Pagé, M. (in collaboration with J. Provencher and D. Ramirez) (1993). *Courants d'idées actuels en éducation des clientèles scolaires multiethniques.* Québec: CSE.

Painchaud, G., A. d'Anglejan, F. Armand, and M. Jesak (1993). Diversité culturelle et littératie. In Pluralisme et éducation: Perspectives québécoises. M. McAndrew, ed. Special issue, *Repères, Essais en éducation* 15: 77–94.

Palmer, H. (1984). Reluctant host: Anglo-Canadian views of multiculturalism in the 20th century. In *Cultural diversity and Canadian education.* J. Mallea and C. J. Young, eds. Ottawa: Carleton University Press.

Parsons, T., and R. Bales, eds. (1955). *Family, socialization and interaction process.* New York: Free Press.

Paulston, C. (1980). *Bilingual education: Theories and issues.* Rowley, MA: Newbury House.

Payet, J. P. (1999). L'école et la question de l'immigration en France. Une mise à l'épreuve. In *Les politiques d'immigration et d'intégration au Canada et en France: Analyses comparées et perspectives de recherche.* M. McAndrew, A. C. Découflé, and C. Cicéri, eds. Pp. 353–369. Paris: Ministère de l'Emploi et de la Solidarité sociale; Ottawa: CRSH.

Phinney, J. S. (1990). Ethnic identity in adolescents and adults: Review of research, *Psychological Bulletin* 108(3): 499–514.

Rawls, J. (1993). *Political liberalism.* New York: Columbia University Press.

Renaerts, M. (1999). Processes of homogenization in the Muslim educational world in Brussels. *International Journal of Educational Research* 31: chapter 3, 283–294.

Sammons, P., J. Hillman, and P. Mortimore (1995). *Key characteristics of effective schools: A review of school effectiveness research.* London: University of London Institute of Education.

Samuda, R., J. W. Berry, and M. Laferrière, eds. (1983). *Multiculturalism in Canada: Social and educational perspectives.* Toronto: Allyn & Bacon.

Schwartz, W. (1996). How well are charter schools serving urban and minority students? *ERIC/CUE Digest* (219).

Shahid, W., and P. Van Koningsveld (1996). Politics and Islam in Western Europe: An introduction. In *Muslims in the margin: Political responses to the presence of Islam in Western Europe*. W. Shahid and P. Van Koningsveld, eds. Pp. 1–14. Kampen, The Netherlands: Kok Pharos.

Smith, A. (1981). *The ethnic revival*. New York: Cambridge University Press.

Suárez-Orozco, C., and M. Suárez-Orozco (2001). *Children of immigration*. The Developing Child series. Cambridge, MA: Harvard University Press.

Suárez-Orozco, C., and I. L. G. Todorova (2003). Understanding the social world of immigrant youth. In *New directions for youth development: Theory, practice, and research*. G. Noam and S. Barry, eds. San Francisco: Jossey-Bass.

Suárez-Orozco, C., M. Suárez-Orozco, and F. Doucet (2003). The academic engagement and achievement of Latino youth. In *Handbook of research on multicultural education*. 2nd ed. J. A. Banks and C. A. McGee Banks, eds. Pp. 420–437. San Francisco: Jossey-Bass.

Stasi, B. (2003). *Rapport au président de la République*. Rapport de la Commission de réflexion sur l'application du principe de laïcité dans la République. December 11. Paris.

Swann, L. (1985). *Education for All*. Final report of the Committee of Inquiry into the Education of Children from Ethnic Minority. CMND 9453. London: Her Majesty's Stationery Office.

Taylor, C. (1992). *Multiculturalism and the politics of recognition*. Princeton, NJ: Princeton University Press.

Thornberry, P., and D. Gibbons (1997). Education and minority rights: A short survey of international standards. *International Journal on Minority and Group Rights* 4(2), 115–152.

Touraine, A (1994). *Qu'est-ce que la démocratie?* Paris: Fayard.

U.S. Department of Education (1999). *The state of charter schools*. Third Year Report. National Study of Charter Schools. May. Washington, DC: Office of Educational Research and Improvement; National Institute on Student Achievement Curriculum and Assessment. www.head.gov/pubs/chartertrdyear/title.html.

Van Haecht, A. (1998). Les politiques éducatives: figures exemplaires des politiques publiques. *Éducation et Sociétés, numéro spécial L'éducation, l'État et le Local*, 1. Revue internationale de sociologie de l'éducation. Paris: INRP; Bruxelles: De Boeck.

Van Zanten, A. (1997). Territerriolisation et recomposition des politiques, des modes de fonctionnement et des pratiques de scolarisation dans les milieux difficiles. In *La scolarisation dans les milieux difficiles: politique, processus et pratiques*. A. Van Zanten, ed. Paris: Institut national de recherches pédagogiques, Centre Alain Savary.

Walford, G. (1996). Diversity and choice in school education: An alternative view. *Oxford Review of Education* 22(2): 143–154.

Waugh, E. H., S. McIrvin Abu-Laban, and R. Burckhardt Qureshi, eds. (1991). *Muslim families in North America*. Edmonton: University of Alberta Press.

Willis, C. W., and M. Alves (1996). *Controlled choice: A new approach to desegregated education and school improvement*. Providence, RI: Education Alliance Press; New England Desegregation Assistance Center, Brown University.

TWELVE

Eugeen Roosens

FIRST-LANGUAGE AND -CULTURE
LEARNING IN LIGHT OF GLOBALIZATION

*The Case of Muslims in Flanders
and in the Brussels Area, Belgium*

EDUCATION IN FIRST LANGUAGE AND CULTURE

In November 2003 the Flanders Forum of Ethnocultural Minorities was
held in the Flemish parliament building. More than three hundred representatives of various immigrant organizations—mostly Muslim—and
their supporters participated. Several topics were identified as priorities,
one of them being education. Although the poor academic performance
of non-EU minority children was widely recognized as problematic (see
Crul; Süssmuth, both this volume), "first-language and -culture education" was selected as the major topic of the day (Ahalli 2003).

Forum participants concluded that L&C1 was never taken seriously
nor incorporated as a full-fledged part of the school program in Flanders
or the Flemish-language schools of the Brussels area. Furthermore, no personnel were professionally trained to teach these subjects. Where L&C1
was introduced, it was left in the hands of teachers hailing from the immigrant students' countries of origin, such as Turkey or Morocco. Generally speaking, these educators were ill prepared, did not know Dutch or
Flemish, and were unable to collaborate with local members of the staff.
Moreover, they lacked familiarity with the social context of immigrant
communities. These negative experiences notwithstanding, nearly all the
participants in the one-day parliament were firmly convinced that L&C1
should be an essential element in present education.

Based on Forum findings, it has been determined that the first step in the field of language and culture is to develop a well-conceived pedagogical project that contributes to immigrant children's well-being. Developing and keeping an emotional attachment to their first language is important for immigrant children since a first language offers emotional support that a second language does not (see McAndrew, this volume). Language courses that focus exclusively on vocabulary and grammar or the study of literature will not suffice. The courses must be adapted to the concrete circumstances of the children attending Flemish-language schools; language must be related to culture and identity formation. Migrant children are confronted with diverse systems of meaning. Successful integration of these systems and their respective components requires, at least, that the most salient elements of the cultures of origin be critically highlighted and analyzed by teachers and students (Süssmuth, this volume). Some of these elements can be used in conjunction with the first language, as building blocks of the students' identities. In this sense, L&C1 can help youngsters to synthesize the various cultural elements that they confront at home, in school, and in their peer group. Making an argument similar to Peter Gärdenfors's in this volume, members of the Forum have stated that understanding cultural patterns should be a primary concern. Intercultural "techniques" will not suffice. Unavoidably, "identity construction" is continually elaborated in the midst of cultural diversity.

Forum members realize that, to make L&C1 fully functional, a renewed intercultural way of thinking is required, putting the present Eurocentrism as well as all other ethnocentrisms in an historical and relative perspective. As compared to a North American context, the Forum's vision comes close to what Alejandro Portes and Longxin Hao (2002, pp. 907–908) are concluding based on their empirical research with American samples:

> We return to the fact that a complete transition towards English monolingualism does not represent the most desirable outcome for immigrant families or their offspring. While popular with the public at large, educational policies that promote complete linguistic assimilation contain hidden costs for these children, depriving them of a key social resource at a critical juncture in their lives. Family relations and personality development suffer accordingly. Nor does the solution lie in accelerating the language assimilation of parents[,] since results show that their linguistic skills play a minor role in children's adaptation outcomes. It is not the ability to communicate in English across generations, but the possibility of learning that language while preserving a cultural anchor

in the family's own past that leads to the most desirable results. Cut these moorings and children are cast adrift in a uniform monolingual world. They, their families, and eventually the communities where they settle will have to pay the price.

What the Forum demands is also in line with the recent work of Carola Suárez-Orozco and Marcelo Suárez-Orozco: "In these pages, we recognize how vitally important to the children's successful adaptation are the parents' ability to maintain respect for family and the child's connection to the culture of origin (2001, pp. 6–7)." Moreover, anthropological fieldwork in Brussels and Flanders shows that parents and grandparents of Moroccan immigrant children, while appreciative of academic education as provided in Belgium, are asking for more cultural and religious recognition in the school setting (Hermans 2002; Roosens 2002).

INTERCULTURAL EDUCATION

The Forum deems "intercultural education," which is practiced in quite a number of Flemish schools, to be fine and useful in its own way, but not to be an adequate replacement for L&C1. To understand this remark, let us take a closer look at intercultural education as it is conceived in Flanders today (Steunpunt Intercultureel Onderwijs 2004).

According to the university center that is supervising, promoting, and monitoring intercultural education, it is designed to teach children and youngsters how to handle "diversity." The term *diversity* as it is used in this context, however, appears somewhat overstretched, covering differences of all kind. In this sense, intercultural education can be practiced in every school, even in towns and villages where no foreigners live. Needless to say, the focus on children with an immigrant background disappears. This definition of *diversity* allows one to conveniently minimize the polarity between "us" and "them."

The advocates of intercultural education do not even care too much about "cultures." According to the supervising center, it may be better for educators not to know too much about the various cultures of the youngsters they educate, because "culture" tends to be represented stereotypically as an "essence," while real culture is always moving and changing. I agree that it is better not to discuss "culture" if conceived of as a frozen, monolithic package. But I sincerely feel that some misunderstanding has occurred here, exactly as in Christopher Clausen's *Fading Mosaic: The Emergence of Post-Cultural America* (2000), in which the author attacks a concept of culture stemming from the days of Margaret Mead. Quite a number of sophisticated books have been written about culture in the meantime. It is certainly true that a culture is unequally spread over a group of people and that it is continuously transformed, from both the inside and the outside, interpreted and reinterpreted by bearers of the culture, and so forth (Shweder 1991; Hannerz 1992). But this is no reason to discard "culture" or "cultures" as pedagogical topics. According to its advocates, intercultural education prepares children and youngsters for adulthood in society. If it avoids critiquing cultural phenomena, however, it may well miss this aim. The media and the world outside the schoolhouse door are full of discourses treating cultures as if they were things, inalterable packages, items of "heritage." Especially in times of interethnic tensions, "culture," "cultural rights," "cultural identity," and "multicultural society"—whether cherished or deplored—are concepts and phenomena that must be critically discussed.

ANTI-MULTICULTURALISM

Given the xenophobia spreading today through the media and political discourse, the L&C1 demands of the Forum may appear naive. The few politicians who still dare to "do something for the migrants" never bring up the issue (see also Süssmuth, this volume). When they do broach education from a migration perspective, they tend to discuss means to improve the academic performance of immigrant students so as to provide them "equal chances" in the labor market (Departement Onderwijs 2004). In fact, this question, more than any other, is of primary concern for immigrant organizations and individuals (Pôle européen 2004). At the moment, unemployment among unskilled and low-skilled non-EU immigrants and their children is four to five times higher than among native Belgians (Manço 2004). As far as I can see, this serious problem is similar to one a number of American academics discuss in various recent studies (Ogbu 2003; C. Suárez-Orozco & M. Suárez-Orozco 1995, 2001; Thernstrom & Thernstrom 2003). Put in this context, "first-language and -culture education" may seem antithetical to school success, as it siphons time from more academic subjects. Even some Muslim circles are convinced that academic courses should be the first priority. A recent example is the Lucerna Colleges, Flemish-language private schools founded by Surcu immigrant Turks in 2003 that require a double load of Dutch- (or Flemish-) language courses in order to improve the academic performance of students (Roosens 2004).

Still other adverse factors must be considered here. In the Netherlands, Pim Fortuyn, before he was murdered in 2002 by a Dutch extremist, proclaimed the Netherlands "full": immigrants were no longer welcome. In November 2004 the deceased Fortuyn was nearly elected in a poll conducted by a popular TV show as the most important Dutchman in history. "Foreigners," especially Muslims, were openly and widely stigmatized as a problem. Two years after Fortuyn's death, Theo van Gogh, a popular Dutch columnist and filmmaker who tended to ridicule Islam and Muslims in his writings and artistic work, was murdered by a young second-generation Muslim in a kind of ritual slaughter. In the Netherlands, the idea was broadcast in the media and through political debates that Fortuyn and van Gogh had paid with their lives for freedom of speech. They were widely considered heroes. Following van Gogh's death, some twenty mosques and Islamic schools were set afire. In the last few years, multiculturalism and so-called cultural relativism have been widely ridiculed.

What happened recently in the Netherlands has strongly influenced the general atmosphere in Belgium, specifically in Flanders. The media have been asking politicians if events in the Netherlands could also occur in Belgium. "Civil integration"—learning the local language, becoming familiar with the main Belgian institutions, and accepting basic local democracy and other values—has been the leading slogan in immigration policy, lip service to "diversity" notwithstanding (Keulen 2004). Indeed, the concept of a multicultural society has not been mentioned in recent elections. In immigration matters, the "clash of civilizations" between Islam and the West has become the dominant issue.

Implementation of L&CI appears an unlikely dream if one considers the policies recently developed and promoted by the Vlaams Belang, which, though condemned as racist (when it went by the name Vlaams Blok), is the largest political party in Flanders, having received 25 percent of the vote throughout Flanders and more than 33 percent in Antwerp. The Vlaams Belang wants to impose a "civil integration" (*inburgering*) procedure. Its policy proposal includes the following (from the leading newspaper *De Standaard*, Dec. 10, 2004):

1. All immigration must be stopped, and all government decrees and rulings that "pamper" migrants must be revoked.

2. All non-EU and non-Belgian migrants (approximately 120,000) who want to stay in Belgium have to take a "civil integration examination." If they fail, they will be forced to enroll in a

course at their own expense and will have to take the examination a second time.

3. Neither Belgian nationality nor the right to become a permanent resident should be extended without examination.

4. A basic examination of "candidate immigrants" must be organized at the Belgian embassies in the respective countries of origin. If the candidate passes, she or he will still have to take the "civil integration examination" after arriving in Belgium.

5. Candidates who pass the exam will be screened in a "neighborhood evaluation" in which native-born neighbors serve as judges.

6. The candidate will have to sign a contract and take an oath in front of a Flemish council of civil integration (still to be established). The contract will stipulate that the newcomer shall respect the law and will adapt to the culture, norms, values, and traditional principles of Western civilization.

7. The official recognition of Islam (effectuated in Belgium in 1974) must be revoked, as Islam is creating a new societal "pillar" impeding integration.

8. All mosques and Qur'anic schools located in the center of cities or towns must be moved to more "neutral outskirts."

In addition to the Vlaams Belang, a large part of the population believes that a "multicultural society" is a leftist illusion (Roosens, working with about fifty discussion groups spread across Flanders and Brussels in 2000–06; *De Standaard,* Jan. 8–9, 2005). The abusive term *multiculti*—a naive leftist activist who still advocates multiculturalism—which is widely used in the Netherlands, is popping up in Belgium as well. With regard to this topic, many Flemings' feelings resemble those of a number of Americans, including such scholars as Huntington (2004), Hollinger (2002), Barry (2001), and Clausen (2000). Even in Canada, where the term *multicultural society* was coined, the Department of Multicultural Affairs has disappeared, and "integration" has become a dominant idea (Kordan 1997). In academic discourse, "assimilation" is no longer a pariah notion (Brubaker 2001; Alba & Nee 2003).

A limited number of academics and intellectuals, however, as well as a rising number of minority leaders, have not given up on multiculturalism (Roosens 1997, 2005; Timmerman et al. 2002), even if in the form of a low-key, "rethought" project in the vein of Parekh's *Rethinking Multiculturalism* (2000).

ANOTHER FACE OF "REALITY": AN ALREADY ESTABLISHED ISLAM

In the field of immigration studies, political discourse and debate, as well as the media and social research, have increasingly focused on Muslims and Islam, especially since the Rushdie affair; 9/11; March 11, 2003 in Madrid; and 7/7 and 21/7/2005 in London. Moreover, extremely high rates of unemployment among Muslims, marked street crime, and relative school failure have been publicized in Belgium as in most other European countries (Pew Forum 2004). For their part, Moroccans and, to a lesser degree, Turks—the major Muslim groups in Flanders—have begun identifying more and more as Muslims first, turning the term *Muslim* into an ethnoreligious notion and thus associating the events in Muslim countries with their identity more closely than before.

The approximately 400,000 Muslims living in Belgium (4 percent of the population) will not go away. Approximately 240,000 of them are already Belgian citizens (Manço 2004); their percentage of the total population is rising as a result of high birth rates. One-third of all Muslims are under the age of fifteen, compared to one-fifth of the general population.

Although a significant number of cultural (including religious) elements imported by the first generation have vanished and hybridization continues, family, ethnic, and religious ties, along with a number of linguistic (Janssens 2001) and cultural traits, have not disappeared, much less transnational bonds with kin and locations of origin (Foblets & Pang 1999; Swyngedouw et al. 1999; Timmerman 1999; Timmerman et al. 1999; Vranken et al. 2001; Roosens 2005).

The media, public debate, policy statements, and the current vogue of anti-multiculturalism all underestimate the resilience of an already established Islamic reality in Brussels and Flanders. What low-educated immigrants hailing from Muslim countries have achieved by founding mosques, Qur'anic schools, cultural centers, and other organizations is still hidden in the shadows. A multifaceted Muslim civil society has developed that is internally fragmented but is becoming more homogeneous and less conditioned by ethnic origins (Renaerts 1999). In light of these undeniable facts, the Forum's demands may be more realistic and reasonable than they look at first glance.

When one takes a closer look at Islam in Belgium, a quite complex picture emerges. In part due to an immigration trend that has continued for more than forty years, a large number of local communities of immigrants who hail mostly from Morocco and Turkey have taken shape. Most first-generation immigrants still keep in touch with the kin they left behind. Many families have a vacation home in their country of origin. Many marriage partners are chosen in the homeland and imported as bride or groom[1] (Lesthaeghe 2000; De Standaard, Dec. 16–17, 2006). The influx of first-generation immigrants has not stopped.

Most Muslim immigrants belong to an Islamic network of people with a specific ethnic or regional background. Due to this diversity, nothing like an "Islamic church" is to be found in Belgium, only a juxtaposition of ethnoreligious groups and networks. Umbrella organizations have been created, but even these are quite diverse in religious tradition and cultural content. The authors of an important recent report counted 328 mosques, 162 of them in Flanders, 89 in Wallonia, and 77 in Brussels. An impressive number of Islamic currents are spread over these various mosques. On the Turkish side the Diyanet, Milli Görüs, Süleymanli, Cemaat-I Nur, Naks ibendi brotherhood, Kadirii brotherhood, and Alevite community are the most important entities. On the Arabophone side, one finds, among others, the following political currents: neo-Islamists, neofundamentalists/Salafii, and Jama'at al-Tabligh (wa 'I-Da'wa) (Kanmaz & El Battiui 2004, pp. 18–22).

There is a second crucial question to consider. Mosques and congregations of mosques are not purely religious institutions in the Christian sense of the term. Numerous mosques also function as cultural centers, language schools, and cafeterias and house voluntary associations (Renaerts 1999; Kaçar 2002, pp. 179–180). Already at the end of the twentieth century, more than seven hundred migrant voluntary associations, many of them founded by Muslims, have been registered in Flanders and Brussels (Intercultureel Centrum voor Migranten 1996). The Vlaams Belang leaders rightly state that a kind of Muslim "pillar," an Islamic civil society, has been developing over the years and that more is at stake than the establishment of a religious body or a kind of church.

In addition, sporadic voices can be heard among immigrant young adults, especially university graduates (Kaçar 2002, pp. 179), who are calling for the development of a European Islam (Bousetta, 2002) along lines suggested by Tariq Ramadan (2004) and studied and described by a number of academics (see chapters in Haddad 2002; Esposito & Burgat

2003; Manço 2004). It is noteworthy that the Catholic cardinal-archbishop of Belgium is openly encouraging this "Europeanization" of Islam.

In relation to these questions, education becomes particularly important. For decades now, youngsters born and raised by Muslim immigrant parents have had only their religious organizations as sources of knowledge about their history, culture, and language of origin. The only other sources are elective courses on Islam taught in schools. As already mentioned, these lessons are provided by teachers most of whom are recruited in the students' respective countries of origin and who have no knowledge of social, political, religious, or cultural realities in Belgium. It is not surprising, then, that some youngsters, lacking solid religious education, turn to their imagination and "invent" their own Islam, opening the door to all sorts of political manipulation (*De Standaard,* Nov. 28–27, 2004).

In other words, while federal and regional policy makers are launching programs to integrate immigrants by making them accept "our values" and learn "our language," they continue to leave the youngsters in the hands of the imported traditional sector, as far as learning their culture and language and the history of their religion is concerned. For the vast majority of children and grandchildren of immigrants, there is no rational, critical counterweight whatsoever.

What Gary Freeman writes about Western democracies in general certainly applies to Belgium: "No state possesses a truly coherent incorporation regime. Instead, one finds ramshackle, multifaceted, loosely connected sets of regulatory rules, institutions, and practices in various domains of society that together make up the frameworks within which migrants and natives work out their differences" (Freeman 2004, p. 946).

And still another urgent question must be looked at: more than 240,000 Turkish and Moroccan immigrants and their children and grandchildren have become Belgian citizens (Manço 2004). They are Belgians now. Many have double nationality. The children and grandchildren of the immigrants, the so-called second and third generations, are addressing the situation in a discourse and style borrowed from the surrounding dominant majority (Bousetta 2002). Sporadically, the question is raised among "new Belgians" what kind of cultural rights they are entitled to. The Flemings have their Flemish Community, their Flemish Region, their Flemish language; the Walloons and the relatively small number (some 71,000) of Germanophone Belgians have their own institutions. What about the "new Belgians"? Will they learn only that they are newcomers and that newcomers must always "adapt"? That they had better forget their own language, cultural traits, ethnic background, and history, or at least consider all this a private matter, while even the color of their skin will continue to mark them in public as different? Will primordial autochthony prevail (Roosens 1998)?

It seems to me that a number of developments point toward a rebirth of multicultural society, this time more low-key but openly supported by hard facts: the mosques and their networks and communities, and an incisive modern European political discourse among better-educated, upwardly mobile children and grandchildren of immigrants.

AN ETHNONATIONALLY ORIENTED ENVIRONMENT

It is understandable, then, that the representatives of ethnocultural minorities are not content with "intercultural education" alone and find "diversity" an almost empty, too fluid a term. What they ask for is substance—language, history, ways of looking at life, family, fine arts, and the like. This is exactly what the Flemings have been fighting for over several decades. In a certain way, native federal Belgium, the host country of immigration, is firmly organized according to "ethnic" principles: locality, language, school, and descent constitute one's identity at the substate level. This native framework strongly suggests to newcomers that sticking to one's "identity" and refusing to be absorbed by "others" is a self-evident necessity.

On top of this, thousands of European civil servants and their families, as well as NATO military personnel, are living in the Brussels and Flemish areas, together with numerous foreign businesspeople and diplomats. Only very rarely has there been any protest against the formidable presence of these well-to-do "strangers" who continue to speak their own languages, visit their home countries, and maintain numerous cultural traits of their own. There are a British School, a Lycée Jean Monnet, an American School, and a Deutsche Schule, not to mention the European Schools that teach main parts of their curricula in the first languages of their "international" students. The three thousand Japanese expatriates and immigrants have there own Japanese School, imported from Japan, with Japanese staff, Japanese curricula, the Japanese language, and even a Japanese school calendar of the academic year (Pang 1995). The natives, both Francophones and Flemings, have been and continue to be tolerant toward foreign residents "who cause no harm in the streets" and contribute to the local economy, whatever their faith, political convictions, dress, or family structure.

Another "unassimilated" minority that has been left undisturbed by the Vlaams Belang and other rightist organizations are the well-to-do Jews of Antwerp, particularly the "visible" Hassidim (Abicht 2004). Between 85 percent and 90 percent of the children of the Jewish community of Antwerp attend separate private schools. Children of this community attend one of three different types of private schools: those that are subsidized by the government and add ten hours of religion taught in Hebrew to the regular curriculum; private schools that are not subsidized and are partly secular and partly religious; or private nonsubsidized schools that are entirely religious. Abicht (2004) claims that these types of schools are not preparing youth for living with their peers from the native community or from other minorities. Moreover, religion is strongly emphasized, much more so than in other schools. On top of this, Antwerp Jews tend to maintain good relations with Israel. They strongly support Israel, spend vacations in that country, welcome visitors from Israel, and speak the official Israeli language in Antwerp.

Immigrants who lack social, economic, cultural, or political capital and who hail from poor countries, especially those who are Muslim, constitute, together with their children and grandchildren, an entirely different category and are kept in this status even after becoming Belgian citizens. Will this situation persist within a thoroughly democratic state?

CONCLUSIONS

To conclude, I offer the following recommendations:

Leading Muslims and local politicians agree that Islamic teachers and imams must be educated in Belgium, by Belgian faculties at Belgian schools, and that their teachings must be controlled and supervized in conformity with Belgian laws, rules, and regulations. Courses for teachers of Islam were started at one local institute of higher education a couple of years ago.

As stated above, the themes developed in this chapter are suitable for pedagogical adaptation for a course on "culture," ethnicity, and the recent history of migration. Classes must take a critical stance. I agree with Unni Wikan when she writes (in this volume) about honor-based violence: "'Honor' gone astray fuels fundamentalist and antihumane practices and processes. By delinking honor from violence and reconnecting it with human rights, we can transcend barriers between cultures and form an agenda for our time."

A course on comparative religion that highlights religions as cultural and historical phenomena must also be offered.

The above-mentioned courses should be compulsory for all youngsters, even in schools where no immigrant children are enrolled.

Language courses may be offered as electives. Johan Leman (1999) has shown through longitudinal studies that adolescents who have attended "bicultural and trilingual" primary education—in their first language, in Dutch, and in French—are neither linguistically, culturally, nor ethnically "disoriented." Nor are they locked up in their ethnoculture of origin; rather, their attitudes toward language and ethnic belonging tend to hybridize.

The study of Islam may remain programmed as an elective, as it has been since 1975.

I thus fully agree with Marie McAndrew (in this volume), who, after a painstaking review of existing theories, concludes: "Whenever family and school hold different norms, values, or codes of conduct, which is unavoidable in the context of migration, the aim should not necessarily be harmonization but respect, or at least avoidance of detrimental judgments about the other party." I would go a step further, however, and join Rita Süssmuth (in this volume) in concluding: "Most school curricula do not consider that today's youth—immigrant or native—are learning, interacting, and living in an environment that is connected (with varying intensity) to different values, cultures, language groups, levels of economic development, and educational systems. . . . To meet this challenge, youth need to develop intercultural skills." This is not naive daydreaming. The Tensta Gymnasium in Stockholm, which serves neighborhoods of underprivileged families and children, shows how this can brilliantly be achieved and combined with academic excellence.

Maurice Crul's contribution to this volume proves how useful cross-national comparisons can be in revealing best practices in programming curricula. It would be very rewarding to find out the extent to which courses in "first language and culture" can be combined with improving the school performance of immigrant youth. Experiments and successful implementations in this field in Canada, the United States, and various European countries, such as the Brussels Foyer Schools and the European Schools, could be retraced and compared (Roosens 1997). It would also be rewarding to find out what proportion of successful precollegiate and undergraduate children of non-EU Muslim immigrant workers are "radicalized," become "Europeanized" Muslims, or simply "lose their faith." A comparison between the United Kingdom, Germany, France, and Belgium would be revealing, given the particular histories and present contexts of these four states.

NOTE

1. Seventy-four percent of the Turkish young men "imported" a bride and 68 percent of the women imported a groom in the 1980s. The figures for the Moroccans were 57 percent and 56 percent, respectively (Lesthaeghe 2000). In 2005, roughly 70 percent of youngsters of Turkish background and 50 percent of their Moroccan counterparts imported their marriage partners from their parents' country of origin (estimates from government circles; research by the University of Antwerp, reported in *De Standaard,* Dec. 16–17, 2006).

REFERENCES

Abicht, L. (2004). *De joden van Antwerpen* (The Jews of Antwerp). Antwerp: Houtekiet.

Ahalli, F., et al., eds. (2003). *Een minderhedenparlement voor een dag: Verslagboek & conclusies* (A one-day minorities parliament: Report and conclusions). Brussels: Forum voor Etnisch-Culturele Minderheden.

Alba, R., and V. Nee (2003). *Remaking the American mainstream: Assimilation and contemporary immigration.* Cambridge, MA: Harvard University Press.

Barry, B. (2001). *Culture equality.* Cambridge: Polity.

Bousetta, H., ed. (2002). *Rompre le silence. Une prise de position citoyenne d'intellectuels belges d'origine maghrébine sur les événements qui ont marqué l'année* (Breaking the silence: A citizens' statement by Belgian intellectuals of Maghreb origin about notable incidents of the year). Brussels: Éditions Labor.

Brubaker, R. (2001). The return of assimilation? Changing perspectives on immigration and its sequels in France, Germany and the United States. *Ethnic and Racial Studies* 24(4): 531–548.

Byram, M. and J. Leman, eds. (1990). *Bicultural and trilingual education: The Foyer model in Brussels.* Clevedon, UK: Multilingual Matters.

Clausen, C. (2000). *Faded mosaic: The emergence of post-cultural America.* Chicago: Ivan R. Dee.

Departement Onderwijs (2004). *Gelijke onderwijskansen voor elk kind . . . scholen maken er werk van!* (Equal chances in education for each child . . . schools work on it!). Brussels: Ministry of the Flemish Community, Department of Education.

Esposito, J., and F. Burgat, eds. (2003). *Modernizing Islam: Religion in the public sphere in Europe and the Middle East.* London: Hurst.

Foblets, M. C., and C. L. Pang, eds. (1999). *Culture, ethnicity, and migration.* Leuven, Belgium: Acco.

Freeman, G. (2004). Immigrant incorporation in western democracies. *International migration review* 38(3): 945–969.

Haddad, Y., ed. (2002). *Muslims in the West: From sojourners to citizens.* Oxford: Oxford University Press.

Hannerz, U. (1992). *Cultural complexity: Studies in the social organization of meaning.* New York: Columbia University Press.

Hermans, P. (2002). Opvoeden in een "multiculturele" samenleving: Opvattingen, idealen, praktijken en problemen van Marokkaanse ouders (Education in a "multicultural" society: Views, ideals, practices, and problems of Moroccan parents). In *Allochtone jongeren in het onderwijs: Een multidisciplinair perspectief* (Allochthonous youngsters in education: A multidisciplinary perspective). Timmerman et al., eds. Pp. 21–43. Leuven, Belgium: Garant.

Hollinger, D. (2002). Not universalists, not pluralists: The new cosmopolitans find their own way. In *Conceiving cosmopolitanism: Theory, context, and practice.* S. Vertovec and R. Cohen, eds. Pp. 227–239. Oxford: Oxford University Press.

Huntington, S. (2004). *Who are we? The challenges to America's national identity.* New York: Simon & Schuster.

Intercultureel Centrum voor Migranten (1996). *Het verenigingsleven van migranten: Een nieuwe dynamiek* (Free associations of migrants: New dynamics). Brussels.

Janssens, R. (2001). *Taalgebruik in Brussel: Taalverhoudingen, taalverschuivingen en taalidentiteit in een meertalige stad* (Language use in Brussels: Language relations, language change, and language identity in a multilingual city). Brussels: VUBPRESS.

Kaçar, M. (2002). *Lucifers schikken: Als gastarbeiders burgers worden* (Ranking matches. When "guest laborers" become citizens). Antwerp: Houtekiet.

Kanmaz, M., and M. El Battiui (2004). *Moskeeën, imams en islamleerkrachten in België. Stand van zaken en uitdagingen* (Mosques, imams, and teachers of Islam in Belgium: The present situation and challenges). Brussels: Koning Boudewijnstichting.

Keulen, M. (2004). *Beleidsnota inburgering 2004–2009* (Policy note on civil integration 2004–2009). Brussels: Flemish Minister of Civil Integration.

Kordan, B. (1997). Multiculturalism, citizenship and the Canadian Nation: A critique of the proposed design of program renewal. *Canadian Ethnic Studies* 29(2): 136–142.

Laevers, F., et al. (2004). *Beter, breder en met meer kleur. Onderwijs voor kwetsbare leerlingen in Vlaanderen, een terugblik en suggesties voor de toekomst* (Better, broader, and more colorful: Education for vulnerable students in Flanders, with a hindsight and suggestions for the future). Rapport (Report).

Leman, J. (1999). Cultural hybridism and self-categorization: Trilingually and biculturally scholarized adolescents in Brussels. In *Education, ethnic homogenization, and cultural hybridization.* J. Leman, ed. Special issue, *International Journal of Educational Research* 31(4): 317–326.

Lesthaeghe, R., ed. (2000). *Communities and generations: Turkish and Moroccan populations in Belgium.* Brussels: VUBPRESS.

Manço, U., ed. (2004). *Reconnaissance et discrimination: Présence de l'islam en Europe occidentale et en Amérique du Nord* (Recognition and discrimination: The presence of Islam in Western Europe and North America). Paris: L'Harmattan.

Ogbu, J. (2003). *Black American students in an affluent suburb: A study of academic disengagement.* London: Lawrence Erlbaum.

Pang, C. (1995). Controlled internationalization: The case of the "kikokushijo" from Belgium. In *Rethinking culture, "multicultural society" and the school.* E. Roosens, ed. Special issue, *International Journal of Educational Research* 23(1): 45–56.

Parekh, B. (2000). *Rethinking multiculturalism: Cultural diversity and political theory.* New York: Palgrave.

Pew Forum on Religion and Public Life (2004). *An uncertain road: Muslims and the future of Europe.* Washington, DC.

Pôle européen des fondations de l'économie sociale (2004). *Économie sociale et intégration dans la société européenne des jeunes issus de la migration* (Social economy and the integration of the children of immigration in European society). Brussels: Éducation et Culture.

Portes, A., and L. Hao (2002). The price of uniformity: Language, family, and personality adjustment in the immigrant second generation. *Ethnic and Racial Studies* 25(6) (November): 889–912.

Ramadan, T. (2004). *Western Muslims and the future of Islam.* Oxford: Oxford University Press.

Renaerts, M. (1999). Processes of homogenization in the Muslim educational world in Brussels. In *Education, ethnic homogenization, and cultural hybridization.* J. Leman, ed. Special issue, *International Journal of Educational Research* 31(4): 283–294.

Roosens, E. (1997). Education for living in pluriethnic societies. In *Preparing adolescents for the twenty-first century: Challenges facing Europe and the United States.* R. Takanishi and D. Hamburg, eds. Pp. 151–176. Cambridge: Cambridge University Press.

Roosens, E. (1998). *Eigen grond eerst? Primordiale autochtonie, dilemma van de multiculturele samenleving* (Own ground first? Primordial autochthony, a dilemma of multicultural society). Leuven, Belgium: Acco.

Roosens, E. (2002). Field research in Brussels.

Roosens, E. (2000–2006). Field research in Brussels and Flanders.

Roosens, E. (2005). Multiculturalism. In: *How to conquer the barriers to intercultural dialogue: Christianity, Islam, and Judaism.* C. Timmerman and B. Segaert, eds. Pp. 163–177. Brussels: Peter Lang.

Shweder, R. (1991). *Thinking through cultures: Expeditions in cultural psychology.* Cambridge, MA: Harvard University Press.

Steunpunt Intercultureel Onderwijs (2004). *Wat is ICO?* (What's ICO?). Gent: Universiteit Gent.

Suárez-Orozco, C., and M. Suárez-Orozco (1995). *Transformations: Migration, family life, and achievement motivation among Latino adolescents.* Stanford: Stanford University Press.

Suárez-Orozco, C., and M. Suárez-Orozco (2001). *Children of immigration.* Cambridge, MA: Harvard University Press.

Swyngedouw, M., et al., eds. (1999). *Minderheden in Brussel: Sociopolitieke houdingen en gedragingen* (Minorities in Brussels: Sociopolitical attitudes and behavior). Brussels: VUBPRESS.

Thernstrom, A., and S. Thernstrom (2003). *No excuses: Closing the racial gap in learning.* New York: Simon & Schuster Paperbacks.

Timmerman, C. (1999). *Onderwijs maakt het verschil. Socio-culturele praxis en etniciteitsbeleving bij Turkse jonge vrouwen* (Education makes the difference: Socio-cultural praxis and ethnicity among Turkish young women). Leuven, Belgium: Acco.

Timmerman, C., et al. (1999). *Integratie van tweede generatie migrantenvrouwen in Vlaanderen: Verschillende wegen tot integratie* (Integration of second generation young women in Flanders: Several ways of integration). Rapport (Report). Antwerp: UFSIA.

Timmerman, C., et al., eds. (2002). *Allochtone jongeren in het onderwijs: Een multidisciplinair perspectief* (Allochthonous youngsters in the school system: A multidisciplinary perspective). Leuven, Belgium: Garant.

Vranken, J., et al., eds. (2001). *Komende generaties: Wat weten we (niet) over allochtonen in Vlaanderen?* (Rising generations: What we know [and do not know] about allochthonous people in Flanders). Leuven, Belgium: Acco.

THIRTEEN

Unni Wikan

RETHINKING HONOR IN
REGARD TO HUMAN RIGHTS

An Educational Imperative in Troubled Times

On January 21, 2002, in the city of Uppsala, Sweden, Fadime Sahindal was shot dead, the victim of an honor killing. When Fadime was buried on February 4, 2002, Sweden set a precedent that would be hard to maintain. Attending the memorial service were the crown princess, the head of parliament, the minister of integration and equality, the minister of justice, the archbishop of Uppsala, and other dignitaries. Ten thousand carnations, Fadime's favorite flower, graced the cathedral. The ceremony was broadcast live on Swedish television.[1]

Fadime's death was a Swedish tragedy, a Swedish trauma. KURDISH WOMAN KILLED ran the morning headlines on January 22, 2002, the day after her death. But Fadime had lived in Sweden from the time she was six years old until her death at the age of twenty-six. Her memorial service testified to a person who was larger than life and who had spent a large part of her life trying to make Sweden see that freedom and liberty should be a basic human right for all people, including the children of immigrants.

"Fadime was one of the martyrs of our times," said the archbishop in her memorial speech. "Let us thank God for Fadime, that with her courage, strength and love of life, she has given heart and hope to so many."[2] The archbishop also reminded the congregation that it had once been the custom for Nordic churches to have a weaponry room where men coming to church would leave their arms before entering the sanctuary. "Let us likewise," she said, "leave feelings of bitterness and anger behind, and look ahead, forward."

It is not common for a Muslim to be given a funeral in a cathedral. But Fadime had willed it, and her family acquiesced. The ceremony transcended religious and ethnic divisions: it consisted mainly of song and music from different corners of the earth and different epochs.[3] Some Muslims insist that by letting Fadime's funeral be held in the cathedral, the family showed themselves to be heretics.[4] But according to the Qur'an it is for God alone to pass judgment. Although, like most Swedes, non-religious, Fadime's family members regard themselves as Muslims. They originate from Turkey, but currently some three hundred members are settled in Sweden. Nearly all attended Fadime's funeral.

As Fadime's coffin was about to be carried out of the cathedral, six women came forth. They were her cousins and friends, all (but one) Kurdish by descent. According to tradition, men should carry the coffin. But the women insisted, and the men had to give in. "She is ours now; you have betrayed her" was the message carried by their quiet procession.

"I know I must live with death threats till their breath expires; it is the only way they can regain their honor, their pride," Fadime had said publicly of the male members of her family, four years before she was killed by her father.

The funeral held on February 4, 2002, was for someone who had struggled for years to alert Sweden to the hazards of its integration policies, or lack thereof. She knew that she might pay with her life. But the price was not too high if she could help others, she said.

The state funeral she was given—though it was not officially labeled as such—was Sweden's way of paying tribute to a person who became an icon after her death, whereas all she had wanted was to be regarded as *en klok människa*—a wise human being.

FREEDOM AND DIGNITY

To develop as competent and responsible citizens of modern, liberal democracies, the youth of today must learn to respect not just differences—among cultures, ethnicities, and religions—but also, above all, the integrity and dignity of the individual human being. *Individual freedom as a social commitment* is Amartya Sen's formulation of what I have in mind (Sen 1990). Freedom (in Arabic, *hurriyya*) is a value that—in my experience as a social anthropologist with fieldwork experience among Muslims, Hindus, and Buddhists in different parts of the world—is uni-

versally shared.[5] This is not to deny that people disagree about what freedom means and about who should enjoy it. Power and privilege also enter
into the equation. But in general, having one's integrity respected is a universal value and is also the basis for international human rights. Hence,
liberal democracies are committed—or should be committed—to teaching and training young people to acknowledge and respect the integral
value of every individual, regardless of race, religion, ethnicity, gender,
or other characteristics.

In my book *Generous Betrayal: Politics of Culture in the New Europe*
(2002), I argue that Western European governments in general, the Scandinavian ones in particular, have failed in this regard. *Misconceived
humanism* is my term for policies that place culture above the individual. Respect for culture has been the basis for numerous official and unof-
ficial policies and projects that recognize the communal aspects of ethnic
groups and minorities but overlook or ignore individual human rights.[6]
The fear of being labeled a racist has at times led many well-meaning
liberals to support practices that have undermined the welfare and
liberty of weaker members of a group. I shall not repeat my argument
here. Instead, I focus on a particular problem related to the integration
of immigrant and refugee youth that urgently needs attention: the problem of honor or honor-based violence. This issue is now receiving increasing attention in Europe, with Sweden playing a key role. Based on my
research, I highlight key elements that must be addressed if we are to help
counter violence in the name of honor among young people, particularly
boys.

WHAT IS THE PROBLEM?

An honor code that underscores the right of the collective (clan, family,
tribe, minority) to loyalty and respect from the individual member has
a long tradition in parts of Europe, the Middle East, North Africa, and
South Asia. A large scholarly literature documents and analyzes such traditions.[7] According to the honor code, power is vested in male leaders
who have judicial authority over other group members. Honor depends
on control over the female body. Violence is endorsed if it is necessary
to maintain that control. Brothers and cousins are their sisters' and
female relatives' keepers. Disgrace or dishonor afflicts not just individuals but the collective as a whole. Honor lost can be regained by resorting to violence. Forced marriage and honor killings are linked to such
conceptions of honor, "honor killings" being the ultimate and most

extreme expression acceptable in *some* of the societies that subscribe to an honor code. Fear and threats of violence are common.

Honor in this conception is not a question of individual integrity or of being true to "one's own self." It is a matter of public opinion and reputation. "Now no one will want to marry girls in my family; with what I have done, they will think that all are whores," said Fadime after she had been spotted on the street with Patrik, her Swedish-Iranian boyfriend. Dishonor accrues when a breach of the rules of honor is exposed; *shame* is too weak a word to describe the result (Wikan 1984). The opposite of honor is no-honor—a state of utter loss of respect (Stewart 1994).

ISLAM VERSUS HONOR

The honor code as just described is not an Islamic phenomenon. It cross-cuts religious affiliations and is found among Christians, Jews, Hindus, Sikhs, and others. It is practiced in only *some* pockets and *some* groups of Muslim as well as Christian, Jewish, Hindu, and Sikh societies in North Africa, the Middle East, South Asia—and Europe. It is the European phenomenon that primarily concerns me here: the presence in Western and Northern Europe of an honor code that contravenes and jeopardizes the human rights of European citizens.

It is not Islam that constitutes the threat to basic values of freedom, liberty, and equality, but particular traditions of honor nourished, revived, and regenerated in segregated settings where all too many immigrants and refugees lead marginalized lives (see Süssmuth; Crul, both this volume). To quote the Danish-Syrian-Palestinian author and politician Naser Khader (2002), "It is the unwritten laws of honor and shame, more than religion, that reinforce the cultural inequalities between males and females, the sexual segregation, the veil, the value of virginity, and so forth. The importance of honor and shame is more problematic for integration in Denmark than the religion of Islam, which in many ways is pragmatic" (p. 143, translation mine).

HONOR AND BOYS

In Europe, as in many other places, boys of immigrant background lag behind girls in school.[8] The girls do not constitute a major problem. They tend to be diligent and committed to going to school, doing their homework, and staying in school—unless, alas, their families remove them from school for an early marriage. With boys it is different. Whereas school for girls constitutes "time off" from chores at home (cleaning, cooking, taking care of younger siblings), boys are left free to roam. While boys have freedom of movement, many girls do not (Mørck 1998). High dropout rates are a problem afflicting mainly boys. Boys "have" honor whatever they do, as long as they keep control of their female kin. Boys struggle for status and prestige among themselves, but in the diaspora the code of honor confers a certain position on them that sets them apart from and above their sisters (Lien 2002). Violence is endorsed and legitimate in defense of honor. Honor requires vigilance, being on guard.

HONOR-RELATED VIOLENCE

Forced marriage and honor killings are just two examples—albeit extreme ones—of practices linked to an honor code. All over Europe, numerous youngsters of immigrant background feel threatened by the possibility of being forced to marry, and thousands have sought protection from municipalities (e.g., social workers, police) and nongovernmental organizations (Sareen 2003; Schlytter 2004). In 2003 the Swedish government appropriated SEK 20 million (c. US $3 million) for the purpose of providing "shelters" (*skyddade boligar*) for women and teenage girls (both immigrant and nonimmigrant) exposed to violence. An amount five times as great was granted for additional action in 2004–06. In London 492 incidents related to forced marriage were reported to the metropolitan police between 2003 and 2005. Most victims were between fifteen and twenty-two years old; one in fourteen was male. In Norway more than four hundred youngsters requested assistance in 2004. "Honor" has come West and, with it, forms of violence that threaten not just the welfare but even the lives of many European citizens and residents.

Fadime had been ostracized by her family and warned, in January 1998, that she would be murdered if she ever returned to Uppsala. Her crime was having chosen her own love—Swedish-Iranian Patrik—and refusing the marriage to a cousin that her family had in mind for her. To make matters worse, she went public with the family's disgrace. She went to the media—though only after being turned down by the police when she sought their protection; and she took her father and brother to court. In the end, she violated the lease on life that her family had granted her: to remain permanently in exile,[9] never to set foot again in Uppsala. She could not endure it. She loved her mother and missed her tremendously. After three years of separation the women—the mother and three of her five daughters—took up secret meetings. They met three or four times in

Uppsala (the only place where the mother, without freedom of movement, could venture). Fadime was killed on January 21, 2002. Fadime was shot in front of her mother and two younger sisters.

Yet at the trial, no one in the family would testify except one sister, Songül. Having been warned by the family to keep silent, she appeared in court with police escort. This is also part of the honor code: to place honor above the law. Honor *is* above the law. Honor is a law unto itself.

This is why I pitied Fadime's mother when, before the court of appeal, she appeared to betray her murdered daughter and testified on behalf of the perpetrator. Fadime's close friend and lawyer, Leif Ericksson, agrees that Fadime would probably have said, "Poor Mama."

HONOR KILLINGS

Fadime was not the first victim of an honor killing in Sweden, nor the last. The Swedish police estimate that there have been one to two such killings yearly over the past twenty years (Älgamo 2004). The first case to gain public attention was that of Sara, fifteen years old, who was murdered by her brother and cousin in December 1996. The boys were sixteen and seventeen years old (Eldén 2004; Wikan 2002, pp. 91–97). The next case to gain notoriety was that of Pela, nineteen years old; her two uncles murdered her in June 1999 (Begikhani 2005; Swanberg 2003). Both Sara and Pela were of Kurdish Iraqi background. In between there were several other murders and attempted murders, but it took Fadime's case to impress upon the authorities that they had failed to give girls like her the protection they needed and, ultimately, had neglected to adequately address the issue of the integration of people like her parents and brothers. Indeed, the concept of honor killing did not gain official recognition in Sweden until after Fadime's death, although the writing had been on the wall ever since Sara's murder five years earlier. But it was deemed racist even to mention the term. Honor killings were just one form of patriarchal violence, which was universal, according to liberals and conservatives alike.[10]

Pela's murder had an awakening effect. After the trial of her killers in December 2000, the minister of integration and equality, Mona Sahlin—one of Sweden's most prominent politicians—said publicly that she had let down (*svekit*) girls of immigrant background out of fear of being called racist.[11] Pela's murder exposed the *transnational* character of honor killings increasingly apparent in many cases. Pela lived in Sweden but was brought to Iraq to be murdered. Eleven persons from three continents were involved in the plot, according to the evidence gathered by the Swedish police: three Australians (Pela's grandfather and two paternal uncles), two Swedes (the two uncles who shot her), and six Iraqi Kurds. All should have been brought to trial, according to the Swedish police. The two Swedish citizens were eventually sentenced to life imprisonment in Sweden.

After Fadime's death, the Swedish police set up a special investigation unit for honor killings, and cases that might have gone undetected as "ordinary" murders, accidents, or suicides were re-examined. The conclusion is that twenty-five to fifty honor killings have taken place over the past twenty years.[12] The British police conducted a similar investigation after the killing of Heshu Yunes in October 2002. Heshu was sixteen years old when her father murdered her.[13] The metropolitan police in London, drawing on the experiences of the Swedish police, have identified for further analysis 109 possible honor-related homicides that occurred between 1993 and 2003. Of the twenty-two cases whose investigation had been concluded by March 2005, nine were judged to be definite honor killings and another nine to be suspected honor killings; still another four were classified as not being rooted in honor-based violence.[14]

Investigation units similar to the Swedish and British may be set up in other European countries as more tragedies gain a public face. In Berlin, twenty-three-year-old Hatin Sürücü is one such critical case. She was murdered by her seventeen-year-old brother in February 2005 after she dishonored her family by divorcing her violent husband, a cousin, by a forced marriage. She may have been the sixth victim of an honor killing in Berlin over the previous four months, according to the police. Human rights organizations report that there have been forty-five honor killings in Germany since 1996.

WHAT IS AN HONOR KILLING?

The critical criterion of an honor killing is that it brings glory. It is murder with the intent of redeeming honor lost, cleansing dishonor. Hence it presupposes an acclaiming community. Without acclaim, there is no honor. It is this above else that distinguishes an honor killing from other sorts of murder. The murderer becomes a hero.

Honor killings, it must by underscored, may be seen as a last resort by those who perform or plan them. We have ample evidence that families often struggle to find ways of covering up disgrace, thus to spare a beloved's life—or to avoid what Fadime's father called "the final solution." Honor killings are not crimes of passion; they are premeditated and carefully planned. The perpetrator is not just an individual but also a collective that has a hand in the planning or even the execution of the murder. Women may also be involved. The murderer is usually a brother, father, cousin, or husband, in that order. The dishonor revenged and cleansed afflicts primarily a female's *natal* family.

Because honor is collective, any member of the group can do the deed or claim responsibility for it. Pragmatic considerations often determine the decision. In Fadime's case a cousin tried to convince the police that he was the murderer; he wanted to become a hero in the family, said some kinsmen. In Sara's case, the two young boys who killed her had evidently been picked for the job by five men, their fathers included. In Pela's case, two uncles shot her, but her father claimed to be the murderer.

A Swedish authority, Jan Hjärpe (2004), explains: "Honor killing is an act of violence with the purported reason to redeem the family's or clan's honor. This is achieved by killing the person who has shown disloyalty to his or her *own* group and thereby damaged the family's reputation. The family and its leaders are then exposed to the contempt and vilification of others within the same social network or community" (translation and italics mine). Men, too, may be victims of honor killings, but it is rare for men to be killed by their *own* families. Men are more likely to be victims of vendettas or blood feuds.[15]

TALET I RIKSDAGEN

Two months before she was killed, Fadime spoke at a conference on integration in the old parliament building in Stockholm.[16] In what has become known as *talet i Riksdagen*—"the speech in parliament"—she tried to make her parents' predicament intelligible, even to shed light on why her brother had attempted to kill her in 1998: "That just he was selected was because he was a minor and didn't risk severe punishment. Moreover, as the only son in the family, it was his duty to see to it that his sisters kept within the rules of the culture." She exonerated her parents, who were trapped in a clan tradition in which the collective good always takes priority over individual happiness. She pitied them their fate: they had lost "both their honor and a daughter." She criticized Kurdish immigrant organizations for failing to help them. But the main responsibility rested, she declared, with the Swedish state:

> Had society taken its responsibility and helped my parents to become more participatory in the Swedish society, then perhaps this might have

been avoided. What has happened to me cannot be undone, but I think it is important that one learns something from it and acts in the future so that such cases are not repeated.

I have chosen to tell you my story today in the hope that it can help other girls of immigrant background so that others need not go through what I have endured. If all carry their straw to the haystack, then things like this need not happen again. Whatever cultural background she has, it should be a matter of course for every young woman to be able to have both her family and the life she wishes to lead. Unfortunately, this is not self-evident for many girls. And I hope that you do not turn your back on them, that you do not close your eyes to them. Thank you for your attention.

IMMIGRANT INTEGRATION

Honor killings have been associated with faraway places and tribal societies. The assumption has been that honor codes as described above would vanish with the development of modern state structures in which the welfare of citizens no longer depends on their ability to derive support and security from kin connections (Hjärpe 2004). Welfare states such as those of the Scandinavian societies should, by this logic, prevent the regeneration of honor as a matter of life or death. Fadime's story is unsettling in many respects.

Her parents did *not* live in a suburban enclave, like many non-Western immigrants in Sweden. They were settled in the city of Uppsala, in an ordinary, ethnically mixed neighborhood. Her father was *not* among the unemployed in a country where non-Western immigrants are four times more likely than other residents to be without a job. Fadime's father had been employed for eighteen years in a small Swedish firm whose workers were almost all Swedish. The family had *not* been living on social welfare, as do the majority of non-Western immigrants in many of Sweden's "enclaves"—a common word for suburbs that contain up to 90 percent immigrants.[17] The Sahindals were moderately well-off.[18]

"We are a normal family," said the eldest daughter, Fidan, to the media. And they were an ordinary, normal family of hardworking people who wanted to lead comfortable, peaceful, prosperous lives and who had seized the opportunity to do so in the West when opportunities in Turkish Kurdistan were limited. Fadime described their lives in their home village as having been happy, if materially not the best. But role expectations were clear: everyone did his or her part, and the family was close-knit and contented.

Problems started in Sweden when she went to school. She was enjoined not to have Swedish friends and not to "become" Swedish. The story she tells resonates with those of numerous other girls—and boys—all over Europe who are under injunctions imposed by parents and their communities not to "become" Swedish or Danish or German or Dutch—even though that's what the children are in many cases, born or raised in Europe.[19]

The horror her family envisioned was of their nice Kurdish girl becoming a Swedish whore. As Fadime tells the story (and many others have, too), there is *no link* between "nice girl" and "Swedish girl." Fadime made it clear why her family reasoned thus: they had no Swedish friends even after a lifetime in Sweden; they lived in *utanförskap*—an evocative Swedish word that conveys the plight of being marginalized—and were horrified by gender stereotypes of Swedes that all too many impressions around them nourished. Who would want their girl to become like that? Without a "language" to speak—after twenty years in Sweden, Fadime's mother does not speak a word of Swedish and her father only a little—Fadime's parents' opportunity for communication with the wider society was limited. This background knowledge is required to understand what she meant when she spoke of society having failed to fulfill its responsibility and make her parents "more participatory" in Sweden.

"Managing difference is becoming one of the greatest challenges to multicultural countries," write Marcelo M. Suárez-Orozco and Desirée Baolian Qin-Hilliard in their introduction to *Globalization: Culture and Education in the New Millennium* (2004): "It is by interrupting 'thinking as usual'—the taken-for-granted understandings and worldviews that shape cognitive and metacognitive styles and practices—that managing difference can do the most for youth growing up today" (p. 4).

It bears mention that Fadime's parents had tried to accommodate her wish to marry Patrik. But people higher up in the family hierarchy warned that "if Fadime gets to marry Patrik, then maybe all the girls will come to marry Swedes." Decisions about marriage are made transnationally. Clan members in Turkey and elsewhere have to be consulted. Helping immigrants to *participate* in the larger society can be a way of building their self-esteem and confidence in making independent decisions. It can help make for "connectivity and cohesion," to borrow Rita Süssmuth's perceptive phrase (this volume). Integration and inclusion are about building bridges and fostering self-worth and empathic understanding.

M. Suárez-Orozco and Qin-Hilliard (2004) use arranged versus love marriage as an example of the need to think outside the box. For many youngsters in a globalized world, arranged marriage is a valuable and valid way of entering into marriage; thus too in Sweden. To be better equipped to deal with the complexities of their lives, it is important that people learn to take multiple perspectives so they can argue "respectfully . . . within a framework of difference" (p. 5). Fadime and Patrik did this when Patrik's (Iranian) father and grandmother came to her parents, asking for her hand in marriage. It was a concession to her parents, a way of respecting their worldview. They on their part accommodated to love marriage, if reluctantly. Here were seeds of hope, prospects for reconciliation and respect such as multicultural societies must nurture.

Veronica Boix Mansilla and Howard Gardner (this volume) underscore the immense importance that a child's social environment plays in her development and education. While the educational system may seek to help youth develop interpersonal intelligence and multicultural understanding by way of direct instruction,

> there is little question that youngsters are most powerfully affected by the examples that they see around them each day. To the extent that parents, teachers, and their respective communities exhibit strong forms of personal relations and cultural sensitivity, we can expect that youngsters will be equipped to participate effectively in working and playing teams. If, however, such forms of sensitivity have not been exhibited regularly by those who are closest to the young, then educational or work institutions face a daunting challenge." (Gardner 2004, p. 253)

This takes me back to the situation in Sweden and that in Europe overall. As Süssmuth observes in this volume, "Only since the mid-1990s has integration become a central political issue in Germany and Europe" (this volume; see also Bawer 2006). The evidence for Sweden, as for most Western European countries, is dismal regarding integration. Marginalization, segregation, discrimination, and racism have engendered enclaves and communities of disadvantaged ethnic minorities (see also Roosens, this volume). Welfare colonialism also plays a part, particularly in Scandinavia. But as Fadime's story shows, integration in the labor market, important though it is, is not a sine qua non of participation in the wider society. In an era of identity politics in which global transnational connections and modern communications steer decisions at the local level more effectively than ever, people must be helped to resist group pressure and the demands of the collectivity. Civic responsibilities must take the place of ethnic affiliation as the primary bond (Maalouf 1998; Sen 2005). Ethnic identity is important. But in Europe today, the great majority of European-born children of immigrants marry *not* another European-born person but a first-generation immigrant from their parent's original homeland. Hence, we have a case of reclanification, retribalization, and re-ethnification; castes and subcastes are also being reinforced. The evidence indicates that the occurrence of such marriages is *higher* among the second and third generation of immigrants than among the first (Charsley 2005; Storhaug 2003). This means that Europe's future children will increasingly have at least one parent who is a recent immigrant from a non-European country.

Honor plays a part in the arrangement of such marriages. Families in Europe are under pressure from kin and acquaintances back home. With family reunification being the only way, besides political asylum, for a non-European to obtain legal residence in Europe now, the pressure on families in Europe is higher than ever. "They will do anything to get a son here," said Fadime. Sweden eventually, in April 2004, nullified a law allowing Swedish girls as young as fifteen to be married if the law in the parents' homeland permitted it; this legislative action bespeaks a belated recognition that "culture" should not take center stage, but that individual freedom and equality must apply to *all* Swedes, irrespective of origin. Now eighteen is the legal minimum age for marriage for all residents in Sweden. (Sweden was unique in Scandinavia in allowing child marriage; see Wikan 2004b). Norway has gone further and criminalized forced marriage.[20] Here also, Fadime's legacy was crucial.

EDUCATION AND LEARNING

With regard to ethnic background, the composition of the Swedish population has changed dramatically over the past fifteen years. Second-generation immigrants—children born in Sweden with at least one foreign-born parent—make up 26 percent of children fifteen and under, as compared to 15 percent of the age group twenty-five to forty-five years old. More and more of these children come from homes with at least one non-European-born parent: 50 percent in the age group five years old and younger, as compared to 16 percent of the age group twenty-one or older. In the age group fifteen and under, 30 percent of second-generation immigrants have two foreign-born parents.

How do children with immigrant backgrounds fare in school? To understand the challenges that Sweden faces concerning education and learning in troubled times, *different* categories of children must be singled out in research, according to the Swedish Welfare Policy Research Institute (Lund 2002). That organization distinguishes four categories; it is *within* the large group of pupils with foreign backgrounds that the crucial differences occur (p. 84). The categories are (1) children who immigrated to Sweden after the age of seven (the beginning of elementary school); (2) children who immigrated before the start of elementary school; (3) children born in Sweden of two foreign-born parents; and (4) children born in Sweden of one foreign-born parent.

The findings are disconcerting, especially for children born in Sweden of *two* foreign-born parents of non-European background. These children are most likely to drop out of school and to score poorly on Swedish reading and mathematics examinations. But the Swedish-language reading ability is significantly poorer for the category of second-generation immigrants as a whole, according to a study undertaken by school authorities in Stockholm in 2000. Nor can one conclude that their poor Swedish is compensated by command of their mother tongue. Only 5 percent of second-generation immigrants reported that they read another language better than Swedish. "If this self-reporting is accurate, the second generation immigrants have not developed any real bilinguality, despite the opportunities offered through the family and mother tongue education" (Lund 2002, p. 102; translation mine).

The challenges faced by countries like Sweden, Norway, and Denmark —small-language nations with a multitude of ethnic groups and languages—are enormous (see Crul, this volume). Many children of immigrant background manage brilliantly in school. But if the conclusions of the Swedish study are valid, the future prospects for children of two foreign-born parents in Sweden are quite poor (*dystre*).

The Tensta Gymnasium is a forerunner in innovative and creative thinking about education for children of immigrants in a globalized world. But in all fairness, the school can only do so much. Many of the new immigrants to Europe—refugees, people seeking political asylum, spouses entering for "family reunification"—hail from societies in which an honor code continues to exist. Many of these immigrants are eager to enjoy the freedom and liberties of the West, having been limited in their life prospects by authoritarian regimes and poverty. Some of them find that their new communities in the West do not allow them the "space" that they had hoped for. Naser Khader is quoted earlier as speaking of the honor and shame complex as hampering integration in Denmark more than Islam does, which is pragmatic. I have heard many similar testimonies from Assyrian and Arab Christians in Sweden and from Hindus in Britain:

it is tradition rather than religion that is the real stumbling block. Identity politics becomes a straitjacket that requires conformity with an honor code that places the good of the collectivity over and above that of individual freedom and liberty. True, religion is steadily being *used* to enforce conformity. It is important to realize that religion is not the culprit and that naming the honor complex, as we might call it, can have a liberating effect. Islam is not the enemy. The real enemy is age-old traditions that occur across religions and that must be changed, for the good of all.

SHARAF HEROES

In Sweden a number of organizations, especially Sharaf Heroes (*sharaf* is Arabic for "honor"), are working in schools and other settings to help youngsters rethink notions of honor that legitimize the use of violence and to replace them with an ethos that makes honor equivalent to the defense of human rights. The entitlement of every individual to dignity and respect is what Sharaf Heroes, along with several other organizations initiated and run by immigrants, is working for.

Sharaf Heroes recognizes boys as well as girls as victims of honor gone astray—of an honor code that compels young men to be the masters and guardians of sisters and cousins, even to use violence to prohibit and prevent girls from enjoying what ought to be inalienable rights: freedom and liberty as equal human beings. The work of this, and other organizations with a similar agenda, is commendable in that it seeks to liberate young people of both sexes from an ideology that ought to have become obsolete in our times, whereas the evidence is that it is, on the contrary, thriving. Males, often cast in the role of mere oppressors, are victims too. Some are compelled to comply with a vision of the collective good that undermines individual welfare and social justice. Liberation in accordance with human rights can be a new formula for honor.

It is not fortuitous that Sweden has come to play a key role on the international scene in efforts to combat violence in the name of honor. Sweden's decision to host an international conference on this issue in December 2004 may be seen as one of the ways the country is making amends for its failure to recognize—in time—the seriousness of the problem. In Sweden, as in several other European countries, it took the honor killings of individual young girls to awaken the public to *patterns* of violence perpetrated in the name of honor.

Violence in the name of honor, or honor-related violence, has become an item on the international political agenda. In November 2002 the

United Nations General Assembly passed a resolution in response to this issue; shortly afterward, the European Council followed suit. Many persons, organizations, NGOs, institutions, and governmental bodies are now "carrying their straw to the hay stack," to use Fadime's words. Her death created a momentum that has affected even places like Jordan and Pakistan. "But for the murders of Fadime and Pela, the West would not have cared about our predicaments," said Rana Husseini, a well-known Jordanian journalist and human rights activist at the Stockholm conference in 2004.

Linking honor with human rights is a way to avoid stigmatizing anyone's culture or identity. Among those who have argued this point is Nazand Begikhani, a prominent human rights spokesperson, journalist, and leader of Kurdish Women Action against Honor Killing, based in Britain (Begikhani 2005). Culture is a very sensitive concept. People who speak out from within their group about honor-related violence tend to be labeled traitors.[21] "What Fadime did was regarded as an offense toward her whole ethnic group," said Masood Kemali, a Swedish-Kurdish sociologist (Swedish Television, program 1, 2002). The language of human rights is now transnational. It supersedes culture and endorses the dignity and liberty of the individual being (Ignatieff 2001; Mayer 1999). It is hard to be against human rights. It can help achieve what Süssmuth (this volume) calls "connectivity and cohesion": "Europe cannot . . . afford to remain passive on integration policies that will help its diverse societies increase their connectivity and cohesion." I contend that teaching human rights is a way of helping to achieve precisely this.

Education in an era of globalization must ever struggle to find new ways to teach and enlighten young people about individual freedom as a social commitment. Liberal democracy, at home and abroad, requires just such an approach. Whether in Iraq or Sweden or the United States, "honor" gone astray fuels fundamentalist and antihumane practices and processes. By *delinking* honor from violence and *reconnecting* it with human rights, we can transcend barriers between cultures and form an agenda for our time.

How to do this in practice, in formal and informal settings, is a challenge for international research and policy collaboration. My contribution has been to map out an empirical terrain that is apparent from contemporary research and to sketch paths that may lead to fruitful practice in the future.

I take my lead from Fadime, whose favorite song was U2's "One." It was played at her funeral in the Uppsala cathedral at the request of her closest friends, who could find no words more fitting for her. It harbors a powerful message about peace and reconciliation—a message for our times.

NOTES

1. Fadime's name is pronounced "Fadîme Shahindál."

2. All translations from Swedish are mine. Originals appear in my book *En fråga om heder* (Wikan 2004a).

3. Among the songs and poems were "Bridge over Troubled Water," Shake-speare's "Shall I compare thee to a summer's day," the Kurdish folksong "Fatime," and Fadime's favorite, U2's "One."

4. The rumor has been widely circulated that the family is Jezidi, a sect not recognized by many Muslims.

5. See, e.g., Wikan 1990, 1991, 1996, 2002, 2003.

6. On this point, see also Finkielkraut 1995; Okin 1999.

7. See, e.g., Ginat 1997; Peristiany 1965; Stewart 1994; Aase 2002.

8. See C. Suárez-Orozco 2004 for an incisive discussion of gendered differences. As she observes, "An emerging body of literature reveals that boys from disparaged minority backgrounds seem to be particularly at risk of being marginalized, beginning in the educational system" (p. 194).

9. Casting out a person and sending her or him into "exile" is a time-honored practice in many honor-bound societies; it enables the family to save honor without resorting to murder (see, e.g., Ginat 1997).

10. Among those who contested this view were a few immigrants, including a member of parliament, Nalin Pekgul (neé Bakshi), who is of Kurdish Turkish background. Demirbagh-Sten (2004) incisively describes the climate of the debate after Sara's death; for a different view, see Eldén 2004, pp. 97–99.

11. What made her realize her mistake, she said, was Pela's younger sister Breen's decision to brave death threats by testifying in court against her uncles as the sole witness.

12. Oral communication by special police investigator Kickis Åhré Älgamo in a lecture at the Nordic Ministers' Council on Honor-Related Violence, Stockholm, Nov. 3, 2004.

13. For a brief but incisive discussion of Heshu's case, see Kennedy 2005, p. 179; Siddiqui 2005.

14. The information was given in a lecture by Commander Andy Baker of the Metropolitan Police at the International Conference on Honour-Based Violence, sponsored by the Metropolitan Police in London, March 21–22, 2005. In an update on April 6, 2007, Commander Baker reported that the police were to review 117 cases believed to be honor killings that are classified as murders "motivated by perceived dishonor to family or community" (*Telegraph*, April 7, 2007).

15. Feuds and vendettas were common in the Nordic countries until the Middle Ages. However, honor killings in the sense of persons (especially women) being killed by their own families are not to be found (see Johansson 2005). In feuds, males were victims, and they were killed by the enemy, not their own family. This was also the case in other parts of Europe (see, e.g., Peristiany 1965).

288 / U. WIKAN

16. Fadime's participation was kept secret due to the threats on her life. She had avoided the media for three years by then. Hence her name did not appear on the program, and she had made sure that the head of the Kurdish national organization in Sweden would not be present. Since her death, her "speech in parliament" has been published in full and is also available on tape.

17. For an excellent in-depth field study, see Carlbom 2003.

18. Fadime's father had income above the national average in 2002; he also bought and sold shares of corporate stock.

19. For several case studies, see Wikan 2002.

20. Belgium followed suit in 2005. The problem of forced marriage is receiving increased attention all over Europe; several countries have passed rules and regulations to counter the practice. Great Britain has made twenty-one years the legal minimum age for bringing a spouse into Britain, whereas Denmark passed an age-twenty-four rule in 2005.

21. See the articles in Mojab & Abdo 2004; Welchman & Hossain 2005.

REFERENCES

Aase, T. (2002). *Tournaments of power: Honor and revenge in the contemporary world*. Burlington, VT: Ashgate.

Älgamo, K. Å. (2004). Confronting honour violence: The Swedish Police at work. In *Violence in the name of honour: Theoretical and political challenges*. S. Mojab and N. Abdo, eds. Pp. 203–210. Istanbul: Istanbul Bilgi University Press.

Bawer, B. (2006). *While Europe slept*. New York: Doubleday.

Begikhani, N. (2005). Honour-based violence among the Kurds: The case of Iraqi Kurdistan. In *"Honour"—Crimes, paradigms, and violence against women*. L. Welchman and S. Hossain, eds. Pp. 209–229. London: Zed Books.

Carlbom, A. (2003). *The Imagined versus the real other: Multiculturalism and the representation of Muslims in Sweden*. Lund: Department of Sociology, Lund University.

Charsley, K. (2005). Unhappy husbands: Masculinity and migration in transnational Pakistani marriages. *Journal of the Royal Anthropological Institute* 11(1): 85–106.

Demirbagh-Sten, D. (2004). Gendering multiculturalism. In *Violence in the name of honour: Theoretical and political challenges*. S. Mojab and N. Abdo, eds. Pp. 143–148. Istanbul: Istanbul Bilgi University Press.

Eldén, Å. (2004). Life-and-death honour: Young women's violent stories about reputation, virginity and honour—in a Swedish context. In *Violence in the Name of Honour: Theoretical and political challenges*. S. Mojab and N. Abdo, eds. Pp. 91–100. Istanbul: Istanbul Bilgi University Press.

Finkielkraut, A. (1995). *The defeat of the mind*. New York: Columbia University Press. Originally published 1987.

Gardner, H. (2004). How education changes: Considerations of history, science, and values. In *Globalization: Culture and education in the new millennium*. M. Suárez-Orozco and D. Qin-Hilliard, eds. Pp. 235–258. Berkeley and Los Angeles: University of California Press; NY, NY: Ross Institute.

Ginat, J. (1997). *Blood revenge: Family honor, mediation, and outcasting.* Brighton: Sussex Academic Press. Originally published 1987.

Hjärpe, J. (2003). Hedersmord. In *Nationalencyklopedin.* http://www.ne.se/isp/search/article.isp?i art id=491725.

Husseini, R. (2004). Address by Rana Husseini, Journalist, Jordan. In *Combating patriarchal violence against women: Focusing on violence in the name of honour.* Report from the International Conference, Stockholm, 7–8 December. Stockholm: Swedish Ministry of Justice and Swedish Ministry for Foreign Affairs.

Ignatieff, M. (2001). *Human rights as politics and idolatry.* Princeton, NJ: Princeton University Press.

Johansson, K., ed. (2005). *Hedersmord: Tusen år av hederskulturer.* Lund: Lagerbringbiblioteket.

Kennedy, H. (2005). *Eve was framed: Women and British justice.* London: Vintage. Originally published 1992.

Khader, N. (2002). *Ære og skam: Det islamiske familie- og livsmønster i Danmark og Mellemøsten.* København: Borgen.

Lien, I.-L. (2002). The dynamics of honor in violence and cultural change. In *Tournaments of Power: Honor and Revenge in the Contemporary World.* T. Aase, ed. Pp. 19–48. Burlington, VT: Ashgate.

Lund, C. et al. (2002). *Arbete? Var god dröj: invandrare i välfärdssamhället.* Välfärdspolitiska rådets rapport. Stockholm: SNS Förlag.

Maalouf, A. (1998). *Les identités meurtrières.* Paris: Editions Grasset & Fasquellle.

Mayer, A. E. (1999). *Islam and human rights.* Boulder, CO: Westview Press.

Mojab, S., and N. Abdo, eds. (2004). *Violence in the name of honour: Theoretical and political challenges.* Istanbul: Istanbul Bilgi University Press.

Mørck, Y. (1998). *Bindestregs-Danskerne: Fortællinger om køn, generationer og etnisitet.* København: Forlaget Sociologi.

Okin, S. M. (1999). Is multiculturalism bad for women? In *Is multiculturalism bad for women?* J. Cohen, M. Howard, and M. C. Nussbaum, eds. Pp. 7–26. Princeton, NJ: Princeton University Press.

Peristiany, J. G.. (ed). (1965). *Honour and shame: The values of Mediterranean society.* London: Weidenfeld & Nicholson.

Pitt-Rivers, J. (1965). Honour and social status. In *Honour and shame: The values of Mediterranean society.* J. G. Peristiany, ed. Pp. 19–77. London: Weidenfeld & Nicholson.

Sareen, Manu. (2003). *Når kærlighed bliver tvang: Generationskonflikter og tvangsægteskaber i Danmark.* København: Manu Sareen; and the People's Press.

Schlytter, A. (2004). *Rätten att själv få välja.* Lund Universität: Astrid Schlytter og Studentlitteratur.

Sen, A. (1990). Individual freedom as a social commitment. *New York Review of Books,* June 14, pp. 49–52.

Sen, A. (2005). *Identity and violence. The illusion of destiny.* Princeton, NJ: Princeton University Press.

Siddiqui, H. (2005). "There is no 'honour' in domestic violence, only shame!" Women's struggles against "honour" crimes in the UK. In *Honour—Crimes,*

Paradigms, and Violence against Women. L. Welchman and S. Hossain, eds. Pp. 263–281. London: Zed Books.

Stewart, F. H. (1994). *Honor.* Chicago: University of Chicago Press.

Storhaug, H., and Human Rights Service. (2003). *Human visas: A report from the front lines of Europe's integration crisis.* Oslo: Kolofon.

Suárez-Orozco, C. (2004). Formulating identity in a globalized world. In *Globalization: Culture and Education in the New Millennium.* M. Suárez-Orozco and D. Qin-Hilliard, eds. Pp. 173–202. Berkeley and Los Angeles: University of California Press; NY, NY: Ross Institute.

Suárez-Orozco, M. , and D. Qin-Hilliard (2004). Globalization: Culture and Education in the New Millennium. In *Globalization: Culture and Education in the New Millennium.* M. Suárez-Orozco and D. Qin-Hilliard, eds. pp. 1–37. Berkeley and Los Angeles: University of California Press; NY, NY: Ross Institute.

Swedish Television, program 1 (2002). Fadime—frihetens pris. Dokument inifrån. First featured October 17.

Swanberg, L. K. (2002). *Hedersmordet på Pela: Lillasystern berättar.* Stockholm: Bokförlaget.

Welchman, L., and S. Hossain, eds. (2005). *Honour—Crimes, paradigms, and violence against women.* London: Zed Books.

Wikan, U. (1984). Shame and honour: A contestable pair. *Man* 19: 635–652.

Wikan, U. (1990). *Managing turbulent hearts: A Balinese formula for living.* Chicago: University of Chicago Press.

Wikan, U. (1991). *Behind the veil in Arabia: Women in Oman.* Chicago: University of Chicago Press. Originally published 1982.

Wikan, U. (1996). *Tomorrow, God willing: Self-made destinies in Cairo.* Chicago: University of Chicago Press.

Wikan, U. (2002). *Generous betrayal: Politics of culture in the New Europe.* Chicago: University of Chicago Press.

Wikan, U. (2003). *For ærens skyld: Fadime til ettertanke.* Oslo: Universitetsforlaget.

Wikan, U. (2004a). *En fråga om heder.* Stockholm: Ordfront.

Wikan, U. (2004b). Deadly distrust: Honor killings and Swedish multiculturalism. In *Distrust.* R. Hardin, ed. Pp. 192–204. New York: Russell Sage Foundation.

Wikan, U. (2008). *Honor and agony: Honor killings in modern-day Europe.* Chicago: University of Chicago Press.

Appendix A

GLOBAL INEQUALITY

Table A.1 Countries by income group

High income	Middle income	Middle income (continued)	Low income
Andorra	Albania	Peru	Afghanistan
Aruba	Algeria	Philippines	Angola
Australia	American Samoa	Poland	Armenia
Austria	Antigua and Barbuda	Puerto Rico	Azerbaijan
Bahamas, The	Argentina	Romania	Bangladesh
Barbados	Bahrain	Russian Federation	Benin
Belgium	Belarus	Samoa	Bhutan
Bermuda	Belize	Saudi Arabia	Burkina Faso
Brunei	Bolivia	Seychelles	Burundi
Canada	Bosnia and Herzegovina	Slovak Rep.	Cambodia
Cayman Islands	Botswana	South Africa Rep.	Cameroon
Channel Islands	Brazil	Sri Lanka	Central African Rep.
Cyprus	Bulgaria	St. Kitts and Nevis	Chad
Denmark	Cape Verde	St. Lucia	Comoros
Faeroe Islands	Chile	St. Vincent and the Grenadines	Congo Dem. Rep.
Finland	China	Suriname	Congo Rep.
France	Colombia	Swaziland	Côte d'Ivoire
French Polynesia	Costa Rica	Syrian Arab Rep.	Eritrea
Germany	Croatia	Thailand	Ethiopia
Greece	Cuba	Tonga	Gambia, The Rep.
Greenland	Czech Rep.	Trinidad and Tobago	Georgia
Guam	Djibouti	Tunisia	Ghana

Hong Kong China
Iceland
Ireland
Israel
Italy
Japan
Kuwait
Liechtenstein
Luxembourg
Macao China
Malta
Monaco
Netherlands
Netherlands Antilles
New Caledonia
New Zealand
Northern Mariana Islands
Norway
Portugal
Qatar
San Marino
Singapore
Slovenia
Spain
Sweden

Dominica
Dominican Rep.
Ecuador
Egypt Arab Rep.
El Salvador
Equatorial Guinea
Estonia
Fiji
Gabon
Grenada
Guatemala
Guyana
Honduras
Hungary
Iran Islamic Rep.
Iraq
Isle of Man
Jamaica
Jordan
Kazakhstan
Kiribati
Korea Rep.
Latvia
Lebanon
Libya

Guinea
Guinea-Bissau
Haiti
India
Indonesia
Kenya
Korea Dem. Rep.
Kyrgyz Rep.
Lao PDR
Lesotho
Liberia
Madagascar
Malawi
Mali
Mauritania
Moldova
Mongolia
Mozambique
Myanmar
Nepal
Nicaragua
Niger
Nigeria
Pakistan
Rwanda

Turkey
Turkmenistan
Uruguay
Vanuatu
Venezuela RB
West Bank and Gaza
Yugoslavia Fed. Rep.

(continued)

Table A.1 (*continued*)

High income	Middle income	Middle income (continued)	Low income
Switzerland	Lithuania		São Tomé and Príncipe
United Arab Emirates	Macedonia FYR		Senegal
United Kingdom	Malaysia		Sierra Leone
United States	Maldives		Solomon Islands
Virgin Islands (U.S.)	Marshall Islands		Somalia
	Mauritius		Sudan
	Mayotte		Tajikistan
	Mexico		Tanzania
	Micronesia Fed. States		Togo
	Morocco		Uganda
	Namibia		Ukraine
	Oman		Uzbekistan
	Palau		Vietnam
	Panama		Yemen Rep.
	Papua New Guinea		Zambia
	Paraguay		Zimbabwe

SOURCES: *University of California Atlas of Global Inequality*; World Bank 2006 (http://web.worldbank.org/WBSITE/EXTERNAL/DATASTATISTICS/0,,content-MDK:20420458~menuPK:64133156~pagePK:64133150~piPK:64133175~theSitePK:239419,00.html),

NOTE: Economies are divided according to 2005 GNI (gross national income) per capita, calculated using the *World Bank Atlas* method. The income groups are low, $875 or less; lower middle, $876–$3,465; upper middle, $3,466–$10,725; high, $10,726 or more.

EXPLANATION OF TERMS

BIRTH RATE The number of live births in a year, expressed as a percentage of the population or per 1,000 people.

DEATH RATE The number of deaths in a year, expressed as a percentage of the population or per 1,000 people.

GROSS DOMESTIC PRODUCT (GDP) The total monetary value of all goods and services produced domestically by a country. GDP includes income earned domestically by foreigners, but not income earned by domestic residents in foreign territory.

GROSS ENROLLMENT RATIO The ratio of total enrollment, regardless of age, to the population of the age group that officially corresponds to one of the following levels of education.

- *Primary education* provides children with basic reading, writing, and mathematics skills, along with an elementary understanding of such subjects as history, geography, natural science, social science, art, and music.

- *Secondary education* completes the provision of basic education that begins at the primary level and aims at laying the foundations for life-long learning and human development by offering more subject- or skill-oriented instruction using more specialized teachers.

- *Tertiary education*, whether or not it leads to an advanced research qualification, normally requires, as a minimum condition of admission, the successful completion of secondary education.

ILLITERACY RATE The percentage of the population aged fifteen years and over that cannot both read and write so as to understand a short simple statement about his or her everyday life.

INFANT MORTALITY RATE The number of infants who die before reaching one
year of age, generally expressed as deaths per 1,000 live births.

FERTILITY RATE The number of children who would be born to a woman if she
were to live to the end of her childbearing years and bear children in accordance with current age-specific fertility rates.

LIFE EXPECTANCY AT BIRTH The number of years a newborn infant would live
if prevailing patterns of mortality at the time of its birth were to stay the same
throughout its life.

SOURCE: *University of California Atlas of Global Inequality* (2006); www.worldbank.org

Notes on Contributors

Kai-ming Cheng is Chair Professor of Education and Senior Advisor to the Vice-Chancellor at the University of Hong Kong. He was also Visiting Professor at the Harvard Graduate School of Education until 2006.

Maurice Crul is a Senior Researcher at the Institute for Migration and Ethnic Studies of the University of Amsterdam.

Antonio Damasio is the David Dornsife Professor of Neuroscience, Neurology, and Psychology and Director of the Brain and Creativity Institute of the College of Letters, Arts, and Sciences, University of Southern California.

Hanna Damasio is the Dana Dornsife Professor of Neuroscience, Neurology, and Psychology and Director of the Dana and David Dornsife Cognitive Neuroscience Imaging Center at the University of Southern California.

Kurt W. Fischer is the Charles Bigelow Professor of Human Development and Education and Director of the Mind, Brain, and Education Program at the Harvard Graduate School of Education.

Peter Gärdenfors is Professor of Cognitive Science at Lund University.

Howard Gardner is the John H. and Elisabeth A. Hobbs Professor of Cognition and Education at the Harvard Graduate School of Education.

Bernard Hugonnier is Deputy Director of the Directorate for Education at the Organisation for Economic Co-operation and Development (OECD).

Tami Katzir is Assistant Professor of Education at the University of Haifa.

Robert A. LeVine is the Roy E. Larsen Professor Emeritus of Education and Human Development at Harvard University.

Frank Levy is the Daniel Rose Professor of Urban Economics at the Massachusetts Institute of Technology.

Marie McAndrew is Professor in the Department of Administration and Educational Foundations of the Faculty of Education and Chair of Ethnic Relations at the University of Montreal.

Veronica Boix Mansilla is a Principal Investigator for Project Zero at the Harvard Graduate School of Education.

Richard J. Murnane is the Juliana W. and William Foss Thompson Professor of Education and Society at the Harvard Graduate School of Education.

Eugeen Roosens is Emeritus Ordinary Professor at the Katholieke Universiteit Leuven and Emeritus Extraordinary Professor at the Université catholique de Louvain.

Carolyn Sattin is a doctoral student at the Steinhardt School of Culture, Education, and Human Development, New York University.

Marcelo M. Suárez-Orozco is the Courtney Sale Ross University Professor of Globalization and Education at New York University, Co-director of Immigration Studies at NYU, and Co-director of the Institute for Globalization and Education in Metropolitan Settings (IGEMS).

Rita Süssmuth is former President of the German Federal Parliament and former Federal Minister for Family Affairs, Women, Youth, and Health.

Unni Wikan is Professor of Social Anthropology at the University of Oslo.

Mary Helen Immordino-Yang is a joint postdoctoral fellow at the Brain and Creativity Institute and the Rossier School of Education at the University of Southern California.

Index

Text: 10/13 Sabon
Display: Franklin Gothic
Compositor: Michael Bass Associates
Illustrator: Michael Bass Associates
Indexer: Herr's Indexing Service